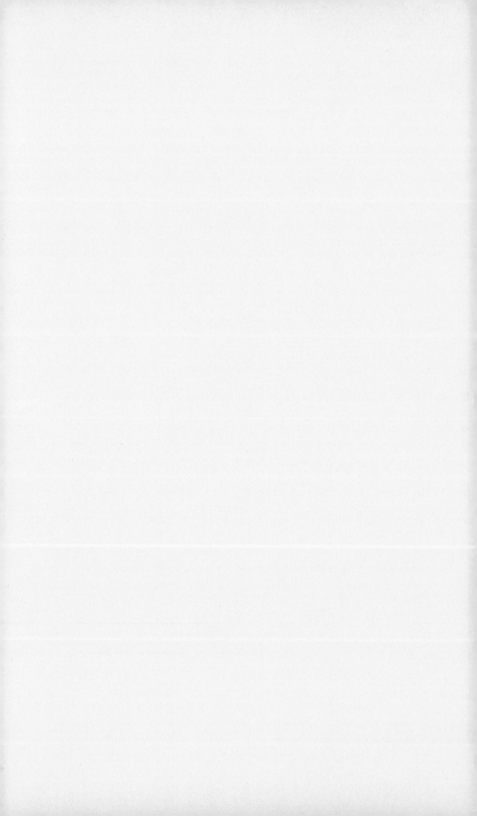

Expressions of Agency in Ancient Greek

Ancient Greek expressed the agents of passive verbs by a variety of means, and this work explores the language's development of prepositions which marked these agents. After an initial look at the pragmatics of agent constructions, it turns to this central question: under what conditions is the agent expressed by a construction other than ὑπό with the genitive? The book traces the development of these expressions from Homer through classical prose and drama, paying attention to the semantic, syntactic, and metrical conditions that favored the use of one preposition over another. It concludes with a study of the decline of ὑπό as an agent marker in the first millennium AD. Although the focus is on developments in Greek, translation of the examples should render it accessible to linguists studying changes in prepositional systems generally.

COULTER H. GEORGE is currently a Research Fellow at Trinity College, Cambridge. He has previously taught at Rice University.

CAMBRIDGE CLASSICAL STUDIES

General editors

R. L. HUNTER, R. G. OSBORNE, M. D. REEVE,
P. D. A. GARNSEY, M. MILLETT, D. N. SEDLEY,
G. C. HORROCKS

'EXPRESSIONS OF AGENCY IN ANCIENT GREEK /

COULTER H. GEORGE
Trinity College, Cambridge

CAMBRIDGE
UNIVERSITY PRESS

CAMBRIDGE UNIVERSITY PRESS
Cambridge, New York, Melbourne, Madrid, Cape Town, Singapore, São Paulo

Cambridge University Press
The Edinburgh Building, Cambridge CB2 2RU, UK

Published in the United States of America by Cambridge University Press, New York

www.cambridge.org
Information on this title: www.cambridge.org/9780521847896

© Faculty of Classics, University of Cambridge 2005

First published 2005

Printed in the United Kingdom at the University Press, Cambridge

A catalogue record for this book is available from the British Library

ISBN-13 978-0-521-84789-6 hardback
ISBN-10 0-521-84789-3 hardback

CONTENTS

vii

ACKNOWLEDGMENTS

In writing this book, I have benefited from the kind assistance of many individuals and institutions, whom I would now like to thank. I am most indebted to my doctoral supervisor, Dr James Clackson. This study is based on a Ph.D. thesis written under his direction, and it would never have advanced without his unfailing words of keen scholarly insight and warm personal encouragement. I am also extremely grateful to my two examiners, Professor Geoffrey Horrocks and Professor David Langslow, both of whom provided me with invaluable comments and suggestions. The Cambridge Faculty of Classics and, in particular, the seminars of the Linguistics Caucus have offered an outstanding forum for presenting and discussing many of the ideas put forward in this book. For financial support as a graduate student, I am indebted to the Marshall Commission and to Trinity College, which generously continues to provide for my material well-being through a Junior Research Fellowship. Equally important was the moral support given by friends and family, especially my parents and grandparents. My fellow graduate students were an indispensable source of good humor and stimulating conversation: Ralph Anderson, Lisa Bendall, Ann Casey, Jenny Davis, Vicky Jackson, Sarah Michael, and Eric Nelson, to name just a few. I am also grateful to my mentors from my undergraduate days, Douglas Mitchell and Harvey Yunis, for their continued advice and friendship. Finally, I owe particular thanks to Daphne, for not turning into a tree, to my sister, Anna, for providing comic relief, and to my mother, Ginger Young, for seeing to my early education in Greek and Latin.

ABBREVIATIONS

The abbreviations of classical Greek authors and works are those found in LSJ, except for the names of the books of the Bible, which are abbreviated as in *The Oxford Dictionary of the Christian Church*, 2nd edn (1974) p. xxv. Fifth-century AD authors are referenced as in Hult 1990, sixth-century authors as in G. W. H. Lampe (ed.) *A Patristic Greek Lexicon* (Oxford, 1961). Where available, Oxford Classical Text editions were used; editions used for other authors are indicated in the footnotes in the relevant sections.

BDB = Brown, F., S. Driver, and C. Briggs (1906) *Hebrew and English Lexicon*. Boston.

Dig. Akr. E/G = Digenis Akritis, Escorial/Grottaferrata versions; text: Jeffreys 1998.

DMic = Aura Jorro, F. (ed.) (1985–93) *Diccionario Micénico*. Madrid.

LSJ = Liddell, H. G., and R. Scott, rev. H. S. Jones (1940) *Greek–English Lexicon*, 9th edn. Oxford.

Nestle–Aland = Aland, K. *et al.* (eds.) (1993) *Novum testamentum Graece*, 27th edn. Stuttgart.

NRSV = New Revised Standard Version

PAC = passive-with-agent construction

Ptoch. = Ptochoprodromos; text: Eideneier 1991.

PASSIVE VERBS AND AGENT CONSTRUCTIONS

Beginning students of Ancient Greek soon learn that the agent of a passive verb is marked with the preposition ὑπό followed by the genitive.[1] Then, of course, the exceptions come to light. The most common of these is the dative of agent, which, for the beginner at least, may be explained away as occurring with perfect passives and -τέος verbals. Later, however, one comes across other irregularities, notably the use of prepositions other than ὑπό$^{+G}$. The conditions that motivate these apparently anomalous agent markers have not yet been satisfactorily explained. The aim of this book is to do so.

I begin with an introductory chapter that lays a theoretical foundation for the work and discusses the reasons why these passive-with-agent constructions (PACs) occur in the first place. In Chapter 2, I move on to Homer, as the *Iliad* and *Odyssey* represent the earliest texts that are syntactically complex enough to have PACs. Because the Homeric data are so different from the later evidence – in particular, these constructions are far less common in Homer – they are best dealt with separately. Next, in Chapter 3, I look at the dative of agent. It is relatively well understood already – it occurs most prominently with perfect verbs – but one question in particular deserves further treatment: When do perfect verbs take ὑπό$^{+G}$ rather than the dative one might otherwise expect? Then, Chapter 4 treats the central issue I shall examine, namely, the conditions motivating the use of prepositions other than ὑπό$^{+G}$ as agent markers in the classical prose authors. Because these conditions were different for poetry than for prose, I reserve discussion of tragedy and comedy for Chapter 5. Finally, in Chapter 6, I trace the development of agent constructions in post-classical Greek, ending with the Byzantine Greek of Digenis Akritis.

---

[1] Henceforth I shall refer to the use of a preposition governing a particular case as e.g. ὑπό$^{+G}$.

Passive voice

If this work is to explain the conditions that influence what agent marker is used in a PAC, it must first set out guidelines for determining what constitutes such a construction. Essentially, such guidelines must be formulated so as to identify the two components of a PAC, a passive verb and an agent. Now the idea of a passive verb at first glance would seem fairly straightforward to most speakers of English, who will be familiar with the passive voice of their native language. If a verb occurs in the passive voice, then the subject of the verb is not the agent, but rather the patient of the action of the verb. Broadly speaking, such an account is sufficient to describe the voice system of English, and, indeed, it is the opposition between active and passive that has dominated the Anglo-American literature on voice. But, while it will be the focus of this study as well, the situation is more complicated in Greek, where, in addition to the active and passive, there is also a middle voice, the general function of which is to indicate that the effects of the action described by the verb in some way affect the subject of the verb.[2] Additionally, it will be crucial to maintain a distinction between the form and function of a voice. For, as the Greek passive was only ever partially independent of the middle, the two could quite easily be confused: a middle form can have a passive function and vice versa.[3] Such contamination is not surprising in light of the overlap between the functions of the middle and passive.

Now the voice opposition most prominent in theoretical linguistics is the contrast of active and passive voice, as proponents of transformational grammar have taken it up as an example of a transformation exhibiting noun-phrase movement in the shift from deep to surface structure.[4] This approach is sensible, because it is,

---

[2] In addition to expressing the active-passive and active-middle oppositions that are of interest here, voice can also be used as a marker of various pragmatic functions, including focus constructions and direct/inverse systems. For a discussion of this type of voice, see Klaiman 1991: 31–5.

[3] Cf. Th. 1.2.1 βιαζόμενοι ὑπό τινων on the one hand, the aorists of the so-called passive deponents like ἐμάνην on the other. Andersen considers the -(θ)η- aorists to be active rather than passive in form and derives their passive significance from a 1-valence value assigned to the suffix -(θ)η- (1993: 198–201). See also the following note.

[4] See Chomsky 1957: 42–3 and 1965: 103–6, Radford 1988: 420–35; Van Valin 2001: 172–225 provides a brief synopsis of recent syntactic theories, with particular attention

in most cases, easy to trace the relation between a passive sentence and its active "prototype." In essence, the passive voice rearranges the relations of the verb to its core nominals (that is, the subject and object), in particular indicating a reduction in the verb's valence (that is, a transitive verb becomes intransitive). Generally, this process involves the demotion of the subject of the unmarked construction (usually the agent) to an oblique relation in the marked construction, typically accompanied by the promotion of the object (usually the patient) to the subject relation.[5] Diagrammatically, with brackets indicating optional elements:

Subj	Vb-Act	Obj		Subj	Vb-Pass	[Obliq]
|		|	→	|		|
Agt		Pat		Pat		[Agt]

The English passive fits in well with this schema:

Achilles killed Hector → *Hector was killed [by Achilles]*

to how they treat the passive. Andersen takes a different view of the passive, arguing that what are commonly called passive markers are in fact usually markers of monovalency (and not valence-reduction) (1994: 27–8). The passive would then be "synergetically" determined by means of contextual inferences from the presence of a monovalent verb, a middle verb, or indeed any other verb whose semantics are potentially passive. He argues this position from the occurrence of (i) non-passive -(θ)η- (see 1993: 99 for examples, most notably in Homer, but also ἐπορεύθησαν, ὡρμήθησαν, ὑπελείφθη in Thucydides), (ii) middle forms used as passives, (iii) active verbs in passive constructions (the type πίπτω ὑπό). However, it must be noted that there are -(θ)η- aorists that are polyvalent, contradicting Andersen's hypothesis. Two examples: *Il.* 4.402 αἰδεσθεὶς βασιλῆος ἐνίπην αἰδοίοιο, Lys. 2.40 ἦ τίς τῆς τόλμης αὐτοὺς οὐκ ἂν ἠγάσθη; Considering that in the aorist, where a three-way opposition exists (e.g. ἔλυσα: ἐλυσάμην: ἐλύθην), the third form functions as a valence-reducing, object-promoting voice, it seems best to call this a passive. Additionally, Andersen places high importance on the Greek dichotomy of active and middle endings in his treatment of voice. Yet in Attic Greek, the futures in -(θ)ήσομαι play roughly the same role as the aorists in -(θ)ην, suggesting that these two formations should be considered as different tenses of the same voice, not as representing two different voices. It was, after all, the existence of the specifically passive forms in -(θ)ην that led to the creation of the -(θ)ήσομαι forms in the first place (Hartmann 1935: 127). Note further that, just as -(θ)ην and -σάμην were interchangeable, so too were -σομαι and -(θ)ήσομαι (Schwyzer–Debrunner 1950: 238).

5 Other variations on the passive include the impersonal passive with a dummy subject "Es wurde im Nebenzimmer geredet" (Palmer 1994: 127–32) and the promotion of roles besides the patient. Malagasy, for instance, in addition to a passive that promotes the patient, also has a "circumstantial" voice that promotes the dative and instrumental (*ibid.* 125, with examples). Similarly, in response to English constructions like "He was given a new tie," Fillmore sees the passive as a means of marking the choice of a "nonnormal" subject: "The verb *give* also allows either O[bject] or D[ative] to appear as subject as long as this 'nonnormal' choice is 'registered' in the V. This 'registering' of a 'nonnormal' subject takes places via the association of the feature [+passive] with the V" (1968: 37).

The primary functions of the passive follow naturally from the syntactic remappings it occasions. First, the passive can be used when it is advantageous for the patient of the action to be the grammatical subject, either pragmatically, because it is a narrative theme, or syntactically, so that it may serve as a pivot. As an example of the first, Palmer offers, "The child ran into the road. He was hit by the car" (1994: 136). The second is illustrated by the frequent use of passive participles in many different Indo-European (IE) languages. As Jamison notes, "A passive *participle* is of far more use in speech [than a finite passive verb], for it provides a more concise and elegant means than a relative clause of embedding into a matrix clause any clause whose object would be coreferential with a noun phrase in the matrix clause" (1979b: 203, italics hers). Secondly, a speaker can use the passive to avoid naming the agent, because it is so obvious as to be unnecessary, or because it is unknown, or even to obfuscate the responsibility for an action. Not all languages, however, are able to express the agent of a passive verb. Latvian provides the textbook IE example of a passive that cannot construe with an agent.[6] Still, Greek can express the agent, and it is precisely the variety of its agent constructions that makes it so interesting.

The middle voice, on the other hand, best known to linguists from its occurrence in Greek and Sanskrit, cannot be reduced to a similarly neat syntactic description.[7] Unlike the passive, which has a relatively clear syntactic function, the middle can only be

---

[6] The agent can, however, be expressed in informal language (Nau 1998: 37).

[7] Cf. Brugmann 1916: 688–9, Delbrück 1897: 428–30 for warnings against neat syntactic divisions among the uses of the middle. Barber 1975 attempts to make just such divisions by positing that the middle voice signals the identity of the subject nominal with various grammatical relations in the predicate. For example, middle marking on a verb with a direct object would indicate that the subject is to be understood as the indirect object (thus, αἱροῦμαι μοῖραν would be equivalent to αἱρῶ μοι μοῖραν). However, Klaiman notes that this model would not account for detransitivizing middle usages such as ὁ κλών κάμπτεται, which by Barber's reasoning would have to be interpreted as reflexive (1991: 28). The position that the middle cannot be readily defined in syntactic terms is lent support by the frequent misuse of the middle by non-native speakers. This difficulty is seen in the deterioration in active-middle distinctions in Koine (Wackernagel 1950: 123–4) as well as the problems foreign speakers of Spanish have in correctly using *se* in constructions like *Juan se cayó del tercer piso* "Juan fell (unintentionally) from the third floor" (example from Arce-Arenales *et al.* 1994: 6).

defined in vague, semantic terms as indicating that the effects of the action in some way accrue back to the subject.[8] Consider the two sentences: ὁ Ἀχιλλεὺς φέρει τὸ δέπας and ὁ Ἀχιλλεὺς φέρεται τὸ δέπας. The difference between the active and middle sentences does not lie in so discrete a factor as the valence of the verb, for, in both sentences, the verb predicates two arguments, an agent-subject and a patient-object. Rather, the use of the middle indicates that the action affects the subject to a greater extent. Achilles does not simply carry the goblet, but rather has an additional interest in the object: he wins it. This definition of voice accounts for all the functions of the IE middle described by Wackernagel, including direct and indirect reflexives, reciprocals, and verbs of taking (the type μισθόω "let out for hire": μισθόομαι "hire") (1950: 124–9).[9] An additional difference between the middle and the passive is that a voice like the IE middle does not seem to be subsidiary to the active: just as there are verbs that only occur in the active, so too there are verbs only found in the middle.[10] Furthermore, passive forms can correspond to a middle as well as an active: αἱρεθῆναι

---

[8] Here are some of the various definitions of the middle. Benveniste: "Dans le moyen . . . le verbe indique un procès dont le sujet est le siège; le sujet est intérieur au procès" (1950: 125). Lyons: "The implications of the middle (when it is in opposition with the active) are that the 'action' or 'state' affects the subject of the verb or his interests" (1968: 373). Strunk argues that the primary function of the middle is to denote "Verhaltensträger-Orientierung" but notes that other verbs exercise this function simply by virtue of their lexical semantics (*moritur* vs. *vivit*) (1980: 323). Andersen has refuted Klaiman's attempt at a rigid definition (1994: 49–61). Still, her initial characterization of the middle is still valid and in line with the other definitions: "[Voice systems like the middle] reflect alternations of the subject's status *vis-à-vis* the denoted action, in terms of whether or not the principal effects of the action devolve upon the subject" (1991: 11). In Andersen's opinion, the middle corresponds to Dionysius Thrax's term πάθος and denotes "the fact that the [subject] stood in an *experiential* 'disposition' to the predication, i.e., it represented that particular participant which experiences the predication" (1994: 35, italics his). Finally, compare Pāṇini's terms for the active and middle, *parasmai padam* "word for another" and *ātmane padam* "word for oneself" respectively.

[9] It is certainly true that some of these functions could be described in syntactic terms. The last type, for instance, could be seen as a remapping of the beneficiary of the active μισθόω to the subject slot of the middle μισθόομαι. But, unlike the passive, which can consistently be defined in terms of a single syntactic remapping, the only common element to the various uses of the middle is the nebulous idea that the subject is somehow more affected by the action in question.

[10] For this reason, Klaiman terms the middle a "basic" voice, as opposed to a "derived" voice like the passive.

5

can mean either "to be captured, taken," as a passive to the active, or "to be chosen," as a passive to the middle.[11] It might seem tempting, then, to view the passive and middle voices as phenomena of quite different natures. The passive, on the one hand, always has a discrete effect on the syntax of the sentence: detransitivization accompanied by promotion of the object. The middle, on the other, need have no visible syntactic consequences: it merely emphasizes the subject's affectedness. To make a clear distinction between the two, however, would be wrong. A voice defined as vaguely as the middle can in fact be used with precisely the same syntactic effect as the passive.[12] Indeed, the passive could be described as an extreme case of subject-affectedness. As proof of the middle's ability to act as a passive, one need only consider the Greek use of the middle outside the aorist and future as the standard passive formation (the type λύομαι ὑπό) or the Russian use of the reflexive as a passive (*Novoe zdanie stroitsja inženerami* "The new building is being constructed by the engineers").[13] Accordingly, I will use the term passive in a functional sense to denote verb detransitivization accompanied by object-promotion, whether this be achieved by a morphologically distinct passive marking or through the use of a middle voice that encompasses other functions as well.

One further debate about the passive has concerned the role of the agent: is it necessary that there be some means of expressing the agent in order for a verb to be called a passive?[14] To some extent, this is a trivial question, as it is simply a matter of nomenclature whether or not one defines the passive so as to include instances of detransitivization with object-promotion that do not allow the agent to be expressed. Still, Klaiman does seek to distinguish sharply between the two types of detransitivization. In her view, the passive voice suppresses or downgrades the subject-agent

---

[11] Kühner-Gerth: "Die Formen des passiven Aorist- und Perfektstammes können ihrer Bedeutung nach ebenso zum Medium, wie zum Aktiv gehören" (1898: 26). Examples from X. *An.*: (passive of the active) 5.4.26 ἐν τῷ πρότερον αἱρεθέντι χωρίῳ, (passive of the middle) 3.1.46 αἱρεῖσθε . . . ἄρχοντας . . . καὶ τοὺς αἱρεθέντας ἄγετε.

[12] See Kemmer 1993: 147–9.   [13] This example is taken from Kemple 1993: 64.

[14] See Schmidt 1963 and Jankuhn 1969: 22–7 for summaries and discussion of the views of Wackernagel, Meillet, Kuryłowicz, and others on the necessity (or not) of the agent-expression in defining the passive.

but does not eliminate the logical notion of an agent; accordingly, it leaves scope for the agent to be expressed by grammatical means. In the sentence *The tree was felled*, an agent (e.g. a lumberjack) causing the falling of the tree is implied, if not explicitly stated, and could be expressed using the preposition *by*. The detransitivizing middle voice, however, termed an anticausative,[15] would have no logical agent assigned, as it "[expresses] spontaneous events, i.e. situations presupposing no participant's control" (Klaiman 1991: 83–4). In the sentence *The tree fell*, the force that brought about the action is not implied, and could not be introduced into the sentence by means of a grammaticalized preposition like *by*.[16]

But while it is valid to distinguish between two types of detransitivization – one that allows for the expression of the agent, one that does not – it is best not to align that difference with the distinction between passive and middle voice. On the one hand, there are voices like the Greek middle and Russian reflexive, best viewed as middles owing to their wide range of uses, that can detransitivize, promote the object, and express the agent with an oblique nominal. On the other hand, there are also voices like the Latvian and Arabic passive, which, as they do little more than detransitivize and promote the object, are best described as passives, but cannot express the agent. Accordingly, one should not consider the inability to express the agent to be particularly characteristic of the middle. It would be better either to call the syntax of detransitivization and object-promotion passive in all cases, noting that some passives allow expression of the agent while others do not, or to call such constructions passive only if the agent can be expressed, and anticausative otherwise. In any event, as this study is concerned with how the agent of a detransitivized verb is expressed, it is of little importance here whether detransitivized verbs that cannot be construed with an oblique agent are to be considered passive.

---

[15] Others use the term "neuter" for such a use of the middle.

[16] I treat both *be felled* and *fall* as intransitive verbs corresponding to the transitive *fell*. The first is a passive; the second, although not a grammaticalized anticausative (*fall*, of course, being the verb from which the causative *fell* was formed secondarily), nevertheless illustrates the point adequately for a language that does not have a middle voice. It is true that, in Greek, agents can be expressed by grammatical means with verbs such as πίπτω and ἀποθνῄσκω. But these intransitives, though active in form, do act as lexical passives to corresponding transitive verbs, such as ἀποκτείνω.

One final point remains. Most frequently it is the semantic role of agent that is mapped to the subject relation of an active sentence and consequently demoted to the oblique in the passive.[17] But there are also other semantic roles that can serve as the subject of a sentence. For example, *Achilles*, in *Achilles saw Hector*, may be labeled an experiencer or a perceiver, rather than an agent, as Achilles' seeing Hector does not involve the same level of deliberate participation on Achilles' part as would, say, his striking Hector. In this work, however, the term agent will not refer in this narrow sense exclusively to the participant that is responsible for effecting an action, but rather will denote more generally the noun that would be mapped to the subject relation in a transitive sentence, whatever its more precise semantic role may be. This broader definition captures better the fact that ὑπο^{+G} performs essentially the same function both in ὤφθη ὑπὸ τοῦ Ἀχιλλέως and in ἐπλήγη ὑπὸ τοῦ Ἀχιλλέως.

Origins and development of the passive voice in Greek

An examination of the passive voice and the expression of the agent in ancient Greek inevitably raises questions about the historical development of voice in the Greek verb. Although many problems remain unsolved, it is generally acknowledged that, by the time of classical Attic, Greek had undergone a transition from a two-voice system, with opposition between an active and middle, to a three-voice system, with the addition of a passive. The transition, however, must be regarded as incomplete, for the passive only became independent of the middle in the aorist and future.[18] A look at this development should begin with Proto-Indo-European (PIE) itself.

---

[17] I use the term semantic role in the same sense as Blake 1994: 64. For further discussion of these points, see Palmer 1994: 8–10, who uses "Agent" to refer to the grammatical relation and "agent" to refer to the semantic role.

[18] The picture is further complicated by the perfect, which, in PIE, probably lay outside the active-middle opposition, but became incorporated into it during the evolution of Greek. Already in Mycenaean, the perfect had begun to be incorporated into the active-middle opposition of the present and aorist stems. As the Greek perfect passive is set apart from the present and aorist by virtue of its construing with a dative of agent, the development of the perfect is treated separately in Chapter 3.

The verbal systems of Greek and Sanskrit suggest that PIE had a two-voice system, with a primary opposition between the active and the middle.[19] First of all, there is a clear historical relation between the morphology of the Greek and Sanskrit middle (e.g. present thematic third singular -εται : -ate, third plural -ονται : -ante), while the distinctively passive forms in each are clearly unrelated formations: Greek's -(θ)η- aorist (and future) passive marker on the one hand, Sanskrit's -i third singular aorist passive and -ya- present passive markers on the other. Second, the middle is used similarly in the two languages: both exhibit a reflexive middle, be it direct or indirect (cf. λούομαι (τὰς χεῖρας) and vahate "(direct reflexive) go; (indirect reflexive) marry"), a reciprocal middle (cf. διαλέγομαι and vivadate "dispute with one another"), and a dynamic middle, indicating the total involvement of the subject (πόλεμον ποιεῖν "cause a war to come about" vs. πόλεμον ποιεῖσθαι "conduct a war," compare tiṣṭhati "stand" vs. tiṣṭhate "hold still").[20] Third, some of the same verbs in both languages inflect either only in the active or only in the middle (the activa and media tantum): βαίνω/gacchati, ἐστί/asti on the one hand, ἧσται/āste, κεῖται/śete on the other. Latin too, though traditionally described as having an opposition between active and passive rather than between active and middle, provides some evidence for the contrasts of voice detailed above, for instance the direct reflexive lavari.[21]

But the lack of a distinct passive morpheme does not imply that PIE could not express the passive, as many languages can use the middle in this function. In both Greek and Sanskrit, the middle was often used to denote passivization.[22] That Latin's inherited middle

---

[19] For a bibliography on voice in PIE, see Szemerényi 1996: 255–7. Standard references include Delbrück 1897: 412–39, Brugmann 1916: 678–711, Wackernagel 1950: 119–44, Schwyzer–Debrunner 1950: 222–42. It suffices here to consider the "classical" reconstruction of the late PIE verbal system, leaving aside the problematic position of Hittite.

[20] Examples from Brugmann 1916: 690, 696, Wackernagel 1950: 127, and Delbrück 1897: 426.

[21] For further description of uses of the Latin passive that resemble the Greek middle, see Hofmann–Szantyr 1965: 288–9 and Joffre 1995: 81–155, especially 115–32. While Touratier takes a different approach in explaining the significance of deponent verbs, he likewise speaks of a mediopassive sense that can be exhibited by Latin passives (1994: 175).

[22] For Greek, see Schwyzer–Debrunner 1950: 237–8; for Sanskrit, see Delbrück 1888: 263–5.

voice (admittedly morphologically different from the Greek and Sanskrit) came to be used primarily as a passive also hints that the PIE middle could assume a passive function. Additionally, several living languages provide evidence that a reflexive construction, similar in function to the PIE middle, can take on the functions of the passive: the Romance languages have a middle that can express an agentless passive (French *la porte s'ouvre*),[23] while the Russian middle can express the passive with the agent.[24]

It does not appear possible, however, to reconstruct a single unified agent expression for PIE, for the daughter languages show a bewildering variety of constructions, presented most recently by Hettrich.[25] This proliferation of agent expressions, it must be noted, does not prove that PIE could not express the agent of a passive verb, let alone that it had no passive. One need only consider the different agent expressions in the Romance languages (Spanish *por*,[26] French *par*, Italian *da*) – none of which directly continues Latin *ab* with the ablative – to find a parallel for the replacement of a single agent expression in the mother language by a variety of constructions in the different daughter languages. Nevertheless, certain patterns do emerge among the attested IE languages: the genitive is frequent with participles, the dative with participles of necessity and perfects, and instrumental and ablatival expressions with finite verbs. Such tendencies can be followed in Greek but must not be pressed too closely. The loss of cases can

---

[23] The Italian equivalent can be used with the agent, if only occasionally: *Il vino si beve dai ragazzi*, "The wine is drunk by the boys" (Maiden 1995: 164).

[24] See the example on p. 6.

[25] Hettrich 1990 concludes that the genitive, dative, ablative, instrumental, and locative could all be used to express the agent. Earlier, Schwyzer had described various similarities of construction among the IE languages but attributed them all to later development: "Nur weniges stammt in dieser besondern Funktion aus indogermanischer Zeit, selbst wenn die verwendeten Mittel die gleichen sind" (1943: 13). Other studies primarily address narrower concerns. Schmidt 1963 notes the frequency of agents with participles, adding that the genitive and dative were common with participles, the instrumental with finite verbs. Jamison has written two articles dealing with this question, one arguing unconvincingly that the instrumental was the sole agentive case in PIE (1979a), the other discussing the use of compounding to express agency with participles (1979b). Finally, Luraghi 1986, 1995, and 2001 explore the relationship between agent expressions and those of similar roles such as instrument.

[26] The agent marker in Spanish had earlier been *de*, which was replaced by *por* in the sixteenth century (Penny 1991: 103).

drastically alter the way a language assigns functions to various prepositions and cases, as seen in the Romance languages. As syncretism reduced the PIE system of eight cases to five in Greek, it is natural to expect that agent expression might have changed as well.

After the comparative evidence from PIE, the next source of data for the development of the Greek language is to be found in the Linear B tablets. Regrettably for syntacticians, the Mycenaean scribes frequently dispensed with such linguistic niceties as verbs for the sake of administrative brevity. An account of voice in Mycenaean is thus all but impossible. Still, enough verbal forms do remain to suggest that the middle functioned in roughly the same way as it did in Homer, although there are no secure attestations of the -(θ)η- aorist to compare it against.[27] First, there are examples of *media tantum* inflected as middles in Mycenaean:

(1) *de-ka-sa-to*	= δέξατο "he received"	KN Le 641.1	
(2) *e-u-ke-to*	= εὔχετοι[28] "he declares"	PY Eb 297.1, Ep 704.5	
(3) *o-ro-me-no*	= ὀρόμενος[29] "watching"	PY Ae 108, 134	

One certainly cannot prove that these verbs were *media tantum* in Mycenaean, as the corpus is too small, but it is reassuring that they are attested in the middle where they do occur. Second, the Mycenaean middle could also be used in two of the middle's differential functions, the dynamic middle and the indirect reflexive middle:

---

[27] There are two possible exceptions. First, Palmer has suggested that the two forms *a-ke* and *pe-re* in PY Tn 316 are the aorist passives ἄγη and φρῆ (from φέρω) (1963: 265–7). Scholarly opinion, however, seems more inclined to take them as present indicatives ἄγει and φέρει (see the respective entries in *DMic*). Second, Chadwick has proposed that *tu-wo-te-to* and *o-je-ke-te-to* (TH Fq 121.3 and Fq 130.1 respectively) are akin to the -θη- aorists of later Greek, though with middle, rather than active endings (1996–7: 294–6). Reconstructed as /thuōthētoi/ and /oie(i)khthētoi/, they would be the passives of θυόω and οἴγνυμι.

[28] The -τοι stands for Attic -ται; the verb here seems to mean "declare" rather than "pray; boast" (Ventris–Chadwick 1973: 547).

[29] Ventris–Chadwick compare *Od.* 14.104, ἐπὶ δ' ἀνέρες ἐσθλοὶ ὄρονται, though it should be noted that the Mycenaean verb is construed with an object after *o-pi* (*qe-to-ro-po-pi*).

(4) *to-ro-qe-jo-me-no* = τροπεόμενος [?][30]   PY Eq 213.1
"turning about"
(5) *u-ru-to*   =Ϝρύντοι "they watch"   PY An 657.1

Third, the middle is found expressing the passive:

(6) PY Ng 319   *de-we-ro-ai-ko-ra-i-ja* SA 1239
                   to-sa-de o-u-di-do-to SA 457
                   "Those from this side of?Aigaleon: [. . .]
                   And so many are not contributed: [. . .]"[31]
                   • *di-do-to* = δίδοτοι, cf. PY Ng 332.2
(7) PY Vn 20.1–2   *o-a₂ e-pi-de-da-to*
                   pa-ra-we-wo wo-no
                   "Thus the wine of Parawe- has been
                   distributed"[32]
                   • *e-pi-de-da-to* = ἐπιδέδασтоι
(8) KN So 4440   *a-mo-ta / pte-re-wa / o-da-twe-ta*
                   'de-do-me-na' WHEEL ZE 6
                   "Six pairs of wheels of elmwood with
                   studs, which have been contributed"[33]
                   • *de-do-me-na* = δεδομένα, cf.
                   de-de-me-no = δεδεμένω PY Sa 287, 794
(9) PY Un 267.1–4 *o-do-ke a-ko-so-ta*
                   tu-we-ta a-re-pa-zo-o
                   tu-we-a a-re-pa-te [[*ze-so-me*]]
                   ze-so-me-no [[*ko*]]
                   "Thus A(r)xotas gave spices to Thuestas
                   the unguent-boiler, for unguent which is to
                   be boiled"[34]
                   • *ze-so-me-no* = ζεσ(σ)ομένω, cf.
                   e-we-pe-se-so-me-na = εὖ ἐψησόμενα MY
                   Oe 127

Although this use of voice is, on the whole, what one would expect
both from reconstructions of PIE voice and the later Greek data, it

---

[30] Ventris–Chadwick call this an "'iterative-intensive' form of τρέπω" and translate "on his tour of inspection" (1973: 269); Palmer suggests either τροqʷεόμενος "causing to plough" or στροqʷηεόμενος "on a tour of inspection" (1963: 459).
[31] Ventris–Chadwick 1973: 300–1.   [32] *Ibid.* 348.
[33] *Ibid.* 372, 518.   [34] *Ibid.* 223–4, 441–2.

would be disingenuous not to note that the passive usages of the middle appear to have been more widespread in Mycenaean than in Homer in two respects. First, the verb δίδωμι is almost never passive in Homer: out of over 450 instances in the poems, only twice is it passive:

(10) *Il.* 5.428   οὔ τοι, τέκνον ἐμόν, δέδοται πολεμήϊα ἔργα
               "the work of war has not been given to you, my
               child"
(11) *Od.* 2.78   χρήματ' ἀπαιτίζοντες, ἕως κ' ἀπὸ πάντα δοθείη
               "demanding back our goods, until everything is
               returned"

It is remarkable, then, that there should be two passive occurrences of it in Mycenaean. Second, in Homer, the future middle participle is not used in the attributive gerundival sense found in the two Mycenaean examples. Rather, future participles are used predicatively with verbs of motion to express purpose.[35]

Two explanations for this disparity are possible. First, it might be that, in administrative documents, there was additional pragmatic motivation for the use of the passive in situations where the agent was unimportant; one need only compare the widespread use of the passive in contemporary bureaucracy. Such an explanation might well account for a passive of δίδωμι meaning "be given, delivered." Second, there remains the possibility that the Mycenaean forms have been misinterpreted in light of the great ambiguities inherent in the writing system. Indeed, alternatives to gerundival readings have been proposed for the two future middle participles.[36] But in the end, however one accounts for these discrepancies, it remains the case that the Mycenaean middle could be used as a passive, lending additional support for the view that the PIE middle could be used as a passive.

For more substantial evidence regarding voice in early Greek, however, we must turn to the works of Homer, where, in addition to the old opposition of active and middle endings, we see the beginnings of a morphologically distinct passive voice, marked by

---

[35] Chantraine 1963: 321.
[36] Palmer denies either of these forms future passive force (1963: 421), while Ventris–Chadwick argue for it (1973: 224, 441–2, 547). See also the relevant entries in *DMic.*

the -(θ)η- suffix. Starting from the inherited middle forms, we find that they can express all the familiar functions of that voice:

(12) *Od.* 6.221   ἄντην δ᾽ οὔκ ἂν ἐγώ γε λοέσσομαι [direct reflexive] "and I will not bathe myself in front of you"

(13) *Il.* 16.230   νίψατο δ᾽ αὐτὸς χεῖρας [indirect reflexive] "and he himself washed his hands"

(14) *Il.* 1.10   ὀλέκοντο δὲ λαοί [anticausative] "and the people perished"

In other cases, however, any difference between it and the active seems impossible for a non-native speaker to determine:

(15) *Il.* 22.32   ὡς τοῦ χαλκὸς ἔλαμπε περὶ στήθεσσι θέοντος "thus the bronze gleamed on his chest, as he ran"

(16) *Il.* 22.134   ἀμφὶ δὲ χαλκὸς ἐλάμπετο εἴκελος αὐγῇ "and the bronze gleamed about him like the light [of a fire or the sun]"

In the absence of native informants to help our understanding, we must base any explanation of the difference between the two on those cases where the middle performs a function clearly distinct from the active: that of marking subject-affectedness. In considering obscure examples like (16), we can only assume that the middle performs the same function here as well, but to a much subtler degree, perhaps even so subtle as to be non-existent and exploitable for metrical ends.[37] Nevertheless, as can be observed in example (14), there are certainly cases where the middle is not likely to be confused with the active. And, indeed, from this anticausative function, it is but a short step to that of the passive-cum-agent:[38]

(17) *Il.* 6.134–5   ὑπ᾽ ἀνδροφόνοιο Λυκούργου θεινόμεναι βουπλῆγι "struck by man-slaying Lycurgus with an ox-goad"

---

[37] See Chantraine 1963: 174. For a Sanskrit parallel, see Whitney 1889: §529a.

[38] Jankuhn's work amply refutes Wistrand's notion that the passive as such did not exist in Homer.

The picture is complicated, however, by a morphological innovation, the suffix -(θ)η-. It appears initially to have been a suffix marking intransitive verbs, associated at first, to judge by the personal endings it takes, with active rather than middle verbs.[39] Nevertheless, by Homer's time at least, it had begun to overlap with some of the functions of the middle. First, some *media tantum* can form their aorist either with the middle endings or with the -(θ)η- suffix:

(18) *Il.* 5.621–2   οὐδ᾽ ἄρ᾽ ἔτ᾽ ἄλλα **δυνήσατο** τεύχεα καλὰ
     ὤμοιιν ἀφελέσθαι
     "but he was not able after that to remove the
     beautiful armor from his shoulders"
(19) *Il.* 23.465–6   οὐδὲ **δυνάσθη**
     εὖ σχεθέειν περὶ τέρμα
     "and he was not able to guide it well around
     the turning-post"
(20) *Od.* 21.28   οὐδὲ θεῶν ὄπιν **αἰδέσατ**᾽ οὐδὲ τράπεζαν
     "and he did not have the proper respect either
     for the watchfulness or for the hospitality of
     the gods"
(21) *Il.* 7.93   **αἴδεσθεν** μὲν ἀνήνασθαι, δεῖσαν δ᾽
     ὑποδέχθαι
     "they were ashamed to refuse, but feared to
     accept"

Second, like the middle aorist, the -(θ)η- aorist can be used as a passive:

(22) *Il.* 5.646   ἀλλ᾽ ὑπ᾽ ἐμοὶ **δμηθέντα** πύλας Ἀΐδαο
     περήσειν
     "but, defeated by me, to cross the gates of
     Hades"
(23) *Od.* 9.66   οἳ θάνον ἐν πεδίῳ Κικόνων ὕπο **δῃωθέντες**
     "who died on the plain, slaughtered by the
     Cicones"

---

[39] See Delbrück 1879: 75.

(24) *Il.* 16.433–4 ὤ μοι ἐγών, ὅ τέ μοι Σαρπηδόνα, φίλτατον
ἀνδρῶν, | μοῖρ᾽ ὑπὸ Πατρόκλοιο
Μενοιτιάδαο δαμῆναι
"O, alas for me, that it is fated that my
Sarpedon, dearest of men, is to be defeated by
Patroclus, son of Menoetius"

It seems clear that voice in Greek was in a transitional state at this point, with the functions of the middle endings and the -(θ)η- suffix overlapping. Chantraine makes the point well in his recital of the various forms of χέω: in the present, χεῖσθαι is usually intransitive (VI), but sometimes transitive (VT); in the aorist, both χύτο and χύθη are VI, while χεύατο is usually VT, but once VI; only the perfect, κέχυτο, is consistently VI (1963: 182).

Identifying passive-with-agent constructions (PACs)

The object of this study is to examine the means by which Greek expressed the agent of a passive verb. We have defined a passive verb as a detransitivized verb that retains the idea of agency, whether or not it is expressed; furthermore, we have defined an agent to be an oblique nominal occurring with a passive verb that would be the subject if the sentence were rewritten in the active voice. Both of these points require further elucidation, especially in light of the peculiarities of ancient Greek, so that relatively consistent guidelines for the identification of PACs may be established.

For the purposes of this study, identifying passive verbs is relatively straightforward. As I am using the term passive in a functional rather than a formal sense, it is generally immaterial whether the verb in question has a peculiarly passive form or one that can also be middle. When, as occasionally will be the case, the syncretism of middle and passive does seem to have affected agent construction (as with ὠφελέω), special mention will be made of the fact. For the most part, however, both morphologically distinct passives and those that share their morphology with middle verbs behave similarly as far as agent marking is concerned. The greatest practical problem with identifying passive verbs in Greek is that there are also a handful of active intransitive verbs that act as suppletive passives to transitive verbs of a different lexical root, e.g. ἀποθνήσκω : ἀποκτείνω or πάσχω : ποιέω. I have, on the whole, disregarded such passives in this study in order to simplify the number of variables that could potentially influence how the agent is marked. Nevertheless, the existence of such constructions as πίπτω ὑπό might well have influenced agent marking with formal passives, and so, where relevant, as in Chapter 5, they will be discussed.[40]

But it is not enough to check that the verb in an intransitive+ oblique construction can be transformed into a corresponding transitive in an active formulation of the sentence. For the oblique expression must also be assessed to ensure that it would be the subject of the corresponding active sentence.[41] One starting point is to determine whether or not the oblique noun (or a semantically similar one) can in fact occur as the subject of the transitive verb corresponding to the intransitive in question.[42] Although this test will not guarantee that the oblique is the agent, it is an easy way to eliminate many that cannot be. Consider:

(25) *Il.* 8.363   τειρόμενον σώεσκον ὑπ' Εὐρυσθῆος ἀέθλων
"I kept saving him when he was being worn down by the labors assigned by Eurystheus"

---

[40] In particular, Schwyzer believes that the adoption of ὑπό with the genitive as the primary PAC can ultimately be traced back to its use with intransitives like πίπτω, with which its meaning "under" fits more easily than with true passives: "Der Gebrauch von ὑπό, der bei eigentlichen Passiva trotz allem befremdet, wird jedoch sofort verständlich bei Verba wie πίπτειν 'fallen', (ἀπο)θνήσκειν 'sterben', (ἀπ)όλλυσθαι 'umkommen', die für die Übersetzungsprache oft eigentliche Passiva vertreten" (1943: 30).

[41] Luraghi defines the role of the agent in more semantic terms, referring to its prototypical features of animacy, volitionality, and control (1995, 2003: 30–1); such a definition would exclude e.g. κύματος in μεγάλου ὑπὸ κύματος ἀρθείς (*Od.* 5.393) from being considered an agent. But because κῦμα can occur as the subject of a verb (as in τοσσάκι μιν μέγα κῦμα διιπετέος ποταμοῖο | πλάζ' ὤμους καθύπερθεν *Il.* 21.268–9) and because this book is, essentially, a study of how Greek marks what would be the subject of an active verb when that verb is passive, I opt for a more syntactic definition of agent that allows such examples as *Od.* 5.393 to be counted as PACs.

[42] Ungrammatical use of a noun that cannot be agentive in a PAC can be exploited for humorous effect. Note from *The Wind in the Willows*: "Stories about . . . steamers that flung hard bottles – at least bottles were certainly flung, and *from* steamers, so presumably *by* them" (Grahame 1908: 25, italics his). To Rat, "steamers" are potential agents of flinging bottles; therefore, their occurrence in an oblique construction (after an ablatival preposition) is automatically interpreted as agentive, thus anthropomorphizing the steamers.

The noun ἄεθλος is not found as a verb subject in Homer. It is best therefore to regard ὑπό in this line as marking a role such as cause. But while this test is good at excluding expressions of cause, origin, and instrument, it is clearly necessary but not sufficient. Consider the false-positive reading it would give for this example:

(26) *Il.* 1.197–8   στῆ δ᾽ ὄπιθεν, ξανθῆς δὲ κόμης ἕλε Πηλεΐωνα
                        οἴῳ φαινομένη· τῶν δ᾽ ἄλλων οὔ τις ὁρᾶτο
                        "and she stood behind, and grabbed Peleus'
                        son by his yellow hair, appearing to him alone;
                        and none of the others saw her"

This would pass the preliminary test, as οἴῳ, referring to Achilles, could be the subject of a transitive φαίνω.[43] However, the sense of the passage is clearly not "made visible by Achilles alone," but rather "appearing[44] to Achilles alone." Achilles is not an agent, but rather fills some other semantic role, such as beneficiary. But if the reason that οἴῳ cannot be the agent has nothing to do with general syntactic restrictions on the noun in question or with its particular syntactic construction in the sentence,[45] it can only be the case that the semantic context is what rules it out as an agent. In particular, an agent should be the entity that performs or exercises control over the action of the verb.[46] Thus, in trying to identify agents, we are left with the following guideline: if an intransitive+oblique construction is to qualify as a PAC, then, first, the oblique nominal must be syntactically capable of serving as the subject of the corresponding transitive verb; second, that nominal must be the entity that performs the action of the verb.

Now this test would give a positive reading not only for Greek agentive expressions with ablatival prepositions like παρά[+G], but

---

[43] Compare *Od.* 18.67f. (subject = Odysseus): φαῖνε δὲ μηροὺς / καλούς τε μεγάλους τε.
[44] This could either be a reflexive middle "making herself visible" or an anticausative middle "made visible."
[45] It is generally agreed that the dative is one possible means of expressing the agent.
[46] Cf. Blake 1994: 69 and Luraghi 2003: 30. Luraghi also lists intentionality as a typical feature of the agent, but, as she notes, natural forces that control an action but do not have intentionality are still treated in Greek in the same way as animate agents (*ibid.* 33). One corollary of this is that, just like animate agents, they can serve as the subjects of transitive verbs. As they are also in such instances the entity that performs the action of the verb, they will be classified as agents here.

also for an English construction like:

(27)   *These gifts were sent from the king.*

Whether or not such an outcome would be considered a false positive depends on whether one takes a narrow or broad view of the agent. If, in the interests of establishing a one-to-one correspondence between sentences with active and passive verbs, the agent is defined narrowly, then one would want a further test to eliminate (27) from consideration. One could stipulate that a language must have only one single grammaticalized means of expressing the agent, the preposition *by* in the case of English. Such a position would better fit the theories of grammar that seek an almost mathematical description of language. However, because agent expressions change over time, it is probably better to follow a broader definition. If a language has a grammaticalized agent marker X at one period, then another grammaticalized agent marker Y at another period, it would follow from the narrow definition that in the intervening period, when X gave way to Y, there was no agent marker. A broad definition, however, would describe the intermediate period more satisfactorily not as a stage when there was no agent marker, but as one when the two agent markers X and Y were in competition with one another. Such will be the case with the post-Classical replacement of ὑπό$^{+G}$ by παρά$^{+G}$ as the leading agent marker of Greek. In line with this model, the Greek equivalents of such constructions as (27) will be treated in this work as PACs.

The pragmatics of PACs

The chief reasons why languages employ passive verbs may be determined from the effects that passivization has on the superficial structure of a sentence.[47] First, it demotes the agent such that it need no longer be expressed. Clearly, this function is pragmatically useful, for there will often be occasions either when the agent is unknown or when it is advantageous for the speaker to suppress the

---

[47] For other accounts of the pragmatic motivation for the passive, see Givón 1979: 185–206, especially 186, Siewierska 1984: 217–54, Desclés *et al.* 1985: 97–105, Klaiman 1991: 21, Dixon–Aikhenvald 2000: 7–8.

identity of the agent. But this function cannot account for the passive constructions of interest to us here: if the passive is being used to eliminate the need to express the agent, then it would be nonsensical to reintroduce the agent in an oblique construction. Rather, we must look to the patient, not the agent, in order to understand why PACs arise. Broadly speaking, there are three overlapping reasons why a speaker might want to promote the patient to become the subject of the verb. First, there are syntactic roles that only the subject of a verb can fulfill. For instance, if one wishes to conjoin the following two sentences into one, the use of the passive allows the speaker to forego repeating the first-person pronoun:[48]

(28) *I went to sleep. But a car alarm woke me up.* → *I went to sleep, but was woken up by a car alarm.*

Second, there are pragmatic conditions under which a patient would be a more appropriate verb subject than would the agent. Speakers tend to structure narratives from the standpoint or perspective of a particular entity, typically a person, but potentially also an inanimate object. Such an entity may be called the narrative theme of the passage.[49] The voice of the verb may then be manipulated by the speaker in order that the syntactic subject of the sentence may be the same as the pragmatic narrative theme as often as possible. For instance, Cicero, as shown by Risselada, chose the voice of the verb so as to have the verbal subject which brought about the most discourse cohesiveness. The fourth Verrine oration provides an example of this: *Segesta est oppidum peruetus in Sicilia, iudices, quod ab Aenea fugiente a Troia atque in haec loca veniente conditum esse demonstrant* (Cic. *Ver.* 4.72). As Risselada notes, "The introductory presentative main clause is followed by a relative clause, in which *quod*, as a relative pronoun, is cohesive with its antecedent and consequently chosen as

---

[48] See also the example from Palmer 1994 cited on p. 4. For accounts of the role of the passive in conjunction reduction and control structures (also known as equi-NP-deletion) see Klaiman 1991: 21, Van Valin 2001: 53–7. Latin also uses the passive to maintain the same grammatical subject from one clause to the next (Rosén 1999: 135).

[49] Another term commonly used to describe this entity is topic, largely in connection with Dik's Functional Grammar (1978: 19, 141–4). I have avoided this term to eliminate confusion due to its alternative use to refer to the initial constituent of a sentence. See Siewierska 1984: 219–20 for a comparison of the two definitions.

perspective of the accusative and infinitive clause *conditum esse*" (1991: 407). In other words, as Segesta is the narrative theme, it is more cohesive for it to be the subject of a passive *conditum esse*, than for Aeneas to have been the subject of an active *condidisse*. A third motivation for the passive is that, by shifting the emphasis from the agent to the patient, it underlines the state of the patient resulting from the action instead of the agent's own participation in the action.[50] This motivation follows naturally from the previous one. If the narrative theme shifts from being the agent to being the patient, thereby triggering the passive, so too the emphasis of the verb will shift in parallel from the action of the narrative theme as agent to the result of the action on the narrative theme as patient.

To what extent, then, do these reasons for promoting the patient account for the instances in Greek where passivization is accompanied by the expression of the agent? First, it is easy to find examples of PACs in Greek where the use of the passive has clearly been motivated by syntactic factors. Foremost among these are many of the PACs with participles. Consider the following sentence:

(29) Pl. *Ap.* 23c   ἐντεῦθεν οὖν οἱ ὑπ᾽ αὐτῶν ἐξεταζόμενοι ἐμοὶ
             ὀργίζονται
             "because of this, then, those who are
             questioned by them become angry at me"

The noun modified by a participle, in this case a notional ἄνθρωποι to be supplied from the definite article, stands in the same relation to the participle as the subject of a sentence does to a finite verb. It would not be possible for the participle here to occur in the active, because of the constraint that the noun it modifies must be, in effect, its subject. Another syntactic environment that can provide motivation for PACs is indirect discourse. As Greek can omit the subject of the subordinate clause if it is the same as that of the main clause, it is more succinct to use the passive if the patient of the verb of the subordinate clause is the same as the agent of the main clause:

---

[50] For this resultative or stative use of the passive, see Dixon–Aikhenvald 2000: 8.

(30) X. *An.* 1.3.10　ὅτι μέντοι ἀδικεῖσθαι νομίζει ὑφ' ἡμῶν οἶδα
"I know, however, that he thinks that he is
being wronged by us"

By using the passive, Xenophon avoids having to introduce an
additional pronoun to represent the patient of ἀδικεῖσθαι. Furthermore, he makes the arguments of the infinitive, otherwise both in
the accusative, rather clearer. In other constructions of this sort, it
may be practically obligatory to use the passive in order to disambiguate the grammatical relations:[51]

(31) Ar. *Nu.* 1340–1　δίκαιον καὶ καλὸν | τὸν πατέρα τύπτεσθ'
ἐστὶν ὑπὸ τῶν υἱέων
"it is right and fair for a father to be beaten
by his sons"

Without the passive, it would be far less clear that it is the sons
who are right to strike their fathers, and not vice versa.

It is but a short step from such syntactic considerations to passages illustrating a more pragmatic motivation for passivization:

(32) Hdt. 1.11.4　ὥρα ἀναγκαίην ἀληθέως προκειμένην (sc.
αἵρεσιν) ἢ τὸν δεσπότεα ἀπολλύναι ἢ αὐτὸν
ὑπ' ἄλλων ἀπόλλυσθαι
"he saw that an inescapable choice truly lay
before him: either he must kill his master, or
himself be killed by others"

Here too, the PAC occurs in indirect discourse. But, in this context,
a rephrasing in the active would be reasonably clear: ἢ ἄλλους
ἀπολλύναι ἑωυτόν. Despite the superficial acceptability of the
active, Herodotus chooses the passive, for reasons connected to
the pragmatics of the sentence. The passage describes Gyges, as he
considers the dilemma with which Candaules' wife has confronted
him. Gyges would therefore be considered the narrative theme: the
sentence is about Gyges, and it is written from his perspective.
Consequently, Herodotus phrases the sentence so as to maintain
Gyges as the subject of all the verbs.

---

[51] Rosén notes that Latin also uses PACs to disambiguate grammatical relations in indirect
discourse (1999: 126, 129).

Setting aside passages like (29), where there is clear syntactic motivation for the passive, we may well ask whether the pragmatic status of the patient in Greek PACs is, as a rule, that of the narrative theme. While I have not conducted an exhaustive investigation of this question, a sampling of the evidence suggests that this is the case. In particular, the patient in PACs may frequently be considered the narrative theme on the grounds that it is the subject of the preceding clause. Consider, for instance, the first twenty PACs with ὑπό in Herodotus 1. Seven of these, primarily involving participles, could not have been easily rewritten into the active and may be excluded.[52] Of the remaining thirteen, the patient is the subject of the preceding verb in seven constructions, at 9.1, 11.4 (example (32) above), 30.1, 51.2, 67.2, 70.3, and 80.6. Here, clearly, the patient is the narrative theme. But even in other PACs, where there is no straightforward test to determine whether the patient is the narrative theme, a case-by-case examination of the sentences suggests that the patient is always considerably closer to that status than the agent.

There are six PACs that remain, then, which could have been rewritten fairly easily as actives, and in which the patient is not the same as the subject of the preceding clause. The first of these occurs at 14.3, in which the patient is the gold and silver dedicated by Gyges at Delphi, while the subject of the preceding verb was a throne dedicated by Midas:

(33) Hdt. 1.14.3   ὁ δὲ χρυσὸς οὗτος καὶ ὁ ἄργυρος, τὸν ὁ Γύγης
ἀνέθηκε, ὑπὸ Δελφῶν καλέεται Γυγάδας
"and this gold and silver, which Gyges
dedicated, is called the Gygadas by the
Delphians"

Despite the change in subject, Gyges' dedications *had* been the subject of the earlier part of the chapter before the brief digression to Midas; clearly, they are more of a narrative theme than

---

[52] Those with participles occur at 26.2, 31.3, 35.3, 40.1, 46.1, 63.2. The final PAC that could not be rewritten into the active is found at 38.1: ἀλλά μοι ὄψις ὀνείρου ἐν τῷ ὕπνῳ ἐπιστᾶσα ἔφη σε ὀλιγοχρόνιον ἔσεσθαι, ὑπὸ γὰρ αἰχμῆς σιδηρέης ἀπολέεσθαι. In indirect discourse, use of the active would be confusing, as, with σε and αἰχμήν as the two participants, it would be more natural to take σε as the agent.

the agent of the sentence, the Delphians themselves. Furthermore, even though the specific treasure referred to is different in the two sentences, both subjects do at least belong to the same class of item. It is far less of a shift of subject to proceed from one treasure to another, than from one treasure to the people who maintained a second treasure. We also see here the stative nuance of the passive. The action of Delphians in calling the treasure the Gygadas is not important; the resulting stative name of the treasure is.

The second of these PACs occurs in a genitive absolute:

(34) Hdt. I.19.I   τῷ δὲ δυωδεκάτῳ ἔτεϊ ληΐου ἐμπιπραμένου
ὑπὸ τῆς στρατιῆς συνηνείχθη τι τοιόνδε
γενέσθαι πρῆγμα
"and in the twelfth year [of the war], when the
crops were being burned by the army, the affair
about to be described happened to take place"

In the previous chapter, Herodotus had been describing the war that the Lydians had waged against the people of Miletus. At the end of the chapter, he writes from the perspective of the Ionians, and the Milesians are the subject of the final sentence. As the Lydian army, therefore, is less immediately a narrative theme than the effects of the war on the Milesians, Herodotus makes the Milesians' crops, not the invaders, the subject of the genitive absolute. What is important in this sentence is that the crops were burning, not that it was the Lydians in particular who had carried out the burning. Again, the passive carries a stative nuance.

Next, another participial construction:

(35) Hdt. I.59.I   τούτων δὴ ὦν τῶν ἐθνέων τὸ μὲν Ἀττικὸν
κατεχόμενόν τε καὶ διεσπασμένον ἐπυνθάνετο
ὁ Κροῖσος ὑπὸ Πεισιστράτου τοῦ
Ἱπποκράτεος
"Croesus found out that, of these two groups,
the Attic population was being oppressed and
divided by Pisistratus son of Hippocrates"

Herodotus has just been speaking of the two groups, Hellenes and Pelasgians, of which the Greeks consisted. In returning to Croesus' inquiries regarding the Greeks, using the Attic population as the subject of the participle in indirect discourse creates a closer tie with the preceding sentence than introducing Pisistratus as the subject would. In the context of a discussion about Greek ethnic history, Attica is more of a narrative theme than Pisistratus is. Once more, the stative nature of the passive can be seen, with the state of Attica more important than the actions of Pisistratus.

The next relevant PAC again occurs at the start of a paragraph:

(36) Hdt. 1.72.1   οἱ δὲ Καππαδόκαι ὑπὸ Ἑλλήνων Σύριοι
ὀνομάζονται
"and the Cappadocians are called Syrians by
the Greeks"

The previous chapter begins with Croesus' plan to invade Cappadocia. Herodotus then spends most of the chapter in a digression detailing an attempt to dissuade Croesus from attacking the Persians. In (36), he resumes his account of the invasion of Cappadocia by describing its location. The sentence with the PAC is little more than a parenthetical remark aimed at giving additional information about the country. Clearly, Cappadocia is the narrative theme here, not the Greeks: the purpose of this sentence is to list another name given to the Cappadocians, and not to emphasize the Greeks' act of naming them Syrians. Again, the state is more important than the action.

Fifth, we have the following construction:

(37) Hdt. 1.87.1   ἐνταῦθα λέγεται ὑπὸ Λυδῶν Κροῖσον
μαθόντα τὴν Κύρου μετάγνωσιν . . .
ἐπιβώσασθαι τὸν Ἀπόλλωνα
"then it is said by the Lydians that Croesus,
after learning of Cyrus' change of heart, called
upon Apollo"

Here the patient is not an object, but rather an entire clause. Still, the subject of that clause is Croesus, who has been the center of attention in the preceding lines: Herodotus is relating how Croesus was nearly burned to death by Cyrus. While the patient as a whole may not be the narrative theme, the subject of the patient-clause is. Additionally, while the stative nature of the passive verb may not be as readily apparent here as in the earlier examples, when the passage is contrasted with instances of the active λέγουσι (see below), it may still be detected.

In the final PAC of this group, the verb is a participle used periphrastically with ἦν that could thus have been easily rewritten as an active:

(38) Hdt. 1.98.1   αὐτίκα δὲ προβαλλομένων ὅντινα στήσωνται
                     βασιλέα, ὁ Δηιόκης ἦν πολλὸς ὑπὸ παντὸς
                     ἀνδρὸς καὶ προβαλλόμενος καὶ αἰνεόμενος
                     "and without delay they started to propose
                     whom they would make king; Deioces was
                     proposed and praised very much by everyone"

At first glance, the passive seems to be employed because the patient, the specific figure Deioces who has been under discussion for the past two chapters, is far more of a narrative theme than the agent, a generic "everyone." Still, it is worth noting that the sentence continues: ἐς ὃ τοῦτον καταινέουσι βασιλέα σφίσι εἶναι "until they consented that he should be their king." Deioces thus is demoted so as to become the object of this subsequent clause. The change of subject is made easier by the precedent of the genitive absolute and third plural subject in the preceding relative clause. In this light, the use of the passive must be due more to the stative aspect associated with the passive. What is important is the fact that Deioces is popular, not the action *per se* of all of those who are praising him. By contrast, the switch to the active in the ἐς ὃ clause underlines the fact that the *state* of Deioces' popularity led in the end to the *action* of others.

So far, the PACs under consideration have all come from Herodotus. The pragmatic status of the patient in other prose authors appears to have been similar. Consider the eighteen PACs with ὑπό in the first book of Xenophon's *Anabasis*. Nine of them involve participles that could not be easily rewritten as actives.[53] In a further seven, the patient is the subject of the preceding verb.[54] The last two resemble the examples from Herodotus, with patients that, though not the subjects of the preceding verbs, were at least to some extent parallel with those subjects:

[53] 1.10, 4.6, 6.6, 6.7, 6.8, 8.21, 9.4, 9.29, 10.3.   [54] 2.25, 3.10 (2×), 4.14, 5.4, 8.29, 9.7.

(39) X. *An.* 1.4.17   καὶ τῶν διαβαινόντων τὸν ποταμὸν οὐδεὶς
ἐβρέχθη ἀνωτέρω τῶν μαστῶν ὑπὸ τοῦ
ποταμοῦ
"and none of those crossing the river was
made wet by the river above the nipples"

(40) X. *An.* 1.9.28   ὥστε ἐγὼ μέν γε, ἐξ ὧν ἀκούω, οὐδένα
κρίνω ὑπὸ πλειόνων πεφιλῆσθαι οὔτε
Ἑλλήνων οὔτε βαρβάρων
"and so I, at least, from what I hear, think
that no one has been loved by more people,
either Greeks or barbarians"

In passage (39), the preceding sentence had had the entire army
as its subject; the patient of the subsequent PAC is "none of the
men crossing the river." While not quite the same as the previous
subject, it is still certainly close enough to be the narrative theme,
especially in comparison with the agent, the river. Example (40)
closes a section in praise of Cyrus. The patient of the PAC, "no one,"
is explicitly compared to and parallel with Cyrus, the narrative
theme of the preceding lines. In short, the patients of Xenophon's
PACs, like those in Herodotus, are typically either the subjects
of the preceding clause or comparable to those subjects in some
respect.

A similar situation obtains in Plato. Of the eleven PACs with
ὑπό in the *Apology*, two may be excluded as they are participial.[55]
In six, the patient is the subject of the preceding clause.[56] Three
PACs remain:

(41) Pl. *Ap.* 30c   ἐμὲ μὲν γὰρ οὐδὲν ἂν βλάψειεν οὔτε Μέλητος
οὔτε Ἄνυτος – οὐδὲ γὰρ ἂν δύναιτο – οὐ γὰρ
οἴομαι θεμιτὸν εἶναι ἀμείνονι ἀνδρὶ ὑπὸ
χείρονος βλάπτεσθαι
"for neither Meletus nor Anytus would harm
me – nor would they even be able to – for I do
not think that it is sanctioned by the gods for a
better man to be harmed by a worse one"

[55] 23c, 27c.   [56] 17a, 17b, 25d, 28d, 30e, 31a.

(42) Pl. *Ap.* 33c   ἐμοὶ δὲ τοῦτο, ὡς ἐγώ φημι, προστέτακται
ὑπὸ τοῦ θεοῦ πράττειν
"and, as I say, it has been assigned to me by
God to do this"

(43) Pl. *Ap.* 41d   οὐκ ἔστιν ἀνδρὶ ἀγαθῷ κακὸν οὐδὲν οὔτε
ζῶντι οὔτε τελευτήσαντι, οὐδὲ ἀμελεῖται ὑπὸ
θεῶν τὰ τούτου πράγματα
"no evil can come to a good man, neither
when he is alive, nor when he has died, nor are
his affairs neglected by the gods"

That the patient is the narrative theme in passages (42) and (43) is
easily established by the presence of the anaphoric pronoun οὗτος
somewhere in the structure of both patients. Example (41), on the
other hand, is rather different. In the clauses preceding the PAC,
the subject had been Socrates' accusers, while Socrates himself
was the object. In the PAC, however, the roles are reversed, with
Socrates, understood to be the "better man," as the subject, and the
"worse man," his accusers, as the demoted agent. Still, the ἀμείνων
ἀνήρ has some claim to be more of a narrative theme: Socrates is
generally going to speak from the perspective of the virtuous more
than from that of the base. Furthermore, the passage bears a strong
resemblance to (31). It could be that the boldness of the statement
prompts the passive in part to make the grammatical relations that
much clearer.[57]

Our next task is to determine the pragmatic status of the *agents* in
these constructions. In English, agents in PACs are generally new
information and, as such, critical to the meaning of the sentence.
Furthermore, they are typically lower on a scale of animacy hierarchy than the patient.[58] In other words, agents in English PACs
are typically nouns, rarely pronouns. Surprisingly, this does not

---

[57] Naturally, as the infinitive has a dative subject, an accusative object would not be ambiguous as it would be in (31).

[58] See Siewierska 1984: 222–3. The animacy hierarchy is discussed at greater length in
Chapter 3; see especially note 16. Essentially, the higher a participant is in the hierarchy, the likelier it is to be an agent. First-person pronouns are highest up, followed by
second-person pronouns, third-person pronouns, animate nouns, and finally inanimate
nouns.

hold true for all Greek authors. Let us start with the first twenty PACs with ὑπό in Herodotus 1, examining them on two grounds: whether the agent is higher on a scale of animacy hierarchy than the patient, and the extent to which the expression of the agent is necessary in order for the sentence to be understood.

Of the twenty PACs in question, in eight, the agent is lower in the animacy hierarchy than the patient, the relative positioning on the hierarchy typical of English PACs as well.[59] In such cases, the patient may be pronominal, the agent nominal, as in 35.3, or both may be nominal, with the patient higher in the hierarchy by virtue of being definite, in comparison with an indefinite agent, as in 70.3 or 72.1. Here we see the Greek passive working like the English passive: the narrative revolves naturally around the more animate entities, which are inherently likelier to be narrative themes and thus promoted to the subject slot when the agent is lower down on the scale. In a further three PACs, the agent and patient are approximately level in the animacy hierarchy.[60] In the remaining nine, however, the agent is higher in the scale than the patient – the type of situation in which English strongly prefers the active.[61] To highlight the significance of this phenomenon, it will be useful to introduce a second parameter, namely, whether the expression of the agent is essential for the understanding of the sentence. Now this is clearly not a criterion that can always be assigned with exactitude, but, even when doubtful cases are set aside, there remain PACs where the agent seems to be omissible, yet is expressed nonetheless. Returning to the nine PACs in which the agent is higher in the animacy hierarchy than the patient, we find three in which the agent is necessary for the sentence to be intelligible, for example:

(44) Hdt. 1.46.1   μετὰ δὲ ἡ Ἀστυάγεος τοῦ Κυαξάρεω ἡγεμονίη
καταιρεθεῖσα ὑπὸ Κύρου τοῦ Καμβύσεω . . .
πένθεος μὲν Κροῖσον ἀπέπαυσε
"afterwards, the toppling of Astyages the son
of Cyaxares by Cyrus the son of Cambyses
forced Croesus to lay aside his grief"

[59] 11.4, 31.3, 35.3, 38.1, 40.1, 70.3, 72.1, 98.1.
[60] 30.1, 67.2, 80.6.   [61] 9.1, 14.3, 19.1, 26.2, 46.1, 51.2, 59.1, 63.2, 87.1.

This passage is the first mention of Cyrus in Herodotus. Accordingly, he is new information and critical to the understanding of the clause. Similar examples may be found at 59.1 and 87.1. In other cases, the agent could be omitted with some loss of intelligibility, but the meaning of the sentence would, for the most part, still be clear. In 14.3 (example (33)), for instance, what is most important is that the treasure is called the Gygadas, not that that name was given to it by the Delphians: as the Delphians are already mentioned in the chapter, it would be natural to supply them as the agent were it not expressly stated. If an alternative name for the treasure were being discussed, then the agent would be critical here; but instead it merely serves to clarify that Gygadas is a name given by the Delphians. PACs in which the agent has similar pragmatic status include 9.1 and 51.2. Finally, in some PACs, the meaning of the sentence would lose virtually nothing if the agent were omitted. In 19.1 (example (34)), it is hard to see what is gained by the presence of the agent: in the context of the war, surely the simple phrase ληίου ἐμπιπραμένου would be understood as a reference to invading armies' practice of burning the crops. One may compare the PACs at 26.2 and 63.2.

In short, when Herodotus decides to express the agent of a passive verb instead of omitting it, that agent need not be critical to the understanding of the sentence, as is generally the case in English. The use of PACs in Herodotus also differs from English in that there is no tendency for agents in passive constructions to be lower than patients in the animacy hierarchy. Not limited to Herodotus, these differences may be found to some extent in Xenophon and Plato as well. The agents in Xenophon's PACs, for instance, do not appear on the whole to be either lower or higher on the animacy hierarchy than the patients. Of the eighteen PACs with ὑπό in *Anabasis* 1, seven have agents that are higher than, three have agents that are level with, and eight have agents that are lower than the patient in the scale.[62] In particular, four of the first group of PACs have first-person pronouns as the agents: quite rare with the English passive, except in contrastive constructions.[63] While the expression of the

[62] 3.10 (2×), 4.6, 6.7, 6.8, 9.4, 9.29; 2.25, 5.4, 8.29; 1.10, 4.14, 4.17, 6.6, 8.21, 9.7, 9.28, 10.3 respectively.

[63] See Siewierska 1984: 224.

agent could be construed as emphatic in these passages, there are other times when Greek authors used ὑπ' ἐμοῦ without any special weight.[64] Xenophon differs from Herodotus, however, in that his agent expressions are more frequently critical to an understanding of the sentence. Only in a handful of these PACs, like that at 1.4.17 (example (39)), does the agent seem omissible: it would be perfectly clear that it is the river that is getting the men wet without the introduction of ὑπὸ τοῦ ποταμοῦ considering that the subject of the sentence was τῶν διαβαινόντων τὸν ποταμὸν οὐδείς. The only other PACs in *Anabasis* 1 in which the agent might be considered omissible are those at 8.21, 9.29, and, possibly, the second of the two PACs in 3.10. This difference between Xenophon and Herodotus may perhaps be explained with reference to the style of the respective authors: the use of apparently otiose agent expressions in Herodotus might be a sign of a style that allows rather looser constructions. In Plato's *Apology*, the agents in the PACs again resemble those of Herodotus more than they do the prototypical English examples. Of the eleven PACs with ὑπό, six have agents that are higher on the animacy hierarchy than the patient of the construction.[65] Furthermore, in four instances, the agent seems omissible (17b, 23c (example (29)), 27c, 28d). The first two of these in particular are good examples of PACs whose pragmatics are quite the opposite of the typical English PAC, with pronominal agents that could be easily supplied from context:

(45) Pl. *Ap.* 17b   τὸ γὰρ μὴ αἰσχυνθῆναι ὅτι αὐτίκα ὑπ' ἐμοῦ
           ἐξελεγχθήσονται ἔργῳ, ἐπειδὰν μηδ'
           ὁπωστιοῦν φαίνωμαι δεινὸς λέγειν, τοῦτό μοι
           ἔδοξεν αὐτῶν ἀναισχυντότατον εἶναι
           "for the fact that they were not ashamed that
           they will immediately be refuted by me in the
           course of my speech when it will be apparent

---

[64] This seems particularly common in the orators; the collocation ὑπ' ἐμοῦ occurs in Lysias 10×, in Demosthenes 34×, but in Plato, in which first-person pronouns should also be frequent, only 27×. Of the examples in Plato, three come from the *Apology* and seven from the *Epistles*, so its occurrence in actual dialogue is even rarer than the simple figures indicate. It is difficult to gauge precisely how much weight should be attributed to the expression of the agent in many cases, but it is at any rate not contrastive in Lys. 3.27, D. 5.4, or Pl. *Phdr.* 243d, to pick one example from each author.

[65] 17a, 17b, 23c, 25d, 33c, 41d.

31

that I am in no way clever at speaking – this
seemed to me to be their most shameless
statement"

Clearly, in all three of these authors, the passive occurs in pragmatic contexts that differ from those in which the English passive is found.[66] Before seeking to explain this, however, it will be instructive to look at the passive constructions in Aristophanes, for the pragmatics of these PACs are far closer to those of the English construction.[67]

There are twelve PACs with ὑπό in the *Clouds*. Only in two of these is the agent higher than the patient in the animacy hierarchy (213 and 624–5). Additionally, the agent is critical to the sense of the clause in every one of the twelve. Typical is the following PAC:

(46) Ar. *Nu.* 169–70 πρῴην δέ γε γνώμην μεγάλην ἀφῃρέθη
ὑπ' ἀσκαλαβώτου
"just now he was robbed of a great idea by
a lizard"

The patient, Socrates, is clearly the narrative theme and higher on the animacy hierarchy than the agent, a lizard. Furthermore, the agent is new information, important for the understanding of the sentence. This is precisely the sort of PAC most common in English: *He was seen by a lizard* sounds far more natural than *A lizard was seen by him*. The PACs in Aristophanes, then, occur in environments far closer to those of English PACs than those of the PACs found in Greek prose of the period.

Leaving aside the data from Aristophanes for now, let us first consider why the passive constructions of the prose authors differ from those found in English. First, why did the Greek prose writers

---

[66] As far as the pragmatic status of the agent is concerned, the Latin passive seems to parallel English more closely than Greek, insofar as Latin authors "exhibit agent expressions in passive sentences as antithetic agents in focus" (Rosén 1999: 133–4).

[67] The passive in the more interactional passages in Plato may also, like the Aristophanic passive, be closer to the English construction. Of the ten PACs with ὑπό in *Republic* 1, five have patients that are higher in the animacy hierarchy (329b, 336b, 336d, 336e, 342d); this is true of only two agents (337e, 340a). Similarly, only once does the agent seem omissible (329b).

not avoid agents that were higher on the animacy hierarchy than the patient, a rare state of affairs in English? Since Greek shows no preference one way or the other, whereas English does, it will be easiest to approach this question from the standpoint of English. To a large extent, this difference stems more from a superficial distinction in the way the two languages treat inanimate nouns than from an underlying dichotomy in the use of the passive. For many of the constructions in English that are analyzed as PACs would not be in Greek because the use of *by* with the passive extends to inanimate participants that would be marked in Greek not by ὑπό but by the dative of instrument or other constructions like διά$^{+G}$. The final phrase in a sentence like *Many people were driven from their homes by the war* would most likely translate into Greek not as ὑπὸ τοῦ πολέμου but as τῷ πολέμῳ. Here are some parallels:

(47) X. *HG* 4.4.19   ἡδομένους δὲ τῷ πολέμῳ
"and delighted by the war"

(48) X. *Cyr.* 3.1.11   ἢ πολέμῳ κρατηθεὶς ἢ καὶ ἄλλον τινὰ
τρόπον δουλωθείς
"either conquered by war or enslaved in
some other way"

(49) Th. 1.2.6   ἐκ γὰρ τῆς ἄλλης Ἑλλάδος οἱ πολέμῳ ἢ
στάσει ἐκπίπτοντες
"for those who were driven out of the rest
of Greece by war or civil strife"

(50) Th. 1.81.6   ὥσπερ ἀπείρους καταπλαγῆναι τῷ
πολέμῳ
"to be terrified by war as if inexperienced
in it"

In contrast, ὑπὸ (τοῦ) πολέμου only occurs once in Xenophon, and not at all in Thucydides. This difference aside, if Greek prose rather frequently demotes high-animacy agents by using the passive, then maintaining the narrative theme as subject must be more important to these authors than structuring sentences from the standpoint of the most animate participant. Such a desire for textual cohesion

33

is perhaps to be expected of a language that so regularly avoids asyndeton. Second, why does English show a tendency for agents to be new information, while the Greek prose writers did not feel this constraint? The two languages must differ here because of the relatively rigid word order of English. In accounting for the greater frequency of the passive in English than in German and the Slavic languages, Siewierska observes that these latter languages dispose of another important means of topicalizing patients that is not available in English: object–verb–subject (OVS) word order (1984: 224–7). Such is the case in Greek as well, where OSV and OVS are both possible:

(51) Hdt. 1.5.3   ταῦτα μέν νυν Πέρσαι τε καὶ Φοίνικες λέγουσι
"now this is what the Persians and Phoenicians say"

(52) Hdt. 1.22.1   ταῦτα δὲ ἐποίεέ τε καὶ προηγόρευε
Θρασύβουλος
"and Thrasybulus did this and ordered it publicly"

Whereas English must generally rely on the passive in order to front the patient to the initial slot, Greek can use either the passive or the active. As passive constructions downgrade the importance of the agent, one would expect Greek to use the active when the agent was new information.

In order to test this expectation, we must find out what circumstances favored the use of the active or passive. To do this, it is best to eliminate as many other variables as possible. One way of doing so is to consider all the expressions in Herodotus similar to 1.5.3 (example (51)), in which various nationalities are depicted as saying something. When does Herodotus write λέγουσι, when λέγεται ὑπό? In Book 1, there are thirty-four instances of λέγουσι, fourteen of λέγεται without an agent expression, and only four of λέγεται with an agent (three times with ὑπό, once with πρός[+G]). Although there is some overlap in the use of the two voices, several important environments can be detected in which λέγεται ὑπό does not appear. The four instances where λέγεται occurs in a PAC are as follows:

(53) Hdt. 1.47.2   ὅ τι μέν νυν τὰ λοιπὰ τῶν χρηστηρίων
ἐθέσπισε, οὐ λέγεται πρὸς οὐδαμῶν
"what the rest of the oracles foretold is not
said by anyone"

(54) Hdt. 1.87.1   ἐνθαῦτα λέγεται ὑπὸ Λυδῶν Κροῖσον ...
ἐπιβώσασθαι τὸν Ἀπόλλωνα
"then it is said by the Lydians that Croesus
called upon Apollo"

(55) Hdt. 1.183.3   ἐγὼ μέν μιν οὐκ εἶδον, τὰ δὲ λέγεται ὑπὸ
Χαλδαίων, ταῦτα λέγω
"I myself did not see it, but I shall report
what is said by the Chaldaeans"

(56) Hdt. 1.191.6   ὑπὸ δὲ μεγάθεος τῆς πόλιος, ὡς λέγεται ὑπὸ
τῶν ταύτῃ οἰκουμένων, ... τοὺς τὸ μέσον
οἰκέοντας τῶν Βαβυλωνίων οὐ μανθάνειν
ἑαλωκότας
"and, because of the size of the city (as is
said by those who live there) those of the
Babylonians who lived in the center of the
city did not learn that it had been captured"

To some extent these may be contrasted with the thirty-four examples of λέγουσι. Consider the first seven of this latter group: they
all occur in the first five chapters, when Herodotus is recounting the
different versions of how animosity arose between the Greeks and
Persians. In 1.1.3, the Greeks say one thing, in 1.2.1, the Persians
say another; they continue to tell their side in 1.3.2 and 1.4.3,
concluding with a final λέγουσι in 1.5.1. Then the Phoenicians
are introduced, and in 1.5.2 give their account. Finally, in 1.5.3,
Herodotus ends the passage with example (51) above. The next
cluster of uses of λέγουσι is similar in the emphasis placed on
who is saying what. At 1.21.1, it is the Milesians in particular to
whom Herodotus in conclusion ascribes the material of 1.20: it is
specifically cited as an addition of the Milesians to an account of
the Delphians in the earlier chapter. Then, in 1.23.1, Herodotus
attributes the Corinthians with telling the story of Arion and the
dolphin. Importantly, the Lesbians are said to agree with them. In all
of these passages, Herodotus has some particular reason for stating

the group of speakers responsible for a version of a story. When he uses the passive, however, the specific source of that which is said is less important, as there is no contrast between different agents. In (53), the specific agent is clearly not important, as it is the indefinite pronoun οὐδαμῶν. Then, in (54), the Lydians' account is given; it is not contrasted with another account, and there are no active instances of λέγουσι in the telling of this episode, the near-death of Croesus. The passive λέγεται does occur, however, without an agent at 1.91.1, though we may presume that ὑπὸ Λυδῶν could be understood. In this episode, Herodotus does not record contrasting stories; hence, the passive is preferred. Finally, the PAC with λέγεται in example (56) also suggests that the distinction between the active and passive phrasing may turn on the importance of the agent's being responsible for the action of the verb. The syntactic context of the construction, occurrence in a ὡς-clause, is paralleled by six other passages in Book 1 with the active. In all these other constructions, the agent is somehow emphatic: in 1.65.4, the Lacedaemonian's view is contrasted with others'; in 1.95.1, Herodotus bases his account on what the Persians say, though he is familiar with three more versions of the story; in 1.105.3 and 1.174.5, the agent is underlined by the intensive αὐτοί; finally, in 1.181.5 and 1.182.2, Herodotus is comparing the stories, which he explicitly says he does not believe, told by both Chaldaeans and Egyptians about their gods' visiting local women. But in (56), the one example of ὡς λέγεται ὑπό, there is no such emphasis laid on the agent: it comes in the middle of a long digression on Babylon, with no indication of contrary sources offering differing accounts.

Although there thus appears to be some difference between the use of λέγουσι and that of λέγεται, the data do not allow too neat a dichotomy. In the PAC with λέγεται in example (55), for instance, the passive follows quite soon after two examples of the active in 1.181.5 (agent: Chaldeans) and 1.182.2 (agent: Egyptians). Clearly, Herodotus has been underlining the sources for each strand of his history. Another motivation may have triggered the passive here. Had Herodotus written τὰ δὲ λέγουσι Χαλδαῖοι, ταῦτα λέγω, he would have equated his own act of λέγειν too closely with that of the Chaldaeans.[68] As it stands, however, the emphasis of the relative clause is on identifying the ταῦτα which Herodotus is reporting with that which is said or current among the Chaldaeans.

In summary, we have seen that, in Greek prose, the passive may be used irrespective of the relative placement of the agent and patient in the animacy hierarchy. Furthermore, there is no strong tendency for the agent to be new information, as is the case in English. Instead, the use of the passive seems to be triggered by far more subjective criteria, in particular a tendency to structure sentences around the standpoint of a narrative theme. If this narrative theme is the patient of a particular verbal action, then the passive may be employed to express the effect of the action on the patient, thereby downplaying the action of the verb and the agent's participation therein. Further support for this explanation arises when the difference between prose and Aristophanes is considered. As mentioned above, the agent in Aristophanic PACs is typically both lower in the animacy hierarchy than the patient and critical to an understanding of the clause. Thus, as in English, passive verbs play a role that complements active verbs from the standpoint of the pragmatic status of the participants. Contrast Greek prose, in which the passive overlaps with the active in this respect. Aristophanes' passive may therefore be considered more natural than that of Greek prose: it occupies a different niche from the active, and is not just a *Luxus der Sprache*. In prose, on the other hand, the author may manipulate the parameter of voice in order to achieve subtle stylistic effects. This difference accords well with the expectation that the genre of comedy would approach the spoken language more closely than would formal prose.

If the typical Greek prose PAC with ὑπό somehow emphasizes the result of the action on the patient, it will next be important

---

[68] One may compare here Panhuis's explanation for the passive in Cicero *Rosc. Am.* 15 *nam patrimonium domestici praedones vi ereptum possident, fama et vita innocentis ab hospitibus amicisque paternis defenditur*: "Two active sentences . . . would create a parallelism, which suggests a similarity in content – which is not what the speaker intends to say" (1984: 239).

to consider the pragmatic status of the participants in PACs with the dative of agent, for in such cases, the verb stands in the prototypically stative aspect, namely, the perfect. Extensive discussion of this construction is reserved for Chapter 3, but one key point should be mentioned here: the dative of agent is used primarily with pronouns, that is, with agents that are high on the animacy hierarchy. These PACs thus fall in line with the typical prose construction, as against that of Aristophanes. Importantly, this also seems true of the PACs with the dative of agent even in Aristophanes. All three datives of agent in the *Clouds* are pronouns:

(57) Ar. *Nu.* 773–4   οἴμ', ὡς ἥδομαι
ὅτι πεντετάλαντος διαγέγραπταί μοι
δίκη.
"Oh, how happy I am that a five-talent
lawsuit has been canceled by me!"

(58) *ibid.* 1276–8   Στρ: τὸν ἐγκέφαλον ὥσπερ σεσεῖσθαί μοι
δοκεῖς.
Αμ: σὺ δὲ νὴ τὸν Ἑρμῆν προσκεκλῆσεσθαί
γέ μοι,
εἰ μὴ 'ποδώσεις τἀργύριον.
"Strepsiades: It seems to me that your
brain's shaken up.
Amynias: And [it seems to me], by Hermes,
that you'll be summoned to court by me if
you don't pay back the money."

(59) *ibid.* 1510–11   ἡγεῖσθ' ἔξω· κεχόρευται γὰρ
μετρίως τό γε τήμερον ἡμῖν.
"Lead the way out: for today at least it has
been danced by us [i.e., we have danced]
enough."

In all of these, Aristophanes' use of the dative of agent occurs in pragmatic contexts that are in two respects comparable to those where ὑπό is found in the prose writers: the agent is higher in the animacy hierarchy than the patient, and it is omissible. Furthermore, in the first of the three, the passive is clearly not being used to allow the agent of one clause to be the subject of a subsequent clause, for the agent is demoted despite being the same as that of the verb that introduces the subordinate clause.

That the passive should be used in two different sets of pragmatic environments in Aristophanes has a parallel in the Mayan language K'iche'.[69] K'iche' has two different passive formations, which Campbell calls "simple" and "completive."[70] The simple passive is reminiscent of the English passive and the Aristophanic constructions with ὑπό, with strong restrictions against high-animacy agents (first- and second-person agents may not co-occur with this passive) and no particular stative nuance.[71] The completive passive, on the other hand, is more like the passive constructions in Greek prose with ὑπό, as well as the dative of agent constructions even in Aristophanes, as it is perfectly compatible with first- and second-person agents and also gives a stative nuance to the verb. The parallel is imperfect insofar as the two passives in K'iche' are signaled by morphologically distinct verb forms; conversely, there is no difference in agent marking, with agents of both passives marked by the relational noun *-uma:l* "by." Nevertheless, the resemblance between the two pragmatically distinct uses of the passive found in ancient Greek and the two passives of K'iche' can be regarded as a typological parallel.

A question related to these pragmatic issues is that of the frequency of PACs.[72] Are they more common in particular genres? The following table sets out the number of PACs per thousand words in selected texts. I have included only PACs with prepositions marking the agent; the frequency of the dative of agent will be discussed in Chapter 3. In listing the number of prepositional

---

[69] The following information about K'iche' is taken from Campbell 2000.

[70] According to Campbell, the latter is called "inchoative-stative" by Mondloch.

[71] Passage (46) provides a representative example of the lack of stative nuance in Aristophanes' constructions with ὑπό. The lizard's action is more important than Socrates' resulting state, as can be seen from the use of the temporal adverb πρῴην specifying the time of the action. This may be contrasted with examples (33) through (38) from Herodotus, which all show verbs with a stative aspect.

[72] Further information about the frequency of PACs as well as of passives generally may be found in Schwyzer 1943: 52–72. Broadly speaking, Schwyzer describes a rise in the frequency both of the passive and of the expression of the agent with the passive, with the latter completely absent in Hesiod and extremely rare in lyric poetry before the fifth century.

PACs, I have also provided subtotals of PACs marked by ὑπό[+G] followed by those marked by other prepositions:[73]

Text	# PACs (ὑπό[+G] + Other)	# Words[a]	PACs / 1,000 Words
Lysias[b]	129 (127 + 2)	32,104	4.02
Hippocrates VM, Aër., Morb.Sacr.	54 (54 + 0)	17,645	3.06
Herodotus 1	60 (43 + 17)	29,065	2.06
Plato Euthyphro, Apology, Crito, Symposium	59 (57 + 2)	35,520	1.66
Xenophon Anabasis 1–3	35 (29 + 6)	23,013	1.52
Thucydides 6–7	49 (45 + 4)	34,902	1.40
Demosthenes 4, 9, 21, 27, 28	40 (33 + 7)	29,473	1.36
Aristophanes Acharnians, Clouds, Birds	34 (32 + 2)	27,617	1.23
Aeschylus Oresteia, Prometheus Bound	28 (8 + 20)	24,858	1.13
Sophocles Trachiniae, Philoctetes, OC	22 (9 + 13)	26,511	0.83
Euripides Alcestis, Medea, IT	16 (1 + 15)	23,048	0.69
Homer (entire)	25 (8 + 17)	199,039	0.13

[a] Most of the word-count data come from the Greek Vocabulary Tool available at http://perseus.csad.ox.ac.uk/cgi-bin/vocab?lang = greek. For authors not included there, word counts are based on the TLG text.
[b] The figure for PACs with ὑπό[+G] includes all the genuine speeches of Lysias; that for other prepositions only includes PACs found in Lys. 1, 3, 4, 5, 7, 14, 31, 32.

[73] To avoid clutter, I have not included authors of the Hellenistic era or later. But note the following frequencies: Euclid 1.1–25 (including the preliminary Horoi etc.): 3.26; Apollonius of Rhodes Argonautica 1, 3: 0.32; Quintus of Smyrna Posthomerica 1–2: 0.29; Nonnus Dionysiaca 1–6: 0.11. None of these figures are surprising: we expect the frequency in the geometer Euclid to resemble that in the similarly technical works of the Hippocratic corpus. As for the late epic poets, they cluster together with Homer, as expected, at the bottom of the list. For more on the figures for late epic, see Chapter 2.

Several observations may be made on the basis of this table. First, PACs are more common in prose than in poetry: the top seven authors are all prose, followed by Aristophanes, also in other respects intermediate between prose and poetry, and finally by the three tragedians and Homer. Second, PACs occur by far the least frequently in Homer – 5.3 times less frequently than in Euripides, who is the next most sparing in his use of the construction. They are the most common in Lysias, but the figure of 4.02 per thousand words, though unusually high, should not be exaggerated: that is still only 5.8 times as frequent as in Euripides. In other words, Euripides' use of the construction is, proportionally, only slightly closer to Homer than to Lysias. Third, aside from the endpoints, the figures are all rather close to one another: even though the poets do use fewer PACs than the prose writers, there is a fairly smooth continuum in the frequency of the construction between, say, Thucydides and Aeschylus. Similarly, one cannot say that this was a construction favored by a particular genre, like history or oratory.[74] Far more striking is the tragedians' infrequent use of ὑπό[+G] as opposed to the other prepositions; that will be discussed in Chapter 5.

But while the overall figures for PAC frequency, taken author by author, do not suggest that any one prose genre particularly favors the construction, a slightly clearer picture arises upon examination of the distribution of PACs within different works of an individual author. Xenophon uses the construction at a rate that is close to the mean for prose authors. Yet he does not use it uniformly within a given work. It is particularly instructive to examine the distribution of PACs in the first three books of the *Hellenica*, in which PACs are significantly more common in passages of direct speech than in those of narrative. In these books, there are twenty-three PACs in direct speech out of fifty-nine total PACs; thus, 39 per cent of

---

[74] Still, it is probably significant that the works attributed to Hippocrates rank relatively high on the list. Taken together with the figures for Euclid (see note[a] to the Table), the high frequency of PACs in these works suggests that technical writers were more partial to the passive construction. As for oratory, forensic speeches might have used the construction more than deliberative speeches. In Demosthenes, the PAC frequency in the two deliberative speeches (*Philippics* 1 and 3) is 1.18, as against 1.42 in the three forensic speeches (*Against Midias* and *Against Aphobus* 1 and 2). If this were so, it would partially explain the high frequency found in Lysias. Further research into the use of the passive by other orators is needed in order to clarify this issue.

the PACs occur in direct speech. Only 22 per cent of these books, however, consists of direct speech.[75] In other words, PACs occur 2.3 times more frequently in direct speech than in narrative.[76]

To explain why PACs might be more common in direct speech, we may turn to another observation. In the data given above, I have counted as PACs all distinct examples of ὑπό used to mark the agent of a passive verb. Such figures, however, obscure the fact that, four times in these books, doubled occurrences of ὑπό are found, indicating two different agents of the same verb. Moreover, all four of these constructions occur in passages of direct speech, for example:[77]

(60) X. *HG* 1.7.19   ἐν οἷς οὔθ' ὑπ' ἐμοῦ οὔθ' ὑπ' ἄλλου οὐδενὸς
 ἔστιν ἐξαπατηθῆναι ὑμᾶς
 "in which it is impossible for you to be
 deceived either by me or by anyone else"

(61) X. *HG* 2.3.32   σὺ δὲ διὰ τὸ εὐμετάβολος εἶναι πλείστοις
 μὲν μεταίτιος εἶ ἐξ ὀλιγαρχίας ὑπὸ τοῦ
 δήμου ἀπολωλέναι, πλείστοις δ' ἐκ
 δημοκρατίας ὑπὸ τῶν βελτιόνων
 "but you, because you changed sides so
 readily, are partly to blame both for the
 killing of many of the oligarchs by the
 people and for the killing of many of the
 democrats by the aristocrats"

In (60), doubled ὑπό is paired with doubled οὔτε; in (61), doubled ὑπό is found in a balanced antithesis. That examples of ὑπό marking the agent occur clustered in passages where the speaker is also using anaphora or antithesis suggests that a speaker might well employ the construction to achieve a certain rhetorical effect of emphasis. This possibility could in turn explain the overall frequency of the construction in direct speech as against narrative.

---

[75] There are approximately 27.5 Loeb pages of direct speech out of 126.5 pages total.
[76] In direct speech, there are about 0.84 PACs per page, while in narrative, only 0.36.
[77] The other two examples occur at 2.3.34 and 3.5.13.

2

AGENT CONSTRUCTIONS IN HOMER

The analysis of PACs in Homer will be quite different from that of those found in later authors. To begin with, there are very few PACs in the Homeric corpus, as seen in the table on p. 40. The independent passive voice was a relatively recent development at that time, and Homer preferred to keep the verb voice in the active, even at the expense of having to change the sentence subject frequently.[1] Additionally, the metrical, formulaic nature of the oral poetry skews the data: the apparent frequency of some PACs might simply result from their metrical utility or occurrence in a formula. Nevertheless, some agent markers can be singled out which seem to have been perceived as characteristic of Homer, to judge from their use in the late epic poets who imitated Homer's language.

The PACs in Homer can, for convenience's sake, be split into two groups: those in which the agent is marked solely by a case, and those in which a preposition marks the agent. Although the former category is said by some to include a genitive of agent,[2] it is argued here that the only case in Homer that by itself can mark the agent is the dative. The PACs with prepositions as agent markers themselves break down into two types. On the one hand, the peculiarly Greek expression of agency with ὑπό is already present, with the preposition governing both genitive and dative objects; on the other, one also finds a host of ablatival prepositions, most commonly ἐκ, but also ἀπό, παρά, πρός, and the adverbial ending -θεν.

---

[1] Note Chantraine 1963: 358–9 on *Il*. 18.32–4. Compare also Jankuhn's discussion of "parataktische Agensangabe" (1969: 109).

[2] The sole instance cited is *Od*. 8.499, which will be seen to be even less convincing a PAC than some of the possessive genitives to be discussed on pp. 48–9.

Problematic cases

As discussed in Chapter 1, there are no objective criteria by which PACs may be definitively identified.[3] This state of affairs results from the difficulty of determining whether a particular intransitive verb is in fact a simple detransitivization of the corresponding transitive and from the impossibility of knowing whether a particular oblique nominal would necessarily be the subject of the sentence if the verb were in the active voice. In connection with Homer, I will discuss four problematic contexts in which the identification of PACs is especially difficult. These grey areas are the greyest in Homer, as the passive is particularly ill-defined at this time, thus increasing the potential for ambiguous interpretation. First, with the verb πείθω and its intransitive counterpart πείθομαι, it is possible that the intransitive verb is semantically different enough from a simple passivization of the transitive that constructions of πείθομαι with an oblique nominal cannot be considered to be PACs.[4] Similarly, with intransitive verbs of emotion such as χολόομαι, it is unclear whether one should regard them synchronically as detransitivized counterparts of transitive verbs (χολόω), when, diachronically, they are the primary forms while the corresponding transitive verbs are secondary causative formations. A third problem is the genitive of agent. Though such genitives are generally considered to be a marginal usage at best, there are in fact many possessive genitives that could be construed as agentive without grossly misrepresenting the semantics of the sentence. Finally, the -ην aorist of δάμνημι needs to be recognized as a passive, not a mere intransitive, as it has been called till now.

---

[3] In his article on agentivity in Homer, De La Villa for the most part uses a broader definition of agent that will be discussed below (see pp. 61–2), but it is narrower in that he excludes agents marked by ablatival prepositions such as ἐκ or πρός (1998: 153). He justifies this exclusion by saying that nouns marked by these prepositions can always be described as having a role other than that of agent. I do not believe this to be the case, cf. my note 52, below.

[4] In this connection, note Matthews on English passives: "the most likely meaning of *She is engaged* does not match that of *He engaged her*, and that of *He was worried* corresponds to only one sense of *It worried him*. In these and many other cases the change of form produces semantic changes that are partly unpredictable" (1981: 15). We must watch out for this in Greek as well.

The first difficulty of interpretation to consider, whether the use of πείθομαι with a dative should be labeled as a PAC, may be illustrated by the two passages below:

(1) *Il.* 1.78–9 ἦ γὰρ ὀΐομαι ἄνδρα χολωσέμεν, ὃ μέγα πάντων
Ἀργείων κρατέει καί οἱ πείθονται Ἀχαιοί
"for indeed I think that I shall anger a man who
wields great power over all the Argives, and the
Achaeans heed him"

(2) *Il.* 1.132 ἐπεὶ οὐ παρελεύσεαι οὐδέ με πείσεις
"since you will not get the better of me nor will
you persuade me"

Traditionally, πείθονται in example (1) is parsed as a middle verb, meaning "obey, heed" and taking a dative object, and πείσεις in (2) as an active verb, meaning "persuade" and taking an accusative object. But note that (1) could be viewed as a passive transformation of Ἀγαμέμνων πείθει Ἀχαιούς, with πείθω detransitivized to πείθομαι and Ἀγαμέμνων demoted to the dative οἱ. The chief obstacle to this interpretation is the requirement that a passive construction be semantically equivalent to the corresponding active construction. If one uses the traditional glosses of "obey" and "persuade" to translate πείθομαι and πείθω, then one could not transform (1) into an active sentence without changing the semantics: one can obey a leader without being persuaded by him. This conclusion, however, might merely be a fallacy of translation. Perhaps there is a semantic field that includes both "be persuaded" and "obey," such as "be put under someone's sway." If that is the case, then it becomes that much more reasonable to consider this a PAC. Still, there is another reason here to retain the conventional wisdom. The compound verb ἐπιπείθομαι, only found in the middle in Homer, governs, like πείθομαι, a dative object. If one interprets the construction with πείθομαι as a passive transformation of πείθω with a dative of agent, then one must either claim that ἐπιπείθομαι is to be understood differently from the simplex (i.e., as a middle verb with a dative object rather than a PAC) or that it is, like πείθομαι, a passive, but of the unattested active

45

*ἐπιπείθω. The latter choice is clearly unattractive considering the rarity of verbs in Homer that are indisputably passive compared to those that must be considered to be middle. As for the former, it is true, to be sure, that the addition of an adverbial prefix can alter the syntactic constructions governed by a verb: ἐπιπέτομαι can occur with a dative object indicating the destination of the flight, whereas πέτομαι does not. Nevertheless, if both πείθομαι and ἐπιπείθομαι with a dative object have approximately the same meaning, then it seems best to view the two constructions as being parallel.

A similar problem in identifying PACs is occasioned by a group of middle verbs, such as κήδομαι and χολόομαι, which denote emotional states and, like πείθομαι above, are traditionally described as middle verbs that take genitive or dative objects, e.g.:

(3) *Il.* 1.56   κήδετο γὰρ Δαναῶν
                  "for [Hera] cared for the Danaans"
(4) *Il.* 1.9–10   ὁ γὰρ βασιλῆϊ χολωθεὶς
                  νοῦσον ἀνὰ στρατὸν ὦρσε
                  "for he, enraged by the king, stirred up a plague
                  throughout the army"

Some of these verbs have active counterparts which are less frequent and generally taken to be secondary causative formations:

(5) *Il.* 5.404   ὃς τόξοισιν ἔκηδε θεούς
                  "who was troubling the gods with his bow"
(6) *Il.* 18.111   ὡς ἐμὲ νῦν ἐχόλωσεν ἄναξ ἀνδρῶν Ἀγαμέμνων
                  "so Agamemnon, lord of men, has angered me
                  now"

As in the previous section, it is not immediately clear whether or not the middle examples of (3) and (4) can be understood as passive transformations of the active (5) and (6), taking the genitive and dative objects as agents. Again, the transformation works well from a formal standpoint, especially between (4) and (6), in both of which Agamemnon is the agent of the anger expressed by the verb.[5]

But here too there are grounds for adhering to the traditional interpretation. Just as construing πείθομαι as a passive would force it to be taken separately from ἐπιπείθομαι, so too the reading of, say, χολόομαι as a passive is hampered by the presence of verbs like σκύζομαι, χώομαι, and ἐπιμέμφομαι. Such verbs lie in the same semantic sphere as χολόομαι and also occur with the dative, but they do not have an active counterpart of which they could be considered a transformation. If we take χολόομαι as a middle, we avoid separating it from these other verbs. Similarly, it is difficult to construe κήδομαι with the genitive as a passive with an agent, when there exist other *media tantum* verbs of grief which, though they take the genitive, cannot be transformed into a corresponding active: ἄχνυμαι, ὀδύρομαι, ὀλοφύρομαι. Furthermore, there is a typological argument against reading χολόομαι as a passive. Verbs of emotion, like χολόομαι, belong to a semantic field that is frequently found with middle marking in the world's languages.[6] It would therefore be economical to regard them as middle in Greek as well. Diachrony supports this view as well, as it is likely that the middle form was original, the active a secondary causative formation.[7]

But, in Homer at least, there is one case in which the passive might still be seen as the best reading of these verbs: in those forms with overt passive marking, e.g. χολωθείς. First, such passive forms contrast with aorist middles like χολωσάμενος (*Il.* 2.195). There is thus a morphological difference that supports the view that the -θη- forms are true passives. Second, the *media tantum* verbs of emotion that lack an active form (σκύζομαι, etc.) also lack forms with -θη-. Since forms like χολωθείς occur only in those

---

[5] One could argue that κήδομαι in (3) is semantically distinct from a passive significance of κήδω in (5), as the first is more "be worried" or "be concerned," while the second is more "harass." Still, one could also use the argument applied to πείθομαι (p. 45) here as well and say that the semantics of the Greek verb are broader than of either of the English equivalents.

[6] See Kemmer 1993: 130–4.

[7] Tucker supports Brugmann's theory that denominative -όω verbs like χολόω developed from adjectives in -ωτός, beginning with perfect middle participles on the model of the ὅσα ἀκίνητα καὶ κεκινημένα pattern (1990: 298).

verbs that also have an active, they may reasonably be regarded as detransitivized actives. Accordingly, in Homer, middle verbs of emotion, when found in ambiguous mediopassive forms, will be judged to be middle, but when marked with an overtly passive ending, to be passive.[8]

We turn now from ambiguities of the verb to those of the noun. In some cases, it is uncertain whether a genitive is to be understood as agentive or possessive.[9] Take the following example:

(7) *Il.* 1.5   Διὸς δ' ἐτελείετο βουλή

"And the plan of Zeus was being accomplished"

One could argue on formal grounds that (7) is a passive transformation of Ζεὺς δ' ἐτέλειε βουλήν, as Zeus is capable of being the subject of τελέω with a noun like βουλή as the object.[10] The line would then translate, "And the plan was being accomplished by Zeus." There is no grossly obvious semantic objection to this interpretation – Zeus was, after all, accomplishing a plan – but it is quite at odds with the traditional analysis of this clause: "And the plan of Zeus was being accomplished." Nevertheless, the reading as a genitive of possession is to be preferred on two counts.

First, one must consider that the Greek genitive resulted from a merger of the IE genitive and ablative. On the one hand, an ablative agent would be typologically sound, but there are no clear examples of ablatival agents in Homer that are not marked by a preposition like ἐκ or παρά. On the other, there are several unambiguous instances of Διός – Verb – Noun word order where the

---

[8] This special case, however, does apply only to Homer. In later Greek, *media tantum* verbs of emotion show an increasing tendency to replace aorist middles with aorist passives, though the middle remains the more common aorist (Kühner–Gerth 1898: 119). Verbs of emotion that have middle presents but passive aorists in post-Homeric Greek comprise three verbs that have only an aorist middle in Homer (ἄγαμαι, ἥδομαι, μαίνομαι (aorist found only in the compound ἐπεμήνατο)), one not attested in the aorist in Homer (ἄχθομαι), one which has an active in Homer (νεμεσάω), and four which do not occur at all in Homer (ἐνθυμέομαι, ἐπιμέλομαι, ὀργίζομαι, προθυμέομαι).

[9] The underlying source of confusion lies in the transitivity inherent in the genitive's important role of marking possession. Allen notes several examples of this, including: "In the Northeast Caucasian language Lakk, for instance, there is a system of ten 'grammatical' cases – and of these it is precisely the 'genitive' (or 'possessive') case that is used to express the subject of a transitive sentence" (1964: 340).

[10] Compare *Il.* 1.523 ἐμοὶ δέ κε ταῦτα μελήσεται, ὄφρα τελέσσω (subject = Zeus) and *Il.* 23.149 σὺ δέ οἱ νόον οὐκ ἐτέλεσσας.

genitive must be taken as possessive.¹¹ The genitive Διός in (7) thus naturally attaches itself to βουλή as a possessive genitive rather than a preposition-less ablative of agent. Second, the identity of the βουλή has not been specified in the previous lines; thus, a nearby genitive is contextually likely to indicate whose βουλή it is.

A similar obscurity is present whenever ὑπό occurs with both a genitive and a dative. It can be ambiguous whether ὑπό governs the genitive with an instrumental dative, or the dative with a possessive genitive:¹²

(8) *Il.* 6.134–5   ὑπ' ἀνδροφόνοιο Λυκούργου
θεινόμεναι βουπλῆγι
"struck by man-slaying Lycurgus with an
ox-goad *or* struck by man-slaying Lycurgus'
ox-goad"

To take the genitives of the previous paragraph as agentive would require adding agency to the functions of the genitive: not an economical approach when other interpretations are not only possible but even likelier. But the situation is different with these genitives after ὑπό. There do exist a few clear cases of ὑπό⁺ᴳ expressing agency,¹³ e.g.:

(9) *Il.* 13.675–6   ὅττι ῥά οἱ νηῶν ἐπ' ἀριστερὰ δηιόωντο
λαοὶ ὑπ' Ἀργείων
"that his people were being slaughtered to the
left of the ships by the Argives"

Therefore, there is a stronger argument for taking ὑπό with the genitive in an example like (8). Whether or not a given construction is agentive has to be argued on a case by case basis.

A final source of difficulty in deciding what to count as a PAC in Homer is the nature of the voice of the -ην aorists. There is a general conception that these are intransitive formations rather

¹¹ For example, *Il.* 5.34 νῶϊ δὲ χαζώμεσθα, Διὸς δ' ἀλεώμεθα μῆνιν; 8.412 Διὸς δέ σφ' ἔννεπε μῦθον; 12.173 οὐδὲ Διὸς πεῖθε φρένα ταῦτ' ἀγορεύων.
¹² Jankuhn suggests that this construction, especially common with ὑπὸ χερσί τινος (15× *Il.*, 1× *Od.*), would have influenced the eventual adoption of ὑπό with the genitive as Greek's main means of expressing agency with a passive verb (1969: 108).
¹³ For more examples, see pp. 62–3.

than passives.[14] For the most part, this view is justified, but it is taken too far in the case of δάμνημι. The -ην aorist of this verb often occurs with an oblique nominal referring to the agent of the subjugation:

(10) *Il.* 18.103   οἳ δὴ πολέες δάμεν Ἕκτορι δίῳ
                     "who, in large numbers, were defeated by *or*
                     succumbed to godlike Hector"

(11) *Il.* 11.309   ὡς ἄρα πυκνὰ καρήαθ᾽ ὑφ᾽ Ἕκτορι δάμνατο
                     λαῶν
                     "thus, in quick succession, (the heads of) people
                     were defeated by *or* succumbed to Hector"

Neither Schwyzer nor Jankuhn includes such expressions as PACs, as they generally treat δαμη- as an anticausative rather than a passive.[15] Jankuhn bases his assessment on Delbrück, whose reasoning is as follows (1879: 78–9). First, there are constructions in which the subject of the verb is not the agent, but rather the "Mittelpunkt" of the action, e.g. "Der Schnee schmilzt." Next, passives can arise from these verbs when an agent is mentioned, e.g. Πηλεΐωνι δαμείς. But such a construction is analogous to lexical intransitives like πίπτω ὑπό, and, as such, is only "nahe an die Grenze des Passivums." Finally, a true passive "ist die neue Ausdrucksweise erst dann, wenn sich an Aoriste wie ἐδάμην analoge Bildungen aus transitiven Verben anlehnen, wie ἐτύπην." As forms like ἐτύπην do occur in Homer (*Il.* 24.241) and as ἐδάμην forms do correspond to a transitive δάμνημι (*Il.* 5.893, 16.103), it seems that the logical conclusion to Delbrück's reasoning is that ἐδάμην is in fact a passive.

In summary, then, it is clear that it is not always easy to distinguish a PAC from various other types of intransitive+oblique constructions. The verbs πείθομαι and χολόομαι with the dative, for instance, are best seen as middle verbs with a dative object, and potential genitives of agent can be safely dismissed as possessive. But -θην forms of χολόομαι and -ην forms of δάμνημι found with

[14] Smyth: "In Hom. all the second aorist forms in -ην are intransitive except ἐπλήγην and ἐτύπην *was struck*" (1920: 395).
[15] Still, Jankuhn does say that *Il.* 16.434 (μοι) μοῖρ᾽ ὑπὸ Πατρόκλοιο Μενοιτιάδαο δαμῆναι "spricht für passive Umdeutung von δαμῆναι" (1969: 68).

agent expressions can be classified as passive verbs, despite a previous reluctance to acknowledge such constructions as PACs. Finally, it should be noted that, even in cases where an intransitive+oblique construction is not a PAC, there can still be contamination from expressions that are. This can be seen particularly clearly when the intransitive+oblique construction is conjoined with a PAC:

(12) *Il.* 5.878   σοί τ' ἐπιπείθονται καὶ δεδμήμεσθα ἕκαστος[16]
        "they obey you and, each of us, we are subject to
        you *or* have been mastered by you"

The personal pronoun σοί, taken with ἐπιπείθονται, is acting as the dative object of a middle verb; but it may also be understood with δεδμήμεσθα, in which case it would be the agent of the passive of δάμνημι.

The dative of agent in Homer

In Homer, the most common means of expressing the agent of a passive verb is the dative of agent. Because PACs with the dative of agent tend to cluster around particular verbs, they are best categorized according to the semantics of the verb. The semantic sphere most frequently found with the dative of agent is that of subjugation, commonly expressed by δάμνημι. The range of meanings exhibited by the passive of this verb extends from its more common sense, "be killed by," for which a parallel construction can be found with κτείνεσθαι to a less common sense, found in the perfect, "be subject to," for which there are parallel usages with ἔχετο and ἀνάσσονται. Both of the meanings, however, can still be subsumed under a broader sense: "be subjugated by." A second sphere includes verbs of accomplishing, such as τελέω and ἀνύω. There remain several datives of agent with τίω and χολόω as well as an isolated example in which the verb is a pluperfect passive, a

---

[16] The change of person is somewhat odd. Leaf 1900 *ad loc.* compares 7.160 and 17.250, but both of these passages involve use of the third person in a relative clause referring to a second person. At any rate, the subject of both verbs here must be "the gods, Zeus excluded," with the third person in ἐπιπείθονται agreeing with ἄλλοι . . . θεοί in the preceding line, the first person in δεδμήμεσθα *ad sensum*, with Ares including himself. Both verbs require σοί to complete their sense.

form of the verb with which the dative of agent is associated in the classical language as well.

We start with the most important class of verbs to occur with the dative of agent, those, especially δάμνημι, that express the subjugation of the patient. Indeed, were it not for these verbs, the dative of agent would not have the numerical predominance in Homer that it does. As they have been established as true passives (p. 50), it is important to include them, but, as they do behave as a block, one must be wary of assigning them the weight suggested by their numbers and proposing that the dative was the unmarked means of expressing agency in Homer without further consideration. Here are the examples of δάμνημι in Homer with the dative of agent, mostly from the aorist stem δαμη- (18×), but also the present (4×) and perfect (2×):

• aorist participle

(13) *Il.* 3.429   ἀνδρὶ δαμεὶς κρατερῷ
"defeated by a strong man"

(14) *Il.* 18.461   Τρωσὶ δαμείς
"defeated by the Trojans"

(15) *Il.* 22.40   Πηλεΐωνι δαμείς
"defeated by Peleus' son"

(16) *Il.* 17.2   Πάτροκλος Τρώεσσι δαμεὶς ἐν δηϊοτῆτι
"Patroclus, defeated in battle by the Trojans"

(17) *Il.* 20.294   ὃς τάχα Πηλεΐωνι δαμεὶς Ἄϊδόσδε κάτεισι
"who, defeated by Peleus' son, will soon go down to Hades"

(18) *Il.* 16.326   ὣς τὼ μὲν δοιοῖσι κασιγνήτοισι δαμέντε
"thus, those two, defeated by two brothers"

(19) *Od.* 24.100   ψυχὰς μνηστήρων κατάγων Ὀδυσῆϊ
                      δαμέντων
"leading down the souls of suitors defeated by Odysseus"

(20) *Il.* 22.55   ἢν μὴ καὶ σὺ θάνῃς Ἀχιλῆϊ δαμασθείς[17]
"unless you die as well, defeated by Achilles"

---

[17] Properly, this aorist belongs to δαμάζω, but as both this verb and δάμνημι share the same root, I place it here.

52

• aorist infinitive

(21) *Il.* 13.603   σοί, Μενέλαε, δαμῆναι ἐν αἰνῇ δηϊοτῆτι
"to be defeated by you, Menelaus, in grim
battle"

(22) *Il.* 20.311–12   ἦ κεν ἐάσῃς
Πηλεΐδῃ Ἀχιλῆϊ δαμήμεναι
"you will allow [him] to be defeated by
Achilles, son of Peleus"

(23) *Il.* 10.402–3   οἵ δ' ἀλεγεινοὶ
(= 17.76–7)   ἀνδράσι γε θνητοῖσι δαμήμεναι ἠδ' ὀχέεσθαι
[of horses] "and it is difficult for them to be
mastered or ridden by mortal men"[18]

(24) *Il.* 20.265–6   ὡς οὐ ῥηΐδι' ἐστὶ θεῶν ἐρικυδέα δῶρα
ἀνδράσι γε θνητοῖσι δαμήμεναι οὐδ'
ὑποείκειν
"that the illustrious gifts of the gods are not
quick to be overcome by mortal men, nor to
yield"

(25) *Il.* 19.416–17   ἀλλὰ σοὶ αὐτῷ
μόρσιμόν ἐστι θεῷ τε καὶ ἀνέρι ἶφι δαμῆναι
"but your own fate is to be defeated by force,
both by god and by man"

(26) *Od.* 4.397   ἀργαλέος γάρ τ' ἐστὶ θεὸς βροτῷ ἀνδρὶ
δαμῆναι
"for it is difficult for a god to be defeated by
a mortal man"

• aorist indicative and optative

(27) *Il.* 9.545   οὐ μὲν γάρ κε δάμη παύροισι βροτοῖσι
"for it would not be defeated by a small number
of men"

(28) *Il.* 18.103   οἵ δὴ πολέες δάμεν Ἕκτορι δίῳ
"who, in large numbers, were defeated by
godlike Hector"

---

[18] It would also be possible to take the dative here and in the next example more closely with
ἀλεγεινοί and ῥηΐδι' respectively, but we would then expect the men to be the subject
of the following infinitives, as in *Il.* 20.356–7 ἀργαλέον δέ μοί ἐστι . . . τόσσουσδ'
ἀνθρώπους ἐφέπειν.

53

(29) *Od.* 3.90   εἴθ᾽ ὅ γ᾽ ἐπ᾽ ἠπείρου δάμη ἀνδράσι δυσμενέεσσιν
"whether he has been defeated on land by
hostile men"

(30) *Il.* 3.301   ἄλοχοι δ᾽ ἄλλοισι δαμεῖεν
"may their wives be subjugated by other men"

- present

(31) *Il.* 13.16   Τρωσὶν δαμναμένους (half-line repeated
at 13.353)
"being defeated by the Trojans"

(32) *Il.* 8.244   μηδ᾽ οὕτω Τρώεσσιν ἔα δάμνασθαι
(= 15.376)   Ἀχαιούς
"do not allow the Achaeans to be defeated
by the Trojans in this way"

- perfect

(33) *Il.* 3.183   ἦ ῥά νύ τοι πολλοὶ δεδμήατο κοῦροι
Ἀχαιῶν
"many young men of the Achaeans are
subject to you"[19]

(34) *Od.* 11.621–2   μάλα γὰρ πολὺ χείρονι φωτὶ
δεδμήμην
"for I was subject to a much inferior man"

These examples may be broken down into three semantic subtypes. The majority refer to the violent death of warriors on the battlefield, or, in example (27), that of a boar. The other two meanings that can be distinguished are the taming of a beast or woman (examples (23) and (30)),[20] and subordination to a superior (the two examples with the perfect, (33) and (34)). The dative of agent with verbs of these meanings is not restricted to δάμνημι. Parallel usages for all three subtypes can be found with different verbs. For the first, compare against (32):

[19] That the dative in this and the following example are agents despite the English translation can be seen if it is borne in mind that the perfect expressed the state resulting from a prior event; in other words, we may translate periphrastically, "many young men of the Achaeans are in the state of having been mastered or subjugated by you."

[20] In (24), the idea of breaking (the will of) an animal has been transferred to Achilles' shield. For δάμνημι used with women and animals, compare the adjective ἄδμης, used to denote unmarried women (*Od.* 6.109, 228) and mules that have not been broken in (*Od.* 4.637).

(35) *Il.* 5.465 ἐς τί ἔτι κτείνεσθαι ἐάσετε λαὸν Ἀχαιοῖς;
"How much longer will you allow the people to
be killed by the Achaeans?"

For the second, compare against (30):

(36) *Il.* 6.398 τοῦ περ δὴ θυγάτηρ ἔχεθ᾽ Ἕκτορι
"whose daughter was possessed [as wife] by
Hector"

For the third, compare against (33):

(37) *Od.* 4.177 αἳ περιναιετάουσιν, ἀνάσσονται δ᾽ ἐμοὶ αὐτῷ
"[cities] which are located around here, and are
ruled by me"

The frequency of the dative of agent with these verbs of subjugation strongly suggests that it is the unmarked PAC for them, at least, whatever its status with verbs of other meanings may be. The basis for this suggestion will become clearer below (p. 64), when the construction with ὑπό will be seen to be rarer with these verbs.

Considerably less frequent is the use of the dative of agent with τελέω and ἀνύω, both verbs that denote the accomplishment of an act:[21]

(38) *Od.* 4.663–4 ἦ μέγα ἔργον ὑπερφιάλως ἐτελέσθη
Τηλεμάχῳ ὁδὸς ἥδε· φάμεν δέ οἱ οὐ τελέεσθαι
"indeed, it is a serious matter that this journey
has audaciously been completed by
Telemachus, although we said that it would
not completed by him"

(39) *Od.* 5.262 τέτρατον ἦμαρ ἔην, καὶ τῷ τετέλεστο
ἅπαντα
"it was the fourth day, and all the
preparations had been finished by him"

(40) *Od.* 5.243 θοῶς δέ οἱ ἤνυτο ἔργον
"quickly, the task was completed by him"

---

[21] Note that, in all three passages, the translation is much smoother if we replace the PAC with a clause containing an active verb, e.g. in (40) "quickly he completed the task."

With so few examples, it is difficult, if not impossible, to assign any exact value to the dative. Indeed, it is just such examples as these that render questionable the exclusive classification of uses of the dative under such headings as datives of interest, possession, and agent. Probably the best analysis of such constructions is simply to note that the inability to distinguish between these different uses explains how the dative came to be used in all of them.

Rather different are the constructions where the dative of agent is used with verbs of carrying or moving:

(41) *Od.* 5.54   πολέεσσιν ὀχήσατο κύμασιν Ἑρμῆς[22]
                    "Hermes was carried by one wave after
                    another"

(42) *Il.* 10.330   μὴ μὲν τοῖς ἵπποισιν ἀνὴρ ἐποχήσεται
                    ἄλλος[23]
                    "that no other man will be carried by these
                    horses"

(43) *Od.* 6.43–4   οὔτ᾽ ἀνέμοισι τινάσσεται οὔτε ποτ᾽ ὄμβρῳ
                    δεύεται οὔτε χιὼν ἐπιπίλναται[24]
                    "it is neither shaken by the winds, nor
                    dampened by rain, nor does snow come near it"

A dative of agent is found in these instances, but the agent is only ever an animal or a force of nature. As it is never human, it is likely that these PACs show the remains of an old instrumental usage.

Another verb that construes with the dative of agent in Homer is τίω, but the construction is restricted to two formulaic usages.[25] The first and most common is the half-line θεὸς (δ᾽) ὣς τίετο δήμῳ, which occurs six times in the poems.[26] The second is a dative of agent found with the perfect participle τετιμένος:

[22] For κῦμα as agent, cf. *Od.* 6.171 τόφρα δέ μ᾽ αἰεὶ κῦμ᾽ ἐφόρει κραιπναί τε θύελλαι.

[23] There is no active *ἐποχέω, but the verb only occurs twice in Homer, so its absence may well be due to chance. Active ὀχέω does exist.

[24] For ἄνεμος as agent, cf. *Od.* 5.368–9 ὡς δ᾽ ἄνεμος ζαὴς ἠΐων θημῶνα τινάξῃ | καρφαλέων.

[25] The only potential example that does not belong to either of these two patterns is *Il.* 4.46 τάων μοι περὶ κῆρι τιέσκετο Ἴλιος ἱρή. Whether κῆρι is taken to be the object of a prepositional περί or as a free-standing locative with adverbial περί (see Kirk 1985 *ad loc.*), it is uncertain whether μοι is better understood as a possessive dative with κῆρι or as an agent. Indeed, as noted above, an ambiguous case such as this shows how the dative came to be used to mark the agent in the first place.

[26] *Il.* 5.78, 10.33, 13.218, 16.605 with δέ, and *Il.* 11.58, *Od.* 14.205 without (both times in relative clauses).

(44) *Il.* 24.533   φοιτᾷ δ' οὔτε θεοῖσι τετιμένος οὔτε βροτοῖσιν
"and he wanders about, honored neither by gods
nor by mortals"

(45) *Od.* 8.472   Δημόδοκον λαοῖσι τετιμένον²⁷
"Demodocus, honored by the people"

Because of their limited distribution, these examples do not support
the case that the use of the dative of agent was particularly triggered
by verbs of honoring. The participial expressions probably should
be grouped together with example (49), as the verb in them is a
perfect passive. As for τίετο δήμῳ, one could see in that an isolated
case of a true dative of agent, an old instrumental usage, or even
a relic of the locative (cf. *Od.* 1.70–1 ὅου κράτος ἐστὶ μέγιστον |
πᾶσιν Κυκλώπεσσι).

As with τίω, the examples of the dative of agent with χολόω
are quite limited:

(46) *Il.* 1.9–10   ὁ γὰρ βασιλῆϊ χολωθεὶς
νοῦσον ἀνὰ στρατὸν ὦρσε κακήν
"for he, enraged by the king, stirred up a
plague throughout the army"

(47) *Il.* 2.629   ὅς ποτε Δουλίχιόνδ' ἀπενάσσατο πατρὶ
χολωθείς
"who, angered once by his father, moved away
to Dulichium"

(48) *Od.* 15.254   ὅς ῥ' Ὑπερησίηνδ' ἀπενάσσατο πατρὶ
χολωθείς
"who, angered by his father, moved to
Hyperesia"

This restricted distribution, however, is greatly due to the method-
ological necessity of discounting PACs of this verb that do not
involve the aorist passive. In fact, there are several examples of
ambiguous mediopassive forms of this verb found with a dative
that could either represent the object of the middle verb or the
agent of the passive verb.²⁸ In light of the late creation of the -θην

---

²⁷ This phrase is also found in the nominative at *Od.* 13.28.
²⁸ (reduplicated future) *Il.* 5.421, *Od.* 24.544; (present) *Il.* 8.407; (perfect) *Il.* 17.710,
Od. 8.276. There are also a couple of aorist middle examples that are unambiguously
non-passive: *Il.* 15.155, *Od.* 6.147.

aorist, it seems best to view the dative with χολωθείς as modeled on the datives found with the verb's middle. That there is a fine line between a middle verb with a dative object and a passive verb with a dative of agent will thus have reinforced the existence of the dative of agent in Homer.

In the final Homeric PAC with the dative of agent, the verb in the construction is a pluperfect passive:

(49) *Il.* 13.168   οἰσόμενος δόρυ μακρόν, ὅ οἱ κλισίηφι λέλειπτο
    "to bring back a long spear, which had been left
    by him in the tent"

There is no reason to dissociate this example from the general tendency of classical Greek to mark the agent of the perfect passive with a dative, especially as it follows the prototypical pattern for such constructions that will be seen in the next chapter: inanimate subject and pronominal agent.

As with most features of Homeric Greek, the dative of agent has generally been viewed from the perspective of PIE. This diachronic bias is understandable and largely justified as the poems clearly incorporate linguistic forms and expressions from a period spanning several centuries. Accordingly, many have seen in the dative of agent a combination of two different usages, resulting from case syncretism between the dative and the instrumental.[29] On the one hand, there are the true dative usages, frequently dismissed as datives of interest. Among these, Schwyzer would count the PACs with the perfect passive (examples (44), (45), and (49)).[30] On the other, the remnants of an instrumental usage have also been descried. Now the search for instrumental agents in Homer can be taken too far: Hettrich argues for such a reading of (22) (*Il.* 20.311–12 ἦ κεν ἐάσῃς | Πηλεΐδη Ἀχιλῆϊ δαμήμεναι ἐσθλὸν ἐόντα) on the basis of an active formulation in which the dative is supposedly instrumental:

---

[29] See Schwyzer 1943: 15–18 and Hettrich 1990: 75 for the dative of interest, 77–80 for the instrumental.

[30] As an example of a true dative, he also gives the τίεσκετο example (see note 25, above). His argument rests on the premise that the verb should be translated as an intransitive ("war mir schätzenswert"). Accordingly, one might infer that he would classify the θεὸς (δ') ὣς τίετο δήμῳ formula the same way.

(50) *Il.* 22.174–6   καὶ μητιάασθε | . . . ἦέ μιν ἤδη | Πηλεΐδη
                      Ἀχιλῆϊ δαμάσσομεν ἐσθλὸν ἐόντα
                      "and consider whether we will defeat him by
                      means of Achilles"

While it could be argued that Achilles is the instrument of Hector's subjugation, it is certainly also possible that here too we have a dative of the beneficiary. In other words, Zeus' words could perhaps be better rendered "and consider whether we will subject him to Achilles, though he is noble." This is not to say, however, that it is wrong to see IE instrumental usage behind some of the datives of agent in Homer: certainly the agents in (41) through (43) are likelier to go back to an IE instrumental than an IE dative. To set up a dichotomy, then, between true datives of agent and those that are relics of the old IE instrumental is legitimate on diachronic grounds. But is there evidence for it within Homer? To pose the question differently, is there any reason, other than historical, to divide all the examples in this section into datives of agent that behave like true datives and those that are clearly instrumental?

Certainly, the division works well to a certain extent, especially regarding a dative usage for the examples with isolated perfect verbs and an instrumental usage for examples (41) through (43). But, in the case of δάμνημι, the evidence is too ambiguous to allow this distinction to be set up for Homer. Even if a dative like that in (22) is to be regarded as instrumental in origin, most of the datives found with δάμνημι are generally considered to be true dative verbal complements in light of the intransitive origin of the -ην aorist. It seems doubtful that the poet would have perceived the two constructions differently: the dative in (50) may reasonably be understood as an instrumental, but it seems far less certain that the dative in (22) would have been seen as such, considering the number of intransitive verbs of this meaning that govern a dative complement.[31] In short the dative of agent in Homer should not be seen as a single, unified construction – (41) through (43) are too different from (44), (45), and (49) to allow that. But neither should we attempt to distinguish too clearly between the different

---

[31] Consider, for example, *Il.* 9.109–10 σὺ δὲ σῷ μεγαλήτορι θυμῷ | εἴξας.

datives of agent on the basis of the supposed antecedents in PIE case usage, for that obscures both the fact that usages where the dative proper is found may have arisen by different paths (δάμνημι versus χολόομαι) and the fact that the ancestral PIE case cannot always be recovered with certainty (θεὸς ὣς τίετο δήμῳ).

The genitive of agent in Homer

Only one example is cited in the standard grammars for a genitive of agent in Homer:[32]

(51) *Od.* 8.499   ὣς φάθ᾽, ὁ δ᾽ ὁρμηθεὶς θεοῦ ἄρχετο, φαῖνε δ᾽
                   ἀοιδήν
                   "thus spoke Odysseus, and Demodocus, getting
                   started, began from [i.e., with] the god, and
                   revealed his song"

As has already been argued by several scholars, it is erroneous to construe ὁρμηθεὶς θεοῦ as "urged on by the god." Calhoun 1938 pointed out that the sense of the line was likelier to be divided at the caesura between ὁρμηθείς and θεοῦ rather than at the awkward diaeresis between θεοῦ and ἄρχετο. As additional support for taking θεοῦ with ἄρχετο, he points to other passages where ἄρχομαι occurs with a genitive marking the starting-point.[33] Downplaying the force of a metrical argument, Koster adds two points. First, taking the genitive with ὁρμηθείς and ἄρχετο absolutely leaves the latter verb weak.[34] Second, in Homer, the genitive with intransitive forms of ὁρμάω designates not the point of departure but rather the goal that is sought.[35] These arguments are sufficient to establish that θεοῦ cannot be a genitive of agent with ὁρμηθείς, but is instead

---

[32] In both cases, the authors are cautious: Schwyzer–Debrunner 1950: 119, Chantraine 1963: 65. Hettrich too classifies this as an agentive genitive (1990: 93 n. 96), calling it a true genitival agent as against the ablatival agents found after prepositions. (However, he does not use this line as his paradigmatic example of an agentive genitive in Greek but cites instead S. *Ph.* 3.)

[33] *Il.* 9.97 σέο δ᾽ ἄρξομαι, *Od.* 21.142 ἀρξάμενοι τοῦ χώρου.

[34] Koster translates this alternative as "*orsus a deo | coepit*" and notes that the beginning of the singing is mentioned twice, "quae tautologia evitatur, si ὁρμηθεὶς ad Demodoci universam actionem, ἤρχετο ad exordium cantus . . . ponimus" (1952: 92).

[35] Koster cites *Il.* 4.335, 14.488, and 21.595.

an ablatival genitive with ἄρχετο.[36] The genitive of agent may thus be removed from grammars of Homer.

ὑπό in Homer

Classical Greek uses the preposition ὑπό with the genitive to express the agent of a passive verb. This usage had already begun at the time of the Homeric poems, though the preposition is found governing the dative as well as the genitive (henceforth, ὑπό[+D] and ὑπό[+G]). According to Schwyzer, the agentive use of ὑπό in Homer is quite rare, limited to only two instances, one with the genitive, one with the dative.[37] He considers the dative usage to be the earlier, as he finds it semantically more natural, especially with intransitive verbs. The genitive then began to be used later, in his view a formal replacement for the dative.[38] Jankuhn, however, is more liberal in counting agentive usages of ὑπό[+G], citing six examples, but considers its use with the dative to be more local than agentive.[39] He accounts for the use of ὑπό[+G] as the primary PAC in classical Greek by positing a weakening of the local "underneath" sense of the preposition, leaving behind only the ablatival force, which could easily serve to express the agent.[40] Additionally, he notes the frequency of the expression ὑπὸ χερσί τινος, which, especially considering how commonly the preposition is placed after χερσί, could have been reanalyzed with χερσί as an instrumental dative and the genitive as the object of the preposition. Finally, De La Villa also examines the agentive expressions with ὑπό in some detail, arriving at a far greater number of examples than either Schwyzer or Jankuhn – seventy-six with the dative, forty-two with the genitive (1998: 173). Some of this higher number is due to his interest in examining all agent markers, not merely those with

---

[36] Recent commentators on the text also take this view. See Heubeck–West–Hainsworth 1988 and Garvie 1994 *ad loc.*

[37] See examples (53) and (61) below.

[38] Schwyzer: "ὑπό cum gen. beim Passiv läßt sich nur als formeller, jüngerer Ersatz für ὑπό cum dat. in gleicher Funktion begreifen" (1943: 29).

[39] The examples are (53), (55), (56), (58)–(60). Jankuhn: "Während man in einigen Fällen ὑπό + gen. bereits als wirkliche Agensbezeichnung auffassen muß, lassen sich die Fälle von ὑπό + dat. meistens noch lokal erklären" (1969: 109).

[40] For the weakening of the semantics of a preposition in respect of vertical movement, cf. Latin *de*; for the use of an ablatival preposition to mark the agent, cf. Latin *ab*.

passive verbs. But he has gone on to include many examples to which it seems unwise to ascribe agentive status. These fall into two main categories. First, he has included expressions with ὑπό χερσί τινος as examples of ὑπό⁺ᴰ marking the agent (e.g. *Il.* 2.374, 860). While it is certainly reasonable to understand the human referent in these expressions as an agent, that human referent is not the object of the preposition ὑπό⁺ᴰ; instead, it is the hands that are the object, and these are better described as an instrument than as an agent. Second, De La Villa has also included expressions in which a woman bears a child to a man, and it is that man that is marked by ὑπό⁺ᴰ:

(52) *Il.* 2.714–15   Εὔμηλος, τὸν ὑπ᾽ Ἀδμήτῳ τέκε δῖα γυναικῶν
                      Ἄλκηστις
                      "Eumelus, whom Alcestis, noble woman,
                      bore to Admetus"

Now De La Villa bases his discussion of semantic roles on the principle that the same semantic role cannot occur twice in the same clause, except by some process of coordination (*ibid.* 150, especially n. 14); if so, then surely Alcestis, as the subject of the active verb, is more properly to be considered the agent in this sentence. In passages such as this one, ὑπό⁺ᴰ must instead mark a role of subjacency, that is, of the mother's physical or hierarchical location underneath the father. In short, then, De La Villa's definition of agency is broader than is justified, and so he is led to overstate the frequency with which ὑπό occurs as an agent marker.

Before analyzing these interpretations, I will list all the passages in Homer in which one might argue that ὑπό is used to mark the agent of a passive verb:[41]

• with the genitive

(53) *Il.* 6.134–5   ὑπ᾽ ἀνδροφόνοιο Λυκούργου
                    θεινόμεναι βουπλῆγι
                    "struck by man-slaying Lycurgus with an
                    ox-goad"

[41] For a full listing of the usages of ὑπό in Homer, see La Roche 1861. The pages relevant to agentive expressions are 347–50 (ὑπό⁺ᴰ) and 356–7 (ὑπό⁺ᴳ).

(54) *Il.* 8.149   Τυδεΐδης ὑπ᾽ ἐμεῖο φοβεύμενος ἵκετο νῆας
                      "Tydeus' son, put to flight by me, returned to
                      the ships"

(55) *Il.* 13.675–6   ὅττι ῥά οἱ νηῶν ἐπ᾽ ἀριστερὰ δηϊόωντο
                      λαοὶ ὑπ᾽ Ἀργείων
                      "that his people were being slaughtered to the
                      left of the ships by the Argives"

(56) *Od.* 9.66   οἳ θάνον ἐν πεδίῳ Κικόνων ὕπο δηωθέντες
                      "who died on the plain, slaughtered by the
                      Cicones"

(57) *Il.* 21.527–8   αὐτὰρ ὑπ᾽ αὐτοῦ
                      Τρῶες ἄφαρ κλονέοντο πεφυζότες
                      "but the Trojans were immediately thrown
                      into confusion by him, and they fled"

(58) *Il.* 21.15–16   ὡς ὑπ᾽ Ἀχιλλῆος Ξάνθου βαθυδινήεντος
                      πλῆτο ῥόος
                      "thus, the stream of the deep-eddying
                      Xanthus was filled by Achilles"

(59) *Od.* 5.393   ὀξὺ μάλα προϊδών, μεγάλου ὑπό[42] κύματος
                      ἀρθείς
                      "looking keenly ahead, lifted up by a large
                      wave"

(60) *Il.* 16.433–4   ὤ μοι ἐγών, ὅ τέ μοι Σαρπηδόνα, φίλτατον
                      ἀνδρῶν,
                      μοῖρ᾽ ὑπὸ Πατρόκλοιο Μενοιτιάδαο
                      δαμῆναι[43]
                      "O, alas for me, that it is fated that my
                      Sarpedon, dearest of men, is to be defeated
                      by Patroclus, son of Menoetius"

• with the dative (not δάμνημι)

(61) *Il.* 16.490–1   ὡς ὑπὸ Πατρόκλῳ Λυκίων ἀγὸς ἀσπιστάων
                      κτεινόμενος μενέαινε
                      "thus, as he was killed by Patroclus, the leader
                      of the Lycian soldiers struggled"

---

[42] Aristophanes and Rhianus read ἐπί here.
[43] Zenodotus rejected this passage on continuity grounds; Leaf accepts it.

(62) *Il.* 5.93–4   ὡς ὑπὸ Τυδεΐδη πυκιναὶ κλονέοντο φάλαγγες Τρώων

"thus the ranks of Trojans, crowded together, were routed by Tydeus' son"

• with the dative (δάμνημι)

(63) *Il.* 5.646   ἀλλ᾽ ὑπ᾽ ἐμοὶ δμηθέντα πύλας Ἀΐδαο περήσειν

"but, defeated by me, to cross the gates of Hades"

(64) *Il.* 11.309   ὡς ἄρα πυκνὰ καρήαθ᾽ ὑφ᾽ Ἕκτορι δάμνατο λαῶν

"thus, in quick succession, (the heads of) people were defeated by Hector"

(65) *Il.* 13.98   νῦν δὴ εἴδεται ἦμαρ ὑπὸ Τρώεσσι δαμῆναι

"now the day is here that will see us defeated by the Trojans"

(66) *Il.* 13.668   ἢ μετ᾽ Ἀχαιῶν νηυσὶν ὑπὸ Τρώεσσι δαμῆναι

"or, amidst the ships of the Achaeans, to be defeated by the Trojans"

(67) *Od.* 4.790   ἦ ὅ γ᾽ ὑπὸ μνηστῆρσιν ὑπερφιάλοισι δαμείη

"whether he would be defeated by the arrogant suitors"

(68) *Od.* 17.252   ἢ ὑπὸ μνηστῆρσι δαμείη

"or be defeated by the suitors"

(69) *Od.* 3.305   δέδμητο δὲ λαὸς ὑπ᾽ αὐτῷ

"and the people were subject to him"[44]

All of these examples meet the definition of a PAC set out in Chapter 1; accordingly, Schwyzer is surely too narrow in accepting only two PACs in Homer, while Jankuhn is right to include the examples with ὑπό[+G] that he does. Yet it is difficult to see how he could make his distinction in seeing a more agentive force in the examples with ὑπό[+G] and a more local force in those with ὑπό[+D]. If we leave aside the examples with δάμνημι, in weighing (53)–(59) against (61)–(62), there is little to differentiate the semantics of the two groups. While (58) and (59) are perhaps sufficiently

---

[44] For the translation of the agent phrase, see note 19.

divorced from a local sense of "from below" that the only possible interpretation of them would be agentive, both (53)–(57) and (61)–(62) refer to warriors being bested in battle such that they could either be beaten "by the enemy" or "under the enemy." To draw a distinction between θείνομαι and δηϊόομαι being associated with a grammaticalized preposition and κτείνομαι with a local one would be unjustified. When one considers the δάμνημι examples, it is noticeable that this verb only occurs 1× with ὑπό$^{+G}$, but 7× with ὑπό$^{+D}$, and 25× with the preposition-less dative. But it is not easy to find any sort of factor that might have conditioned the choice of one construction over another. Neither the tense or mood of the verb, nor position in the line, nor obvious semantic distinctions seem to favor the presence or absence of ὑπό.[45]

As a further complication, there are several cases in which both the genitive and the dative are found with ὑπό, and it is not clear whether the preposition governs the genitive with an instrumental dative, or the dative with a possessive genitive:[46]

(70) *Il.* 11.821   ἦ ἤδη φθίσονται ὑπ᾽ αὐτοῦ δουρὶ δαμέντες;
                 "will they perish now, defeated by him with a
                 spear *or* defeated by his spear?"

(71) *Il.* 17.303   ὑπ᾽ Αἴαντος μεγαθύμου δουρὶ δαμέντι
                 "defeated by great-spirited Ajax with a spear
                 or by Ajax' spear"

(72) *Od.* 3.234–5   ὡς Ἀγαμέμνων
        ὤλεθ᾽ ὑπ᾽ Αἰγίσθοιο δόλῳ καὶ ἧς ἀλόχοιο
        "thus Agamemnon was killed by the
        treachery of Aegisthus and his wife"

---

[45] Compare (60) and (65) with (25) and (26), (64) with (31) and (32), (67) and (68) with (30), and (69) with (33) and (34), in which the distinct meaning of δάμνημι in the perfect appears both with and without ὑπό. The only example with ὑπό which does not have a counterpart among the preposition-less constructions is (63), as the aorist passive participle δμηθείς does not occur with the dative alone. If we assume that the PACs with ὑπό come from a later stratum of the language than those with the dative (witness their spread in classical Greek), there is a slight chance that δμηθείς occurs with ὑπό because the -θην aorist is itself morphologically younger than the other forms. But a line like (20) shows that the dative of agent could be used with at least some -θην aorists.

[46] Note also (53) above. I list it as a certain example of a PAC with ὑπό$^{+G}$ because ὑπό is distant enough from the dative βουπλῆγι that it is far more natural to understand the preposition as governing the genitive Λυκούργου.

Jankuhn notes on (72) that there are several examples of δόλῳ being used as an instrumental dative, but none of its use with ὑπό. Although this observation would suggest that ὑπό is here an agent marker, the position of ἧς ἀλόχοιο seems more likely to be that of a possessive genitive (parallel to Αἰγίσθοιο) than that of a second object of ὑπό.

One last means by which ὑπό could express the agent is in the phrase ὑπὸ χερσί τινος (15× Il., 1× Od.):

(73) Il. 2.860   ἀλλ᾽ ἐδάμη ὑπὸ χερσὶ ποδώκεος Αἰακίδαο
                   "but he was defeated at the hands of the
                   swift-footed grandson of Aeacus"

Although this phrase's frequency is generally ascribed to its being a formula, it is possible that it was in fact acting as a compound preposition, grammaticalized to express the agent. The strongest argument for this view is that, in this usage, χερσί never occurs with an epithet, though it frequently combines elsewhere with adjectives like στιβαρῇσι or κρατερῇσι. Blake notes that in the expressions *on top of* and *in front of*, *top* and *front* "differ from the common nouns *top* and *front* in that they cannot be modified by an indefinite article nor by adjectives" (1994: 16). As such, they attain the status of relator nouns. This seems to be the case with χερσί as well. Furthermore, the preposition and χερσί always occur directly next to each other: the genitive never occurs sandwiched between them, as in (70) and (71). Two further cross-linguistic parallels might be cited: the use of *kiššari*[+G] in Hittite to denote the agent, and the English periphrasis *at the hands of* to express agency with an intransitive verb.[47]

There are, however, reasons to believe that this phrase had only begun to be grammaticalized as an agent marker. First, the form of

---

[47] For the Hittite, see Hettrich 1990: 27. As for the English example, because *hands* could be modified by an adjective, I would not consider it to be a compound preposition. Still, it shows how a phrase involving this particular body part can become at least a partially grammaticalized means of expressing agency. Also relevant are three passages in which periphrases with παλάμη are used in a similar capacity: Il. 3.128 οὓς ἔθεν εἵνεκ᾽ ἔπασχον ὑπ᾽ Ἄρηος παλαμάων; 5.557–8 ὄφρα καὶ αὐτώ | ἀνδρῶν ἐν παλάμῃσι κατέκταθεν ὀξέϊ χαλκῷ (followed in the next line by τοίω τὼ χείρεσσιν ὑπ᾽ Αἰνείαο δαμέντε); and 7.104–5 φάνη βιότοιο τελευτὴ | Ἕκτορος ἐν παλάμῃσιν. The word order in the first example is reminiscent of the ὑπ᾽ αὐτοῦ δουρί examples.

χερσί can vary: one finds χερσί(ν), χερσ', and χείρεσσιν, a feature that points to poetic variation rather than rigid grammaticalization. Still, this argument is certainly not conclusive, as it would be unwise to go on to suggest that the dative plural was also not yet grammaticalized owing to its multiplicity of forms. More importantly, the preposition may be placed before or after χερσί. This flexibility strongly suggests that this phrase had not yet been grammaticalized as a unit. Considering the inherent impossibility of establishing a clear boundary between what is and is not a PAC, it is best to regard these constructions with ὑπὸ χερσί as occupying ground in the middle between the two: a sort of embryonic agent marker that never reached complete grammaticalization.

To return to the question of ὑπό$^{+G}$ and ὑπό$^{+D}$ as agent markers, the following conclusions seem sound. First, both prepositions can mark the agent, and they do so in approximately equal numbers. Second, although the numbers alone do not allow us to establish which preposition, if either, was a preferred agent marker, it is nevertheless significant that ὑπό$^{+D}$ almost always marks the agents of δάμνημι, whereas ὑπό$^{+G}$ occurs with a wider range of verbs. This distribution suggests that, even in Homer, ὑπό$^{+G}$ was already on its way to approaching its fifth-century status as the primary agent marker of classical Greek; the question of how it reached its later predominance is accordingly that much less problematic. No doubt Jankuhn is right to account for this as at least in part due to the weakening of the preposition's function towards that of marking a purely ablatival motion. So too De La Villa's argument that it expanded into the territory of ὑπό$^{+D}$ because it was more uniquely an agent marker also rings true. But, seen in light of these initial conditions, the later primacy of ὑπό$^{+G}$ seems not so much an unexpected development as it does a natural reduction in the diversity of agent markers available to Homer.

Ablatival prepositions in Homer

Many languages use ablatival prepositions to denote the agent of a passive verb, e.g. Latin *ab*, German *von*, Old English *fram*. Such prepositions are also found in Greek's palette of agent markers. In Homer, the most common is ἐκ, but ἀπό, παρά, πρός, and the adverbial ending -θεν also occur. I will first list all the examples by preposition. Next, as roughly half of the examples involve a verb denoting the accomplishing of an act, I will discuss those PACs as a group. Lastly, I will turn to the remaining examples, which can only be labeled as miscellaneous.

- ἐκ[48]

(74) *Il.* 5.652–3   σοί δ' ἐγὼ ἐνθάδε φημὶ φόνον καὶ κῆρα
         μέλαιναν
         ἐξ ἐμέθεν τεύξεσθαι
         "and I say that your death and black fate will
         be accomplished here by me"

(75) *Il.* 18.74–5   τὰ μὲν δή τοι τετέλεσται
         ἐκ Διός
         "these things have been accomplished for you
         by Zeus"

(76) *Il.* 2.668–9   ἠδ' ἐφίληθεν
         ἐκ Διός
         "and they were loved by Zeus"

(77) *Od.* 7.69–71   ὣς κείνη περὶ κῆρι τετίμηταί τε καὶ ἔστιν
         ἔκ τε φίλων παίδων ἔκ τ' αὐτοῦ Ἀλκινόοιο
         καὶ λαῶν
         "thus she has been and continues to be
         honored very much in a heartfelt way by her
         own children and by Alcinous himself and
         the people"

- πρός/προτί

(78) *Il.* 6.56–7   ἦ σοὶ ἄριστα πεποίηται κατὰ οἶκον
         πρὸς Τρώων;[49]

---

[48] As PACs with ἐκ, I reject the three examples of ἐκ used with ἐφῆπται (*Il.* 2.32–3 = 2.69–70 and 21.512–13, discussed below), as there is no transitive ἐφάπτω or ἐφάπτομαι, and these verbs are better classified as middle. So too, the examples with ἔχομαι should be dismissed: *Od.* 6.197 τοῦ δ' ἐκ Φαιήκων ἔχεται κάρτος τε βίη τε and 11.346 Ἀλκινόου δ' ἐκ τοῦδ' ἔχεται ἔργον τε ἔπος τε. This usage of ἔχω is not paralleled by any transitive active usages (the closest seems to be *Od.* 2.22 δύο δ' αἰὲν ἔχον πατρώϊα ἔργα), and is best taken as a middle "depend on" (so LSJ ἔχω C4).

[49] I have reservations about including this as a PAC, for there is no Homeric active corresponding to this usage of ποιέω ("be done"): in Homer, this verb nearly always means "make" rather than "do." Still, this example is probably best interpreted as passive, for

"has excellent treatment been given to you in your house by the Trojans?"

(79) *Il.* 11.831–2   ἐσθλά, τά σε προτί φασιν Ἀχιλλῆος
                       δεδιδάχθαι
                       ὃν Χείρων ἐδίδαξε
                       "wonderful [medicines], which they say that you were taught by Achilles, whom Chiron taught"

• παρά

(80) *Il.* 15.122   πὰρ Διὸς ἀθανάτοισι χόλος καὶ μῆνις
                     ἐτύχθη[50]
                     "anger and wrath were formed against the immortals by Zeus"

• ἀπό[51]

(81) *Od.* 4.522–3   πολλὰ δ᾽ ἀπ᾽ αὐτοῦ
                      δάκρυα θερμὰ χέοντ᾽
                      "and many hot tears were shed by him"

• -θεν

(82) *Il.* 15.488–9   δὴ γὰρ ἴδον ὀφθαλμοῖσιν
                       ἀνδρὸς ἀριστῆος Διόθεν βλαφθέντα βέλεμνα
                       "for I saw with my own eyes the arrows of one of their leaders damaged by Zeus"

Four of these passages involve a verb of bringing about or accomplishing: τεύχω in (74) and (80), τελέω in (75), and ποιέω in (78). For verbs of this meaning, it is natural to see the agent as

---

no good parallels suggest that it should be seen as a middle, unlike ἔχομαι in the previous note, where a middle reading is supported by e.g. ἅπτομαι.

[50] Schwyzer cites this as a PAC (1943: 25). Jankuhn disagrees, arguing that the prepositional phrase is the "Angabe des Ausgangspunktes" (1969: 102 n. 13). Still, a sentence such as Ζεὺς ἔτευξε χόλον is not unreasonable, cf. *Il.* 1.110 ἑκηβόλος ἄλγεα τεύχει and *Od.* 24.475–6 ἢ προτέρω πόλεμόν τε κακὸν καὶ φύλοπιν αἰνὴν | τεύξεις.

[51] I reject Jankuhn's reading of χειρῶν in *Il.* 23.714–15 τετρίγει δ᾽ ἄρα νῶτα θρασειάων ἀπὸ χειρῶν | ἑλκόμενα στερεῶς as agentive: "[Die] Bewegung des (ständigen) Hin- und Hergezogenwerdens geht von den Händen aus, die hier durchaus den Wert des Agentes haben" (1969: 74). The noun χείρ is only extremely rarely a verbal subject, and then not with a strongly transitive verb like ἕλκω. As an alternative, Chantraine takes ἀπό with τετρίγει (1963: 94).

the source of the action and, accordingly, to express the agent with an ablatival preposition. This usage can also be seen in non-passive constructions, such as:

(83) *Od.* 2.134   ἐκ γὰρ τοῦ πατρὸς κακὰ πείσομαι
"for I will suffer ill at the hands of my father"

(84) *Il.* 2.32–3   Τρώεσσι δὲ κήδε᾽ ἐφῆπται
(= 2.69–70)   ἐκ Διός
"and sorrows are fastened upon the Trojans by Zeus"

(85) *Il.* 21.512–13   Ἥρη,
ἐξ ἧς ἀθανάτοισιν ἔρις καὶ νεῖκος ἐφῆπται
"Hera, at whose hands strife and quarrels are fastened upon the immortals"

The use of ἐκ in (85) is close to that in (74) and even closer to that of πάρ in (80).

The remaining examples are quite diverse. In (76) and (77), one might see a common semantic ground of "being esteemed by." But it is strange, in (77) at least, that the dative is not used, considering the instances where the related verb τίω is found with a dative of agent. Perhaps a prepositional construction was used because the agent spilled over on to the next line: at any rate, ἐκ occurs as an agent marker only at the beginning of a line, and in three of the four examples, the verb is part of the previous line. The word order in (79) is striking, with a verb, albeit an enclitic, sandwiched between the preposition and its object. Although it might be tempting to dismiss this PAC as an aberration, the presence of an active transformation of δεδιδάχθαι προτί in the next line makes the agentive reading particularly attractive.[52] In (81), the use of ἀπό may have been conditioned by its occurrence in other scenes of tear-shedding, such as *Il.* 23.385 and *Od.* 14.129. Indeed, the possibility can hardly be excluded that the prepositional phrase denotes not the agent, but the source of the tears, with the verb understood as a middle. As for (82), the -θεν suffix is

---

[52] An example such as this one seems a particularly good reason, *pace* De La Villa (1998: 153), to argue that ablatival prepositions could indeed mark agents in Homer.

best understood as agentive, as the verb βλαφθέντα, in contrast to χέοντο in (81), does not denote a sufficient amount of movement for the suffix to be marking source in a strictly spatial sense.[53] Still, the line is awkward and is perhaps best seen as a clumsy expansion of 15.484: Ἕκτωρ δ᾽ ὡς εἶδεν Τεύκρου βλαφθέντα βέλεμνα.

Later Greek epic

The evidence for PACs in Homer is meager enough that any conclusions about the factors that motivated the use of one agent marker rather than another must necessarily be tentative. Important as an additional source of information, however, is the way in which epic poets of the post-classical period marked the agents of passive verbs. Influenced by Homer in other respects, they might well be expected to have imitated his language in passive constructions as well. While their use of agent markers cannot directly help us to understand the Homeric data in its own right, it at least can give us insight into what later Greeks perceived to be Homeric peculiarities in prepositional use. The following section, accordingly, discusses the prepositional PACs in selected books of Apollonius of Rhodes (*Argonautica* 1, 3), Quintus of Smyrna (*Posthomerica* 1–2), and Nonnus (*Dionysiaca* 1–6). To judge from these works, it seems as if all three of these poets, including the rather distinctive Nonnus, marked the agent in ways that are reminiscent of the Homeric data presented already. Their debt to the language of Homer is clear in the overall rarity of PACs, the avoidance of ὑπό$^{+G}$, the frequent use of ὑπό$^{+D}$, and the sporadic use of the other non-standard agent constructions found in Homer.

Determining frequency figures for PACs in the late epic poets is not a task where complete precision can be achieved, for there is no way to delineate in all cases what constitutes a PAC. This difficulty is of course present in all authors, but it is particularly problematic when considering epic because the absolute number of potential PACs in epic is so small that a different decision as to whether a handful of uncertain cases should be considered as PACs can change the relative rankings of the frequency of PAC use

---

[53] Lejeune: "Il y avait là l'amorce d'une expression du complément d'agent. Ce tour, pourtant, ne s'est pas développé" (1939: 87–8).

in these authors. Nevertheless, no matter how broadly or narrowly
one defines PACs, the frequency of their occurrence in these three
late epic poets is significantly lower than it is in classical prose, or
even than it is in tragedy – and comparable to their frequency in
Homer. The constructions I have counted as PACs in these authors
are as follows:

Text	Location of PACs[a]	# PACs	# Words in text	PACs / 1,000 Words
Apollonius of Rhodes 1, 3	1.520* 1.794 1.1098–9* 3.469 3.702 3.1343	6	18,545	0.32
Quintus of Smyrna 1, 2	1.433 1.805 1.817	3	10,276	0.29
Nonnus 1–6	3.38* 5.465–6	2	18,769	0.11

[a] As with the frequency table at the end of Chapter 1, I only include
PACs with prepositions as agent markers. For all PACs listed, the agent
marker is ὑπό[+D], except for those with asterisks, for which it is ἐκ.

There are other passages that one might also include as PACs, such
as the following:

(86) Nonn. 3.241–2 ὑπὸ πλήκτρῳ... | ... ἐλελίζετο χορδή
"and the string quivered at the touch of
the plectrum"

But although it is just conceivable that we should understand
ἐλελίζετο as a passive from ἐλελίζω "set in motion, cause to
quiver" with the plectrum as the agent, the construction here seems
closer to that at e.g. 6.21 (καὶ τυπόων ἑλικηδὸν ὑπ' ἀγκυλόδοντι
σιδήρῳ), with the prepositional phrase denoting a combination of
instrument ("with the plectrum/iron") and subjacency ("under the
plectrum/iron"). Such an interpretation also seems likely in light

of the rarity of the active ἐλελίζω, which suggests that ἐλελίζετο is best understood as a middle. Similarly ambiguous cases may be found at 5.154–5 and 6.90–1. What is important, however, is that even if these three borderline passages are included in the figures for Nonnus, that still results in only five PACs in the first six books of the *Dionysiaca*, or a frequency count of 0.27 per 1,000 words, still well below the frequency seen in prose authors or tragedy. The frequency of PACs in late epic, therefore, is demonstrably low, and closer to that of Homer (0.13 / 1,000 words) than classical prose (from 1.36 to 4.02 / 1,000 words).

It is not just in terms of their frequency that the PACs of late epic resemble Homer more than classical prose. Both during the Hellenistic period, when Apollonius was writing, and during the late Imperial period, when Quintus of Smyrna and Nonnus were active, the usual agent marker was ὑπό$^{+G}$. It is hardly to be found, however, in the works of these poets. In the books investigated, the closest any of them came to using ὑπό$^{+G}$ as an agent marker is the following passage in Quintus:

(87) Q. S. 2.51–2   μηδ' ἐνὶ πάτρῃ
           μίμνοντες κτεινώμεθ' ὑπ' Ἀργείων ὀρυμαγδοῦ
           "and let us not, remaining in the country, be
           killed amidst the din of the Argives"

While this passage is certainly reminiscent of Homeric examples where ὑπό$^{+G}$ is used as an agent (cf. (55)), Quintus still shies away from a straightforward agent expression with this construction, for the object of the preposition is not the Argives, but rather the din made by their fighting. Thus, the prepositional phrase as a whole indicates not the agent of the verb κτεινώμεθα, but rather the circumstances under which the action of the verb takes place.

This paucity of agent constructions with ὑπό$^{+G}$ in later epic was no doubt due to the desire to avoid a prosaic construction; such an avoidance must have been especially tempting in light of the alternative provided by ὑπό$^{+D}$, which would have been an easy way to add a Homeric color to one's language. Indeed, as indicated in the table above, ὑπό$^{+D}$ is the preferred means of marking the agent in late epic, accounting for eight of the eleven PACs in the texts in question. At times it occurs in passages which are quite reminiscent of its use in Homer, for example:

(88) A. R. 3.468–9   εἰ δέ μιν αἶσα | δμηθῆναι ὑπὸ βουσί
"and if it is his fate to be defeated by the oxen"

(89) Q. S. 1.804–5   ὅσσαι . . . | . . . ὑπ᾽ Ἀργείοισι δάμησαν
"as many as were defeated by the Argives"

While βουσί does not occur in Homer as an object of ὑπό, the fact that, in both examples, the verb in the PAC is the passive of δάμνημι lends them a decidedly Homeric feel. At other times, however, ὑπό$^{+D}$ is used in PACs in contexts which have gone beyond those where it is found in Homer. Sometimes, its occurrence, though without exact Homeric precedent, nevertheless is understandable in light of the general semantics of the preposition:

(90) A. R. 3.1343   τῆμος ἀρήροτο νειὸς ὑπ᾽ ἀκαμάτῳ ἀροτῆρι
"then, the fallow field was plowed by the tireless plowman"

In (90), for instance, the fact that the field could be viewed as plowed not just *by* the plowman but also *under* the plowman renders the choice of ὑπό$^{+D}$ to mark the agent a natural one. Contrast this with (91):

(91) A. R. 1.794   οὐ μὲν ὑπ᾽ ἀνδράσι ναίεται ἄστυ
"the city is not inhabited by men"

In this example, the use of ὑπό$^{+D}$ seems less motivated by the spatial semantics of the preposition – it is unlikely that the poet should wish to emphasize the location of the city underneath the men that inhabit it – and more by the fact that ὑπό$^{+D}$ is frequently used as an agent marker in Homer and so could be consciously adopted by a later writer as a feature of epic diction.

Nor is ὑπό$^{+D}$ the only Homeric agent marker to be employed by later epic poets. In Apollonius, we also find ἐκ used once in a way that resembles examples (74) to (76) from Homer:[54]

---

[54] The other two examples with ἐκ that I have included in the frequency figures given above are both only marginal PACs, as the agent in both cases is ἄνεμος.

(92) A. R. 1.1098–9 ἐκ γὰρ τῆς ἄνεμοί τε θάλασσά τε νειόθι τε
χθών | πᾶσα πεπείρανται
"for the winds and the sea and all the earth
below have been created by Rhea"

While the exact reading of the verb is in doubt, the most likely
interpretation of this passage is to understand that all the earth has
been made by Rhea. As in (75) and (76), ἐκ is used to denote a
divine agent; as in (74) and (75), the verb is one of accomplishing.
In addition to this Homeric use of ἐκ, the use of the compound
agent marker ὑπὸ χερσί$^{+G}$ also continues in later epic. As was the
case with ὑπό$^{+D}$, it sometimes occurs in contexts similar to those
where it is found in Homer:

(93) A. R. 1.814–15 εἰ καὶ ἐν ὀφθαλμοῖσι δαϊζομένην ὁρόῳτο
μητρυιῆς ὑπὸ χερσὶν ἀτασθάλου
"even though he should see her killed
before his eyes at the hands of her wicked
stepmother"
(94) Q. S. 1.494–5 αὐτὰρ ἐπεὶ καὶ νῆες ἐνιπρήσεσθαι ἔμελλον
χερσὶν ὕπο Τρώων
"but when even the ships were about to be
burned at the hands of the Trojans"

But, again like the later use of ὑπό$^{+D}$, the construction has been
extended to include nouns other than χερσί. Quintus, for instance,
uses παλάμῃσι, which does not occur with ὑπό$^{+D}$ in Homer,[55] but,
as another word for (a part of) the hand, also does not represent a
significant departure from Homeric usage:

(95) Q. S. 1.588–9   ὅσων ὑποκάππεσε γυῖα
Ξάνθου πὰρ προχοῇσιν ὑφ' ἡμετέρης
παλάμῃσιν
"how many people's limbs fell at our hands
besides the streams of Xanthus"

The use of ὑπό with ποσσί also occurs (Q. S. 2.201). Indeed,
the distinction between this class of agent constructions and the

---

[55] It does, however, occur with ὑπό$^{+G}$ once and with ἐν twice; for the passages in question,
see note 47.

use of ὑπό⁺ᴰ to mark the instrument (cf. (86)) or the attendant circumstance can be a fine one:

(96) A. R. 1.6–7   τοῦδ' ἀνέρος ὅντιν' ἴδοιτο
δημόθεν οἰοπέδιλον ὑπ' ἐννεσίῃσι δαμῆναι
"to be defeated at the bidding of the man
whom he would see coming from the people
wearing just one sandal"

While this is not a passage that should be counted among PACs proper – ὑπό⁺ᴰ is not an agent marker here as ἐννεσίῃσι is not the agent, and ὑπ' ἐννεσίῃσι⁺ᴳ conveys too much semantic information to be considered a compound agent marker – it does at least show one way that an epic poet could circumvent the need to employ a PAC altogether.

Conclusion

Homer used PACs too infrequently for the exact conditions that motivated one agent marker over another to be recovered. Nevertheless, the outlines of some general trends are apparent, which, though perhaps tenuous on the basis of Homeric evidence alone, receive further confirmation in light of the practices of later epic poets, as well as those of classical prose, as will be seen in Chapter 4. The chief conclusions may be summarized as follows:

- Both of the agent markers standard in later Greek, the dative of agent and ὑπό⁺ᴳ, were already used by Homer but were not yet grammaticalized in the functions they assumed in Attic prose.
- Another common means of marking the agent was ὑπό⁺ᴰ, which occurs especially with the passive of δάμνημι. That this agent marker was seen as particularly Homeric may be inferred from its frequent use in later epic poets.
- Various ablatival prepositions could also be used. The most frequent of these is ἐκ, which, like ὑπό⁺ᴰ, was taken up by later epic poets as an agent marker.
- The semantics of the verb seem to play a role in determining what agent marker is used: ὑπό, both with the genitive and with the dative, is often found with verbs of subjugation; the

ablatival prepositions, especially ἐκ, are frequently found with verbs of accomplishing or bringing about. Because of the paucity of examples, it might seem tenuous to propose that the semantics of the verb have influenced the choice of agent marker. Nevertheless, that this is the correct interpretation of the data is suggested by the semantic naturalness of using ὑπό, a preposition whose spatial function is to denote subjacency, to mark an agent that is a subjugator, and the ablatival prepositions, whose spatial function is to denote source, to mark an agent that is a creator. This interpretation will be further supported in Chapter 4 by the evidence of classical prose, in which the greater number of PACs allows us to see more clearly how verbs of particular semantic fields could trigger particular prepositions as agent markers.

3

AGENT CONSTRUCTIONS WITH PERFECT PASSIVE VERBS

Most passive verbs in Greek express their agent by means of the preposition ὑπό with the genitive. The most common exception to this rule is that passive verbs in the perfect generally construe with an agent in the dative case:

(1) Hdt. 1.18.2   ὡς καὶ πρότερόν μοι δεδήλωται
    "as has earlier been shown by me"

Because of this anomaly, many scholars have denied that the dative found with perfect passives is an agent at all. Instead, they would describe this usage as a dative of interest. What is less clear, however, is the reason why the perfect is distinguished from the other aspects of the Greek verb in this way. The answer seems to lie in the stative nature of the perfect: if no dynamic action is being described, what place is there for an agent? Furthermore, while it is quite plain that the usage of the Greek perfect changed significantly over the period from Homer to Koine, the effects that this change had on the expression of the agent with the perfect passive have not been fully examined. As early as Herodotus, some perfect verbs have ὑπό$^{+G}$ rather than the dative marking the agent, notably when the subject (that is, patient) of the verb was animate. This use of the perfect passive with an animate patient becomes more frequent by the time of Polybius. At the same time, the construction of perfect passives favored earlier, with inanimate patients and animate agents in the dative, is increasingly replaced by the new, resultative perfect *active*. The greater frequency with which ὑπό$^{+G}$ marks the agent of perfect passive verbs in later Greek can thus be attributed to the growing use of the perfect passive with animate subjects, which expressed their agent with ὑπό$^{+G}$, at the expense of the perfect passive with inanimate subjects, which favored the dative of agent.

The origin of the dative of agent

The dative of agent is problematic for the standard grammars of Greek because of the tension between equating it with the use of ὑπό$^{+G}$ and dissociating it from the prepositional agent constructions. If they were equivalent, then why did Greek maintain two separate means of expressing the agent? If they performed two different functions, then why did the dative occur in what approximates complementary distribution with ὑπό? Kühner–Gerth is closer to the position of equating the two constructions: "Der Dativ steht bei passivischen Ausdrücken scheinbar in gleicher Bedeutung wie ὑπό c. gen. Er bezeichnet auch hier die Person, in deren Interesse eine Handlung vollzogen wird; dass dies zugleich die die Handlung hervorrufende Person ist, ist formell nicht angedeutet" (1904: 422). Somewhere in the middle lies Schwyzer–Debrunner: "Auch in der bes. häufigen Verwendung dieses Dativs beim passiven Perfekt ist er für das Sprachgefühl nicht völlig gleichwertig mit dem später geläufigen Ausdruck des Agens beim Passiv (ὑπό c. gen. et dat.)" (1950: 149). And Humbert sees a significant difference between the two constructions: "On dit ordinairement que le datif équivaut à ὑπὸ suivi du génitif dans les autres thèmes: mais en réalité, le parfait exprimant un état acquis, τὰ πεπραγμένα ἡμῖν ne peut pas signifier: 'les choses qui ont été faites *par* nous,' mais: 'le travail fait *en ce qui nous concerne, pour notre part*'" (1960: 287). He is right to call attention to the perfect's function as a stative. As Hettrich notes, regarding *Od.* 8.472 Δημόδοκον λαοῖσι τετιμένον, "Da keine Handlung im eigentlichen Sinne bezeichnet wird, kann die beteiligte Person auch nicht die Agensrolle ausfüllen" (1990: 75). Thus, at first, the stative perfect was incompatible with the idea of an agent, and the so-called dative of agent was in fact just a dative of interest. Over the centuries from Homer to Polybius, however, the perfect stopped acting exclusively as a stative,[1] and there was no longer any reason for the perfect passive not to construe with an agent. What had been simple datives of interest were then free to be understood as agents, in competition with ὑπό$^{+G}$. In the following paragraphs, I will describe more fully the beginnings of this dative of agent, covering first the nature of the

---

[1] See pp. 81–3 for fuller details.

79

Indo-European perfect, then the force of the dative when construed with the perfect.

In all probability, the PIE perfect of most verbs was originally a stative, although with some verbs it served as an intensive instead.[2] Employing endings distinct from those of the active and middle,[3] it expressed neither action directed at an object nor an action affecting the subject, as did the other two voices, but rather an absence of action, that is, the state resulting from a previous action. One may compare it to German *Die Tür ist geöffnet*, in which it is only important that the door is open, as against *Die Tür wird geöffnet*, in which the action of opening the door comes into play.[4] To continue the analogy with German, it may be noted that only the latter of the two sentences above may be construed with the agent, e.g. *von mir*. As the first sentence describes not an action but a state, there is no logical basis for referring to an agent. So too it must have been with the PIE and, by extension, early Greek perfect. Still, though it could not be construed with an agent, it could occur with a dative.[5]

---

[2] Most scholars agree that the PIE perfect had a stative function, although they dispute the exact nature of the relationship between the perfect and mediopassive endings. Stative function is well-attested across the IE family: for IE generally, see Kuryłowicz 1964: 57–61; for Greek, Wackernagel 1950: 166–71 and Schwyzer–Debrunner 1950: 263–4; for Latin, Hofmann–Szantyr 1965: 317–20; for Sanskrit, MacDonell 1916: 341–2; for Germanic, Meid 1971: 32–4. If the semantics of the verb, chiefly durativity, precluded the strict function of state-resulting-from-an-action, then the function became intensive (Meid 1971: 33).

[3] Many think that the middle endings were originally related to the perfect, as initially proposed by Kuryłowicz 1932 and Stang 1932. Rix 1988, however, would construct a three-voice system, with both active and middle distinct from the stative (later, perfect). Stempel too would construct a three-voice system, comparing IE with Semitic (1995: 525), but sees the middle endings as ultimately derived from a contamination of active and perfect endings (1996: 43–67).

[4] The examples come from Jankuhn (1969: 21). He quotes them in the context of Reichenkron's distinction of four different diatheses (active, middle, stative, passive).

[5] It is possible, of course, that this Greek dative is not an original dative, but rather an instrumental. Certainly, in light of examples (41) to (43) (and possibly (22) and (50)) in Chapter 2, the original instrumental might well have had some role in the creation of the Greek dative of agent. Two facts, however, militate against an instrumental origin for the datives of agent found with perfect verbs. First, there is the very co-occurrence of the dative of agent with the perfect; if the dative of agent is to be explained as an original instrumental, then there should be some link between the perfect and the use of the instrumental. But while there are, to my knowledge, no grounds for connecting the perfect with the instrumental, there is a relationship between the perfect and dative, seen in the similar Latin construction of the type *mihi facta sunt* (Green 1913: 73, Kuryłowicz 1964: 57). Second, the dative of agent with perfect verbs is chiefly found with personal pronouns as agents. If it had been primarily instrumental in origin, we would have expected the

What was the force of this dative? All the related constructions in Greek can be loosely characterized as datives of interest: datives with verbals of necessity, datives with adjectives like φίλος (quite similar to the dative with τετιμένος), and the dative of possession. Indeed, all these functions come quite close to Schwyzer–Debrunner's description of the Greek dative: "Die Hauptfunktion des echten Dativs ist nämlich die Bezeichnung der persönlichen Beteilung an der Verbalhandlung oder die Stellungnahme zu derselben" (1950: 139). So long as the perfect indicated a state rather than an action, the dative could not be an agent, but was instead some manner of dative of interest. As the role of the perfect changed, however, it did begin to describe actions. Two clues then point to a growing equivalence of the dative of agent to ὑπό[+G]. First, the increasing use of ὑπό with the perfect suggests that, *pace* Humbert, it did reach the point where the expression of an agent was not incompatible with the semantics of the perfect. Still, one could argue for a dual function of the perfect, retaining stative function where construed with the dative, but having acquired true passive function where construed with ὑπό. The second point, however, meets this objection: one increasingly sees phrases like εἴρηταί μοι replaced by εἴρηκα.[6] If these two constructions are as interchangeable as λέγεται ὑπ' ἐμοῦ and λέγω, then there is a good case for arguing for the equivalence of the dative of agent and ὑπό, at least in this later stage of Greek.

The development of the Greek perfect system

As mentioned in the previous section, the PIE perfect had endings distinct from the active and mediopassive endings. With these endings, characterized in Greek by the letter α, the perfect could express either a stative, that is, the state of the subject resulting from a prior action, or an intensive, used to indicate emphatic or repeated

range of nominals found in these expressions to have ranged more evenly from inanimate nouns through animate nouns to pronouns.

[6] A similar change may be seen in Latin, where constructions with *mihi est* are replaced by those with *habeo* (Bauer 1996, 1997: 288–90). While the Greek evidence is different in that the starting-point is not a perfect participle with the copula, there is still the movement from a stative construction with a dative agent to a transitive construction with a nominative agent.

action. Both these functions are present in early Greek, although the Mycenaean evidence is quite slim.[7] For the stative function, consider Mycenaean *a-ra-ru-wo-a* (KN Ra 1541 and others), equivalent to ἀρηρώς, or Homeric *Il.* 18.12 ἦ μάλα δὴ τέθνηκε Μενοιτίου ἄλκιμος υἱός, *Il.* 2.135 καὶ δὴ δοῦρα σέσηπε νεῶν καὶ σπάρτα λέλυνται. The intensive perfect, though not found in Mycenaean owing to the nature of the texts, can be found in Homer at e.g. *Il.* 17.264 βέβρυχεν μέγα κῦμα, *Il.* 8.559 γέγηθε δέ τε φρένα ποιμήν.[8] However, as is clear from λέλυνται in *Il.* 2.135, the mediopassive endings could also be used with the perfect stem in the same stative function. In fact, these mediopassive perfects are the more common type in Mycenaean, found both in a finite form like *e-pi-de-da-to* (PY Vn 20.1), "a été distribué," which represents ἐπιδέδασται, as well as in several participles, like *a-pu ke-ka-u-me-no* (PY Ta 641.1), equivalent to κεκαυμένος. Chantraine ascribes the advent of these mediopassive perfects to an imbalance in the system, with present middles aligned anomalously with the old "alphatic" perfect forms (e.g. γίγνομαι/γέγονα and ὄλλυμαι/ὄλωλα), once the latter were reinterpreted as actives rather than as a third voice distinct from the active-middle opposition (1927: 24–36).[9]

At this point, both the old alphatic and new mediopassive endings were in competition to mark the (usually intransitive) stative perfect. Then, in the fifth century, the alphatic endings were increasingly reinterpreted as active *transitive* endings paired with the mediopassive intransitive. Although intransitive significance

[7] For instance, there are no finite perfects in Mycenaean with -α endings. For a full study of the perfects in Mycenaean, see Chantraine 1967.

[8] Sauge appears to take this type of perfect as the starting-point for his investigation of the perfect, in which he links together several types of construction as "factitif" (2000: ix). His terminology is very confused, however, with his factitive including not only a causative ("je fais crier quelqu'un"), but also distinct agentive reflexives ("Je fais que je crie" = "je crie de toutes mes forces") and ergatives (!) ("je suis fait crier" = "je crie-sous l'effet de la douleur, par exemple") (*ibid.* ix n. 1). In the end, he is led to absurdities, as seen, for instance, in his description of the perfect as ultimately causative: "Ainsi, la structure de base est celle d'une construction transitive (causatif) devenant absolue *par effacement* soit de l'agent (agentive-refléxive), soit de l'incitateur ('passif'), c'est-à-dire de l'un des deux rôles. C'est ce que l'examen du verb τέθνηκα permettait de confirmer: à la construction transitive τέθνηκε τίς τινα (X fait mourir Y) répondent la construction réflexive-agentive (τέθνηκε τίς) 'X fait mourir [lui-même]' et la construction 'passive': 'τέθνηκε τίς' 'X [est fait qu'il] meurt'" (84).

[9] See also Kuryłowicz 1964: 63.

was retained in some common verbs like γέγονα, many new perfects with alphatic endings were transitive, especially aspirated and
kappatic perfects such as τέταχα and λέλυκα. The exact force of
this perfect is subject to some debate. It is usually called the resultative perfect, as the emphasis is believed to have shifted from the
state of the subject to the result of the action on the object. Wackernagel introduced the term in explaining why Attic Greek could
form δέδωκα and τέθηκα, but Homeric Greek could not. He pointed
out that the semantics of these verbs were not compatible with the
primarily stative usages of the perfect in Homer. These forms were
not possible until the perfect had acquired an additional sense, as
it did in Attic, in which "das Perfekt von einer vergangenen Handlung gebraucht wird, deren Wirkung im oder am Objekt noch in der
Gegenwart fortdauert" (1904: 4). In such cases, it was no longer
the state of the subject that mattered, but the effect of the action on
the object. Chantraine continues this view (1927: 119–45). McKay,
however, questions it in two articles on the Greek perfect, one dealing with literary Greek, one with non-literary papyri (1965, 1980).
In his opinion, throughout the history of the Greek perfect, it is the
state of the subject that remains important (1965: 9–11; 1980: 33).
He explains the change in the perfect instead as "an increasingly
conscious implication of the past and present time relationship in
the essential state idea of the perfect" (1965: 11). Still, whether
one takes Wackernagel's or McKay's position, it is adequate for
this study simply to note the increase in transitive perfects (compare Slings 1986: 11 n. 15). For, with the alphatic endings reinterpreted as active transitives, and the mediopassive endings function-
ing as intransitives, the perfect system began to act more like the
present and aorist: the increasingly common transitive active was
opposed to an intransitive mediopassive.[10] This shift in the perfect
system was to affect the expression of the agent with the perfect
passive.

---

[10] For the widespread use of the transitive perfect in post-classical Greek, see Mandilaras for
the evidence from non-literary papyri (1973: §461–81). Both his "extensive" (§465–6)
and resultative (§467–9) categories come into play. As for the NT evidence, see Blass–
Debrunner 1961: §342–3. Moulton does note that the resultative perfect had begun to
wane slightly by the NT, which shows far fewer innovative forms than the Septuagint
(1976: 83–4).

The development of the dative of agent

With the growth of the transitive perfect active and the consequent opposition of active and passive in the perfect, one might well expect the expression of the agent to change. In general, there is a growing tendency to use ὑπό⁺ᴳ rather than the dative to express the agent. In the following section, I will examine the expression of the agent with perfect verbs, starting with Herodotus, to illustrate the gradual rise of ὑπό⁺ᴳ. An analysis of the data will follow.[11]

In Herodotus, the dative is the most common means of expressing the agent of a perfect passive verb. Of the twenty-six PACs in Book 1 involving verbs of the perfect system, nineteen express the agent with the dative, compared to six with ὑπό⁺ᴳ (and one with ὑπό⁺ᴰ).[12] Typical examples include:

(2) Hdt. 1.123.2   πρὸ δ' ἔτι τούτου τάδε οἱ κατέργαστο
"and even before this, the following things had been done by him"

(3) Hdt. 1.130.3   ὡς εἴρηταί μοι πρότερον
"as has been said by me earlier"

It is found with a wide range of verbs: three times with ἐξευρίσκω, κατεργάζομαι, and λέγω, twice with νομίζω, and once each with αἱρέω, δηλόω, ἐκτοξεύω, ἐξεργάζομαι, καταστρέφω, κοσμέω, ὀρύσσω, ποιέω:

[11] I pass over the perfect PACs in Homer as they have already been discussed in Chapter 2, and, more importantly, they are extremely rare: there are only thirteen in all of Homer (about 200,000 words), as opposed to twenty-six in the first book of Herodotus (about 30,000 words). Thus, they can do little to further the interpretation of the classical construction. Still, I will offer a short account of their distribution. Seven of the thirteen perfect PACs are with the dative, but five of these do not resemble the classical construction as the subject is personal: in three cases, the verb is τετιμένος (or -ον) (Il. 24.533, Od. 8.472, 13.28), in two it is δεδμη- (Il. 3.183, Od. 11.621–2). It seems likely that the use of the dative is to be connected with the semantics of the verbs rather than their being perfects. As for the other two perfect PACs with the dative, they do look more like the later construction (Il. 13.168, Od. 5.262). The two examples with ὑπό still show the local sense of the preposition (Il. 21.318, Od. 3.305), the two with πρός are very unusual (Il. 6.56–7, 11.831), and only the two with ἐκ look like later constructions with ὑπό. The dative might have been avoided in Il. 18.74–5 because there could have been ambiguity with the τοι already present, and in Od. 7.69–70, because the subject is animate.

[12] The nineteen examples with the dative are found at 8.4, 18.2, 68.6, 77.2, 86.3, 100.2, 123.2, 123.3, 130.3, 138.1, 165.2, 169.2, 185.5, 201.1, 202.1, 202.2, 214.2, 216.3; the six examples with ὑπό⁺ᴳ at 35.3, 40.1, 59.1, 63.2, 114.5, 148.1; the one example with ὑπό⁺ᴰ at 94.7.

(4) Hdt. 1.185.5   ἐπείτε δέ οἱ ὀρώρυκτο
"and when it had been dug by her"

(5) Hdt. 1.214.2   ὡς σφι τὰ βέλεα ἐξετετόξευτο
"when their arrows had all been shot by
them"

While the agent is usually a pronoun, two of the nineteen agents
are nouns:

(6) Hdt. 1.8.4   πάλαι δὲ τὰ καλὰ ἀνθρώποισι ἐξεύρηται
"and that which is noble has been known by
men for a long time"

(7) Hdt. 1.201.1   ὡς δὲ τῷ Κύρῳ καὶ τοῦτο τὸ ἔθνος
κατέργαστο
"and when this nation too had been defeated
by Cyrus"

The subject of the verb is often impersonal or a demonstrative
pronoun, as in examples (2) and (3).[13] Finally, only five of the
nineteen PACs involve participles.[14]

PACs with ὑπό are less frequent, exceptions where ὑπό is used
instead of the dative falling into two well-defined groups. First, a
dative of agent is avoided when it would be ambiguous, generally
because the semantics of the verb would cause the dative to be
understood as an indirect object. Two of the PACs with ὑπό fall
into this category:

(8) Hdt. 1.63.2   ἔλεγον τὰ ἐντεταλμένα ὑπὸ Πεισιστράτου[15]
"and they said what they had been told to say
by Pisistratus"

(9) Hdt. 1.148.1   κοινῇ ἐξαραιρημένος ὑπὸ Ἰώνων Ποσειδέωνι
Ἑλικωνίῳ
"dedicated jointly by the Ionians to Poseidon
of Helicon"

---

[13] There are four PACs in explanatory ὡς clauses (18.2, 86.3, 130.3, 169.2), and four with
demonstrative pronouns as subjects (123.2, 123.3, 165.2, 216.3); one could probably
also include 100.2 in this group.

[14] 68.6, 86.3, 123.3, 185.1, 202.1.

[15] For ἐντέλλω with the dative, compare Hdt. 7.149.2 περὶ δὲ ἡγεμονίης αὐτοῖσι ἐντετάλθαι
ὑποκρίνασθαι.

Second, ὑπό is used when the subject of the verb is personal or quasi-personal. The other four PACs with ὑπό meet this criterion:

(10) Hdt. 1.35.3   ἐξεληλαμένος τε ὑπὸ τοῦ πατρὸς καὶ
ἐστερημένος πάντων
"banished by my father and deprived of
all I had"

(11) Hdt. 1.40.1   ὡς ὤν νενικημένος ὑπὸ σέο μεταγινώσκω
"as I have been prevailed upon by you, I'll
change my mind"

(12) Hdt. 1.59.1   κατεχόμενόν τε καὶ διεσπασμένον
ἐπυνθάνετο ὁ Κροῖσος ὑπὸ Πεισιστράτου
"Croesus found out that [the population of
Attica] was being oppressed and divided by
Pisistratus son of Hippocrates"

(13) Hdt. 1.114.5   ὑπὸ τοῦ σοῦ δούλου, βουκόλου δὲ παιδὸς
ὧδε περιυβρίσμεθα
"we have been outraged in this way by one
who is your slave and the child of an
herdsman"

In contrast to the perfect PACs with the dative, the majority of these PACs are participles. Furthermore, the agent is, except in 1.40.1, a noun rather than a pronoun.

It is self-evident that the use of ὑπό in passages (8) and (9) is motivated by a need to clarify the roles of the nouns in the sentence. But the same need, if less obviously, also explains the use of ὑπό in examples (10) through (13), when the subject of the verb is personal. For one may rank nouns and pronouns in an animacy hierarchy according to the likelihood of their occurring as the agent of a sentence: at the top of the scale, first- and second-person pronouns are most likely, then third-person pronouns and demonstratives, then human nouns, other animate nouns, and finally, at the bottom, inanimate nouns.[16] Such a hierarchy can have a tangible influence on the morphology and syntax of a language. Languages

---

[16] This analysis originated from a study of split-ergativity in Australian languages (Silverstein 1976) and has been taken up by Dixon in his works on ergativity (1979: 85–91 and 1994: 83–97). Wierzbicka 1981 offers the cautionary note that, when one looks solely at sentences describing interactions between humans, first-person pronouns may actually be more frequent as patients than agents. Although they question the validity of

with inverse systems, for instance, show special marking whenever the noun that is lower down on the hierarchy is the agent instead of, as expected, the patient.[17] In Greek too, the use of ὑπό with certain perfect passives can be explained in this way. If the agent is animate, and the patient is inanimate, then the two participants are fulfilling their expected roles, and even a relatively ambiguous agent marker like the dative of agent is sufficient to signal these roles. But if both agent and patient are animate, then both participants have equal potential to be the agent, and ὑπό is necessary to clarify which is the patient, which the agent. Similarly, the animacy hierarchy can explain why the dative of agent is so common with pronouns: because pronouns are prototypical agents, the dative is likelier to be a sufficient indication of the agentive status of a pronoun than of a noun. At this point, it is also worth recalling the pragmatic evidence from Aristophanes discussed in Chapter 1. In prose, the agent in a PAC is likely to be high-animacy, whether the agent marker is ὑπό or the dative of agent. But the situation is different in Aristophanes, where there is a dichotomy between ὑπό marking low-animacy agents, and the dative of agent marking high-animacy agents. It is not surprising, then, to find that, in prose too, the exceptional circumstance where ὑπό marks the agent with perfect verbs typically occurs when that agent is relatively low-animacy.

One may then summarize the data from Herodotus as follows. Perfect PACs generally cluster at two ends of a continuum with the following characteristics:

dative of agent ⟵⟶ ὑπό$^{+G}$

dative of agent	ὑπό$^{+G}$
• subject is inanimate	• subject is animate
• agent usually pronoun	• agent usually noun
• verb rarely a participle	• verb frequently a participle

Wierzbicka's including only human–human interactions in her data, Mallinson–Blake agree that it may be best not to see the hierarchy in terms of the likelihood of being the agent, but rather of being the topic (1981: 80–91). While this latter formulation may work well for English, the data presented in Chapter 1 – in particular, Greek's readiness to demote the first-person pronoun to an oblique, non-topical agent expression – suggest that, for Greek at least, the hierarchy describes the likelihood of a participant's being the agent. At any rate, whatever the best theoretical description may be, the parallel between Greek and languages with inverse systems seems clear.

[17] For examples, see Palmer 1994: 207–11.

In Herodotus, PACs at the left end of the scale are more common. As the perfect becomes more integrated with the present and aorist, we might expect more PACs at the right end, as it is closer to the PAC usage found with these other tenses. The evidence presented below will show that this is indeed true.

In classical Attic, the nature of the PACs found with perfect verbs varies widely from author to author. Based on numbers alone, sample texts from Thucydides and Demosthenes have more PACs with the dative, Xenophon more with ὑπό, and Lysias and Plato lie somewhere in between, as seen in the middle column below:[18]

Author	% PACs with dative	% PACs with dative (modified)
Thucydides	83 (10/12)	83 (10/12)
Demosthenes	75 (21/28)	50 (7/14)
Lysias	48 (15/31)	33 (8/24)
Plato	39 (9/23)	18 (3/17)
Xenophon	11 (1/9)	11 (1/9)

These numbers, however, are misleading. While Thucydides does employ the dative of agent in a wide range of usages, the figures for Demosthenes and Lysias are inflated by the frequency of such participial constructions as τῶν πεπραγμένων αὐτῷ, and the count for Plato by the common occurrence of PACs with ὁμολογέω. If these constructions are left out of the tally, the figures for Thucydides and Xenophon remain the same, but those for Demosthenes, Lysias, and Plato drop, as indicated in the right column. Before examining these figures in light of the parameters mentioned above – whether the subject is animate, whether the agent is a pronoun, and whether the verb is a participle – I must first discuss two issues regarding participles. Two phenomena appear related, but are in fact probably distinct. First, in Herodotus, it will be seen that substantivized participles, i.e. participles used

---

[18] The texts examined were Thucydides 6, 7, Lysias 1–8, 14, 31, 32, Xenophon *Anabasis* 1.1–4.5, Plato *Euthyphro, Apology, Crito, Symposium*, and Demosthenes 4, 9, 21, 27, 28.

with the definite article as nouns, behave anomalously in their agent constructions. In Chapter 4, I will ascribe their behavior to the disruption of the verbal category of voice that occurs when a verb is used in a predominantly non-verbal way. A different discrepancy, however, is discussed in the following section: substantivized neuter participles behave more like *finite* verbs, usually taking the dative of agent, as against other, more adjectival participles, which are found more often with prepositions. I would suggest that the dative was the original usage, but that, as the perfect passive mimicked the present and aorist more and more, use of ὑπό spread rapidly with most participles, as this was a favored context for present and aorist passives. At the same time, the dative survived most persistently in set phrases that could involve either finite verbs, such as ὡς εἴρηταί μοι, or substantivized neuter participles, like τὰ πεπραγμένα αὐτῷ. Let us consider now each author in turn.

The dative of agent with perfect verbs is well established in Thucydides. In Books 6 and 7, it is found ten times, compared to two instances of ὑπό. It is found with nine different verbs, mostly resembling the verbs used by Herodotus in perfect PACs.[19] Twice the agent is a noun, elsewhere a pronoun. In all cases, the subject of the verb is either impersonal or neuter. It is not found with the participle, only with the indicative. That Thucydides should be so prone to use the dative of agent with perfect passives is only to be expected, considering his fondness for the construction with other tenses as well.[20]

At first glance, Demosthenes too would seem to favor the dative of agent, with twenty-one of the twenty-eight PACs with perfect verbs taking a dative of agent. However, fourteen of them – half the total number of perfect PACs – belong to a limited class, namely, participles used with the definite article as neuter substantives. Furthermore, in twelve of these, the verb is πράσσω, with

---

[19] These are ἁμαρτάνω, ἀποτελέω, διαπολεμέω, ἐξεργάζομαι, ἑτοιμάζω, εὑρίσκω, λέγω (2×), παρασκευάζομαι, and πράσσω.

[20] Examples are found at 6.16.3 (maybe), 87.3; 7.11.2, 26.1, 27.3, 34.4; see also 7.70.7 for a striking example with a verbal noun. Rusten 1989 points out instances at 2.7.2, 35.3, 41.4, 43.5, 46.1, 77.2, and 101.5.

only two instances of other verbs.[21] Curiously, this construction does not appear to have been used by Herodotus or Thucydides. In Herodotus, PACs containing such nominalized participles are often marked by non-standard prepositional usages and are quite rare in the perfect anyway; substantivized perfect participles with agents are not found in Thucydides 6 or 7, though a present passive participle does occur – with a dative agent (6.87.3). It should also be noted that, of PACs in Demosthenes with perfect participles, all fourteen neuter participles with the definite article take the dative, never a preposition, while the participles that are not substantivized always take a preposition, never the dative: good evidence for distinguishing between the two types of participles. The PAC at 21.195 might appear to be a counter-example, for it does show a substantivized participle used with a preposition. This participle, however, is masculine plural and should be regarded separately from the more common construction with the neuter participle. Its patient, after all, is animate, rather than inanimate, and it therefore falls naturally into the prepositional category. Still, the dative of agent is clearly prominent in Demosthenes even if these participial constructions are disregarded on the grounds that, as a quasi-formulaic expression, they skew the data in favor of the dative of agent: the remaining seven examples include one with a noun agent[22] and five verbs other than πράσσω.

The situation in Lysias is similar. Of fifteen PACs with the dative, seven involve neuter participles used as substantives (4× πράσσω, 2× ποιέω, 1× ἀσεβέω). If these are omitted, the ratio of PACs with the dative of agent to those with prepositional agent markers is 8:16. As in Demosthenes, there is a tendency, though not as absolute, for substantivized participles to take the dative (seven of nine) and non-substantivized participles to construe with a preposition (ten of twelve).

In Plato, the ratio of PACs with the dative of agent to those with ὑπό is similar to that of Lysias. While the number of PACs with

---

[21] 21.18 τοῖς ἑαυτῷ νενεανιευμένοις, 21.169 τοιαῦτ᾽ ἦν αὐτῷ τὰ λελητουργημένα καὶ πεπραγμένα.

[22] 9.25 πάνθ᾽ ὅσ᾽ ἐξημάρτηται καὶ Λακεδαιμονίοις ἐν τοῖς τριάκοντ᾽ ἐκείνοις ἔτεσιν καὶ τοῖς ἡμετέροις προγόνοις ἐν τοῖς ἑβδομήκοντα.

the dative is not as swollen by substantivized participles as it is in the orators – only two of nine fall into this category – it does seem to be inflated by a number of PACs with ὁμολογέω, which, as will be seen in Chapter 4, often shows peculiar behavior in its agent constructions, favoring the dative of agent even with verbs that are not perfect passives. If one leaves out the PACs with ὁμολογέω, which include the two involving substantivized participles, only three PACs with the dative remain, as against fourteen with ὑπό.[23]

As for Xenophon, the number of PACs with perfect passives is, as a whole, quite low, with only eight found in 122 OCT pages, approximately the same sample size as used for the other authors. Of these, only one involved a dative of agent, *An.* 1.8.12 κἂν τοῦτ', ἔφη, νικῶμεν, πάνθ' ἡμῖν πεποίηται.

If the authors are arranged chronologically, with Thucydides and Lysias born in the mid-fifth century, Plato and Xenophon in the late fifth century, and Demosthenes in the early fourth century, the pro-portion of PACs with ὑπό does gradually rise – with the notable exception of Demosthenes, who uses the dative of agent quite fre-quently. It might seem arbitrary to discount Demosthenes as an exception, were it not for the general rarity of ὑπό in Homer and its frequency in Polybius and, even more so, in the New Testament, discussed below. There is thus evidence for a trend of increasing use of ὑπό in perfect passive constructions.

In conjunction with this spread of ὑπό, one should also look at the other parameters that vary according as the agent is marked by ὑπό or the dative: the animacy of the subject, whether the agent is a noun or a pronoun, and whether or not the verb is an adjectival participle.[24] Consider the following two charts:

---

[23] Among the PACs with ὁμολογέω, I include *Cri.* 49a ἢ πᾶσαι ἡμῖν ἐκεῖναι αἱ πρόσθεν ὁμολογίαι ἐν ταῖσδε ταῖς ὀλίγαις ἡμέραις ἐκκεχυμέναι εἰσίν. It is unclear whether ἡμῖν is to be understood as an agent of ἐκκεχυμέναι εἰσίν. Even if it is, the construction is likely to have been influenced by the noun ὁμολογίαι as well as the preceding clause, in which the *aorist* of ὁμολογέω is construed with a dative of agent: ὡς πολλάκις ἡμῖν καὶ ἐν τῷ ἔμπροσθεν χρόνῳ ὡμολογήθη.

[24] Here and in the following table, I define "adjectival" to mean all participles except for neuter participles used with the definite article.

PACs with dative	% inanim. subject	% pronom. agent	% adjl. ptcl.
Thucydides	100 (10/10)	80 (8/10)	0 (0/10)
Lysias	100 (15/15)	80 (12/15)	13 (2/15)
Plato	100 (9/9)	89 (8/9)[a]	11 (1/9)
Xenophon	100 (1/1)	100 (1/1)	0 (0/1)
Demosthenes	100 (21/21)	90 (19/21)	0 (0/21)

[a] The one agent that is a noun occurs at *Smp*. 201d ἐκ τῶν ὡμολογημένων ἐμοὶ καὶ Ἀγάθωνι. Willingness to have a noun be a dative of agent probably results from the fact that the verb is ὁμολογέω. Furthermore, use of the dative could well have been motivated by the pronoun ἐμοί.

PACs with preps.	% anim. subject	% noun agent	% adjl. ptcl.
Thucydides	50 (1/2)	100 (2/2)	50 (1/2)
Lysias	44 (7/16)	63 (10/16)	62 (10/16)
Plato	71 (10/14)	64 (8/14)	57 (8/14)
Xenophon	63 (5/8)	75 (6/8)	50 (4/8)
Demosthenes	71 (5/7)	14 (1/7)	57 (4/7)

For the entire period, it is clear that, while the dative of agent is most often limited to the prototypical context of an inanimate subject and a pronominal agent and is rarely found with participles (except for those that are neuter substantives), the prepositional PACs often extend into situations involving one or more of the conditions typical of PACs with the dative. Determining the motivation for prepositional PACs with inanimate subjects is particularly important. Without fail, an animate subject requires a prepositional PAC.[25] But what causes a perfect passive with an inanimate subject to construe with ὑπό$^{+G}$ rather than with the dative of agent?

If we take the dative as the default construction with inanimate subjects, we find that the PACs with prepositions usually fall into certain categories. First, a prepositional PAC can occur when the

[25] This statement holds absolutely true for my own corpus. Smyth only notes two counter-examples, at D. 19.247 and 57.10, where "the subject is personal and the person is treated as a thing in order to express scorn" (1920: 344).

semantics of the verb make it more natural for the dative to be interpreted as an indirect object. At Pl. *Smp.* 183c and 188c, we see that the dative with the perfect passive of προστάσσω refers to the person *to* whom, not *by* whom something was ordered. Thus, at *Ap.* 33c, it is not surprising that the agent is expressed with ὑπό, especially as there is already a dative, ἐμοί, indicating the person to whom the command was given: ἐμοὶ δὲ τοῦτο, ὡς ἐγώ φημι, προστέτακται ὑπὸ τοῦ θεοῦ. Seven of the nineteen prepositional PACs with perfect verbs and inanimate subjects belong to this category.[26] Still, Thucydides does not shrink from ambiguity in this respect: with εἴρηται, the dative can refer either to the agent (6.2.1, 6.94.1) or to the indirect object (6.42.2, 67.1; 7.4.7, 10.1, 20.1, 2).

There are three other cases in which the dative is avoided because it would be ambiguous, not because the semantics of the verb prompt interpretation as an indirect object, but because another dative is present: Lys. 14.19 (τοῖς ὑπὸ τούτων περὶ τὴν πόλιν πεπραγμένοις), where a dative of agent might be confused with the dative of the participle, and Pl. *Euthphr.* 6b (καὶ ὑπὸ τῶν ἀγαθῶν γραφέων τά τε ἄλλα ἱερὰ ἡμῖν καταπεποίκιλται) and *Smp.* 177a (ἄλλοις μέν τισι θεῶν ὕμνους καὶ παίωνας εἶναι ὑπὸ τῶν ποιητῶν πεποιημένους), where datives of interest are present. Lys. 1.24 (ἀνεῳγμένης τῆς θύρας καὶ ὑπὸ τῆς ἀνθρώπου παρεσκευασμένης)[27] might also belong in this category, as a dative might be interpreted as dative of interest – though, unlike the other examples just mentioned, there is no directly competing dative.

Occasionally, the preposition, especially when it is other than ὑπό, is used to add a nuance associated with the particular meaning of the preposition. At Lys. 1.2 and D. 21.41, παρά[+D] is used with γιγνώσκω, as often occurs with this verb, indicating that what is known is not so much effected by someone as present with them.[28]

---

[26] In addition to the example from the *Apology*, instances can be found at Lys. 3.15 and 3.37 (μαρτυρέω), 7.29 (προστάσσω), D. 21.170, Pl. *Smp.* 183b, and X. *An.* 1.1.6 (all with δίδωμι).

[27] Francken suggests that the text here is corrupt and deletes ὑπό, presumably because it is otiose to say that the door was opened *and* prepared by the maid and therefore better to suppose that the maid herself was prepared. I disagree, as I think it is possible for the speaker to have emphasized both the physical opening of the door as well as the conspiratorial complicity of the maid in doing so.

[28] For further discussion of παρά[+D] as an agent marker, see Chapter 4.

Note especially the parallelism in the Lysias: καὶ ταῦτα οὐκ ἂν εἴη μόνον παρ' ὑμῖν οὕτως ἐγνωσμένα, ἀλλ' ἐν ἁπάσῃ τῇ Ἑλλάδι. Furthermore, at two places in Lys. 7, διά[+A] and ὑπό are used because the guilt of the speaker depends on whether or not he was the agent of the verbs in question.

There remain four prepositional PACs which, taken together, suggest that another important condition motivating the use of a prepositional agent marker was the fact that the agent was a noun, rather than a pronoun. Two of these examples are found in Xenophon, at *An.* 2.2.16 and 4.2.10. In both cases, the agent is a noun. The only dative of agent that does occur in my sample of Xenophon is the pronominal ἡμῖν. Xenophon may well have restricted the use of the dative of agent to pronouns in favor of a more widespread use of ὑπό. In the other two PACs as well, Th. 6.96.2 (καὶ ὠνόμασται ὑπὸ τῶν Συρακοσίων διὰ τὸ ἐπιπολῆς τοῦ ἄλλου εἶναι Ἐπιπολαί), and Lys. 5.1 (τὰ παρὰ τῶν ἄλλων εἰρημένα), the agent is a noun, not a pronoun. Though these authors were certainly capable of using the dative of agent with nouns, it seems likely that in these two passages, their choice of prepositional agent markers is indicative of a general tendency to prefer prepositions when marking nouns as agents.

By the time of Polybius, the New Testament (NT), and Plutarch, the dative of agent with the perfect passive has become much rarer.[29] In the particular texts selected for study, only four of the nineteen PACs (21 per cent) with perfect passives in Polybius and none of the eight in the NT or the three in Plutarch have a dative of agent. Those datives of agent that are present in Polybius are restricted to the canonical form: all have inanimate subjects, all have pronominal agents, and only two different verbs are found (3× λέγω, 1× παρασκευάζομαι). To some extent, the decline in the use of the dative of agent results from the fact that the use of prepositional agent markers had started to encroach on what in

---

[29] Texts searched exhaustively for PACs with perfect verbs were Book 3 of Polybius (in Foucault's Budé edition), *Mark* and *Acts* (in the Nestle–Aland edition), and Plutarch's *Life of Antony* (in the Mondadori edition of Amandini *et al.*). Additional information on the PACs with specific verbs was collected by means of TLG searches of all of Polybius and the NT and of all of the *Lives* of Plutarch.

classical Attic would have been the domain of the dative. But, as the dative of agent frequently continues to be used in the circumscribed contexts where it was found earlier, the greater part of its decline should be attributed to the reduction in the occurrence of those contexts, largely as a result of the increased use of the perfect active.

Consider the six times in Polybius 3 that a preposition marks the agent in a PAC with an inanimate subject. Two of these PACs probably would have had a prepositional agent marker in Attic as well: 3.33.18, where the verb, κατατάσσω, induces the use of ὑπό, as the dative could be interpreted as the beneficiary, and 3.44.5 (καὶ δι' ἑρμηνέως τὰ δεδογμένα παρ' αὐτῶν διεσάφει τοῖς ὄχλοις), where the presence of an additional dative, τοῖς ὄχλοις, could have motivated the use of a prepositional agent marker to avoid ambiguity. But, in the other four cases, one might well have expected an Attic author to have used the dative of agent. Certainly the PACs at 3.9.1 and 3.33.17, both with substantivized participles (from γράφω and πράσσω), the first with a pronominal agent, resemble the many in Lysias and Demosthenes that have the dative. So too, it is conceivable that the PAC at 3.21.2 (ταύτας . . . ἤδη συνωμολογημένας ὑπὸ Λυτατίου), with the verb συνομολογέω, would have taken a dative in Plato. The construction at 3.40.8 (κατέσυραν τὴν κατακεκληρουχημένην χώραν ὑπὸ Ῥωμαίων) is less clear. A dative would have been ambiguous, as it could have been read as a dative of possession, but such ambiguity would not have significantly altered the semantics of the sentence. Indeed, it is the ambiguous interpretation of a dative of interest, closely connected with the dative of possession, that led to the dative of agent in the first place.

Mark and *Acts* provide only three examples in which a preposition marks the agent of a perfect passive whose subject is inanimate, but here too the construction with ὑπό may have spread to contexts that formerly elicited the dative. The PAC with προστάσσω at *Acts* 10.33 would have called for ὑπό in Attic; such might also be the case with *Acts* 16.4 (τὰ δόγματα τὰ κεκριμένα ὑπὸ τῶν ἀποστόλων). But *Mark* 5.4 provides a good example of an environment that would probably have called for a dative of agent in classical Greek: διὰ τό . . . διεσπάσθαι ὑπ' αὐτοῦ τὰς ἁλύσεις καὶ τὰς πέδας συντετρῖφθαι.[30]

Plutarch's *Life of Antony* offers only three examples of PACs with perfect verbs, at 46.4 and 76.2 with ὑπό and at 61.2 with παρά[+G]. In both PACs with ὑπό, the verb's subject is animate and ὑπό is thus expected. As for the PAC with παρά[+G] (ἦν δὲ καὶ παρὰ τοῦ Μήδων βασιλέως ἀπεσταλμένη βοήθεια), the dative of agent might have been avoided in classical Attic as well, considering that the agent is a noun, not a pronoun. The use of παρά[+G] is due to the semantics of the verb.[31] This evidence from Plutarch, then, is insufficient to settle the question as to whether his avoidance of the dative of agent represents a significant departure from the standards of Attic.

Thus, while these initial figures give some support to the view that the use of the dative to mark the agent of perfect passives gradually declined in favor of ὑπό and other prepositions, it is necessary to examine a somewhat wider corpus in order to ensure that the data can be more conclusive. The remainder of this section, then, singles out ten verbs that construe with the dative of agent in Herodotus or Thucydides and describes, on the basis of an examination of the entire corpus of Polybius and the NT and all of Plutarch's *Lives*, the frequency with which the perfect passives of these verbs continue to construe with the dative of agent. On the whole, it will be seen that the dative of agent continues to be a agent marker, and that the infrequency with which it occurs in these later authors results not so much from a move towards ὑπό as the agent marker with perfect passives as from the increased use of the perfect active, eliminating the need for an oblique agent marker altogether.

Consider, then, the following ten verbs, all of which construe with a dative of agent in Herodotus or Thucydides: ἁμαρτάνω, γράφω, δηλόω, ἐργάζομαι (and its compounds), ἑτοιμάζω, εὑρίσκω (and its compounds), λέγω, νομίζω, ποιέω, and πράττω. First, we must consider the general frequency in Polybius, the NT,

---

[30] One of the uncial manuscripts has a different text here, with the verb rephrased in the active voice, but its presence in the other manuscripts suggests that it was legitimate Greek of the period.

[31] See Chapter 4 for further details about the use of παρά[+G] with verbs of sending.

and Plutarch's *Lives* of the dative of agent with these verbs. The only three which occur more than twice with the dative of agent are δηλόω, λέγω, and πράττω. The first of these, δηλόω, occurs four times with a dative of agent in Polybius, and never with a dative of agent in the NT or Plutarch's *Lives*; furthermore, in all four of the occurrences of the dative of agent with δηλόω in Polybius, the agent in question is the personal pronoun ἡμῖν, and the verb itself is always the indicative form δεδήλωται. This distribution gives the strong impression that, in this expression at least, the dative of agent is preserved as a fossilized form. The second verb, λέγω, occurs twenty-three times with the dative of agent in these authors: twenty-one times in Polybius, never in the NT, and twice in Plutarch's *Lives*.[32] Despite its frequency in Polybius, the dative of agent with λέγω seems nearly as fossilized as that with δηλόω: in one PAC (10.11.4), the agent is πολλοῖς, but in all the others (excluding the participial PACs discussed below) it is either ἡμῖν or, once, μοι. As for the two examples in Plutarch, one occurs close to the beginning of *Phocion*, in a context that suggests that the dative of agent, by now rare, could be used as a high-register rhetorical device:

(14) Plut. *Phoc.* 1.2   τοῦτο δ' εἰ καὶ τῷ ῥήτορι θρασύτερον
                          εἴρηται
                          "and if this has been said by the speaker
                          rather boldly"

The other occurs in a passage where the dative of agent with λέγω is parallel to one with πράττω, the verb with which, it will be seen shortly, the dative of agent was most persistent:

(15) Plut. *Ct. Mi.* 52.3   Πομπηΐου δ' εἰπόντος, μαντικώτερα μὲν
                             εἰρῆσθαι Κάτωνι, φιλικώτερα δ' αὐτῷ
                             πεπρᾶχθαι
                             "and when Pompey said that more
                             prophetic words had been spoken by
                             Cato, but that friendlier actions had been
                             carried out by himself"

---

[32] I have restricted these data to perfects formed from the stem εἰρη-.

The third verb, then, which is found more than twice with the dative of agent in these texts, is indeed πράττω, with which this construction is found thirty times, nineteen times in Polybius, once in the NT, and ten times in Plutarch's *Lives*. As the raw numbers suggest, it is with this verb that the dative of agent remains the most productive. In Polybius, found only twice with finite verbs (4.80.4, 9.34.11), it is mostly restricted to participial forms, where it occurs in a curious distribution to be discussed below. The one dative of agent with πράττω in the NT is, according to Blass–Debrunner, the only dative of agent in the entire NT with any verb (1961: §191):

(16) *Luke* 23.15   οὐδὲν ἄξιον θανάτου ἐστὶν πεπραγμένον
αὐτῷ
"nothing deserving of death has been done
by him"

Here too we see the dative of agent occurring with a participle. Both in Polybius and in the NT, then, the dative of agent with πράττω is found in environments that are reminiscent of those in which it typically occurred in Demosthenes as well. In Plutarch, however, the datives of agent with πράττω are more frequently found with the non-participial forms of the verb, with only three of the ten examples occurring with participles. As a result, the dative of agent in this instance still seems to be productive – or, at any rate, to have been revived on the basis of Attic models.[33]

Indeed, with the other seven verbs examined as well, it is only Plutarch who employs the dative of agent with any regularity. None, of course, occurs with the dative of agent in the NT; but Polybius too has no datives of agent with γράφω (which occurs four times with ὑπό, once with παρά[+G] as agent markers), νομίζω (which occurs in one PAC with παρά[+D] as the agent marker), ἁμαρτάνω, ἐργάζομαι, or εὑρίσκω (the latter three of which do not occur in any PACs). As for ποιέω and ἑτοιμάζω, the former only occurs in

---

[33] Though Plutarch himself shied away from deliberate Atticizing (Horrocks 1997: 82), his contemporaries' general awareness of Attic precedent could well have encouraged his use of the construction.

one PAC, where it does, to be sure, occur with the dative of agent (34.2.10), the latter in three PACs, of which two have the dative of agent (2.69.11 and 15.27.4), the other ὑπό (9.17.8).

In Plutarch, on the other hand, in addition to one dative of agent with ποιέω (and also one PAC with ὑπό), γράφω, νομίζω, ἁμαρτάνω, and ἐργάζομαι also all occur with the dative of agent (2× each, except for νομίζω, with only one example), unlike in Polybius. While γράφω does occur seven times in PACs with ὑπό, and ποιέω in one with ὑπό, the other three verbs are only found in these PACs with the dative of agent. (Of the other two remaining verbs, ἑτοιμάζω does not occur in any PACs in the *Lives*, and εὑρίσκω only occurs in one, with ὑπό.) In short, the impression given by these data is that the dative of agent is used only rarely in Polybius, almost never in the NT, and, while it continues to serve as an agent marker with perfect passive verbs, PACs with perfect verbs are themselves relatively rare, if, for example, there are only three found with the perfect passive of ποιέω in all of Polybius and the *Lives* of Plutarch.

Thus, the decisive factor in the decline of the dative of agent seems to have been more a reduction in PACs with the perfect passive altogether than an overwhelming shift to the use of ὑπό as an agent marker with these verbs. Indeed, in Polybius at least, despite the apparent prejudice against the dative of agent, both agent markers seem to be viewed as nearly equivalent to one another insofar as the choice of which one is used with participles seems to have been governed to a large extent by the case of the participle. If the dative of agent is still available in this way as a stylistic feature that can be controlled by the author, it seems less of a fossilized usage. Consider, for instance, the following two charts, which show the effect that the case of the participle can have on the expression of the agent:

• agent markers in Polybius with the participle εἰρημένος

	G participle	N participle	A participle	D participle
D agent	4	0	1	1
ὑπό agent	2	5	2	5

• agent markers in Polybius with the participle πεπραγμένος

	G participle	N participle	A participle	D participle
D agent	12	0	5	0
ὑπό agent	1	0	0	3

In the case of both εἰρημένος and πεπραγμένος, the dative of agent is preferred if the participle is in the genitive (thus avoiding the confusion, or at any rate, the repetition of a double genitive), while ὑπό is preferred if the participle is in the dative (again, thus avoiding a double occurrence of the dative). The picture is less clear if the participle is in the nominative or accusative; thus, we cannot ascertain which agent marker would have been preferred if the particular stylistic consideration of avoiding the repeated use of a given case were not an issue: with εἰρημένος, ὑπό is preferred, seven to one, while with πεπραγμένος, the dative of agent is preferred, five to zero. Such a pattern is consistent with the observation that, generally, the dative of agent was most persistent with πράττω.

The dative of agent, then, survived into these authors, but only under reduced circumstances. Now the chief reason for its decline does not seem to have been that it lost ground to ὑπό. Take Polybius, for instance: with finite forms of the perfect passive of λέγω, the fifteen examples of the dative of agent do, to be sure, look fossilized, as mentioned above. But there is only one corresponding example of such a form construing with ὑπό as the agent marker. As for πράσσω, finite forms of the perfect passive only occur twice with the dative of agent, but never at all with ὑπό. Furthermore, while there is only the one instance of the dative of agent in the entire NT (example (16)), of the ten verbs mentioned above, only one of them, ἑτοιμάζω, occurs in a PAC with ὑπό as an agent marker, and that only once. The perfect passives of the other nine verbs are never found with ὑπό marking the agent. In Plutarch's *Lives*, there are rather more PACs of perfect verbs with ὑπό: seven times with λέγω, once with ποιέω, eight times with πράσσω, nine times with γράφω, and once with εὑρίσκω: but the perfects of δηλόω and ἑτοιμάζω are not found in any PACs, and those of νομίζω, ἁμαρτάνω, and ἐργάζομαι are found only with the dative of agent.

Rather, the decline of the dative of agent is due to the reduction in the number of PACs of perfect passives altogether, a reduction enabled by the rise of the perfect active. Again, consider Polybius first. The construction δεδήλωται ἡμῖν occurs four times – a clear descendant of the Herodotean example at the start of this chapter. But the active counterpart is far more frequent, with δεδηλώκαμεν occurring fifteen times. Contrast Herodotus, where δεδήλωκα and δεδηλώκαμεν do not occur at all, and the perfect active of δηλόω only occurs once in the *Histories* in any form. As for the perfect of λέγω, εἴρηται ἡμῖν/μοι occurs fourteen times in Polybius as against εἴρηκα/εἰρήκαμεν twelve times. This ratio is a significant change from Herodotus, where the passive construction also occurs fourteen times, but the active only three times. In the NT, this ratio becomes even more skewed in favor of the active: active forms of εἰρη- occur twenty-one times, the passive only five times. Furthermore, the perfect active of ποιέω occurs sixteen times in the NT, as against only one example of the perfect passive (*Hebrews* 12.27). Finally, in Plutarch's *Lives*, while there are no examples of δεδήλωταί μοι or δεδήλωται ἡμῖν, the active δεδηλώκαμεν is found twice. In the first six *Lives*, he does continue to use the perfect passive of λέγω more frequently than the active (by a 20:11 ratio), but even this represents an increase over Herodotus and Thucydides in the frequency of the perfect active as against the passive: in the first two books of Herodotus' *Histories*, there are twenty-seven examples of the perfect passive against only three of the perfect active; in the whole of Thucydides, there are fifty-three perfect passives, but only eight perfect actives. These figures suggest that, in the fifth century BC, the perfect active was a verbal form that had not yet reached the full extent of its potential use; indeed, it spread in the Greek of Polybius, the NT, and Plutarch at the expense of the perfect passive, and, in doing so, caused a decline in the frequency of the environment in which the dative of agent occurred. Accordingly, the dative of agent itself then went into decline as well.

Conclusion

The anomalous use of the dative of agent with the perfect first arose because the perfect expressed a state rather than an action. As such, it could not be construed with an agent in the same way that dynamic aspects like the present or aorist could. Later in Greek, however, the function of the perfect active changed so as to become the transitive counterpart of an intransitive passive. The perfect thus came into alignment with the present and aorist, and, in consequence, ὑπό⁺ᴳ was no longer excluded as a possible agent marker with the perfect passive. The dative of agent did remain, however, but its use became restricted, for the development of the perfect active gave Greek the ability to rephrase the older passive construction εὕρηταί μοι with the rather pithier εὕρηκα.

4

AGENT CONSTRUCTIONS WITH PREPOSITIONS OTHER THAN ὑπό: PROSE

While ὑπό is by far the most common agent marker in classical Greek prose, other prepositions do occur in its place.[1] In this chapter, I will explore the linguistic motivation for these non-standard agent markers. Generally speaking, there are two factors that affect the selection of agent markers. The more important is the semantic field to which the verb belongs: verbs of sending and giving often use an ablatival preposition like ἐκ or παρά$^{+G}$; verbs of thinking often use a locatival preposition like πρός[2] or παρά$^{+D}$. The second, lesser factor concerns the syntax of the verb: participles sometimes take different agent markers than would finite verbs. The body of this chapter will examine the works of six major prose authors in turn (Herodotus, Thucydides, Xenophon, Lysias, Plato, and Demosthenes) to demonstrate how these two factors affect the expression of the agent.

Survey of earlier literature

Scholarship on this question has been surprisingly scarce. Aside from the section in Kühner–Gerth (1898) on the uses of prepositions generally, the chief existing studies are Schwyzer's lengthy article on agent constructions (1943) and a brief article on agenthood by Luraghi (2000). Both Kühner–Gerth and Schwyzer suffer from a failure to address the conditions under which non-standard agent markers are used. They merely offer lists of examples, and vague statements as to their distribution in the various authors. Luraghi's article, on the other hand, while offering a good starting-point for understanding the motivations for non-standard agent

---

[1] For the frequency of ὑπό relative to other agent markers, compare the two bracketed figures in the chart on p. 40.

[2] In this study, πρός refers exclusively to the use of the preposition with the genitive, as this is the only case with which it could mark the agent.

markers, is too cursory to provide a thorough understanding of these prepositions. Still, it will be useful to examine the findings of all these works in order to lay the foundation for a more complete study of this subject.

The section in Kühner–Gerth (henceforth, KG) that deals with prepositions gives examples of prepositions other than ὑπό used to mark the agent. Although the examples are helpful, the descriptions given to distinguish the various prepositions are too vague to be useful. Still, a brief look at the labels given to ἀπό, ἐκ, παρά⁺ᴳ, παρά⁺ᴰ, and πρός provides a starting-point for a more detailed investigation.

- ἀπό is said to occur only rarely, and ἀπό τινος may be translated "von Seiten jemandes, *aliquo auctore*" (1898: 457). Aside from one example with γενέσθαι from Herodotus, and one with δέδοται from Xenophon, the only passages cited are from Thucydides. The assessment that this is a rare usage is correct, but the translation offered only accounts for one of the two main uses of ἀπό in Thucydides, as will be seen below.
- ἐκ is described as primarily limited to Ionic, being rare in Attic prose, though occasionally found in tragedy (*ibid.* 460). KG cite several examples from Homer and Herodotus, several from Sophocles and Xenophon, and one each from Plato, Lycurgus, and Isaeus. This account of the distribution is misleading, inasmuch as it understates the frequency with which ἐκ occurs in tragedy: it is nearly as common as ὑπό. True, this could be an Ionicism, but its surprisingly common occurrence should be noted all the same.[3] KG also fail to give any account of why it is used either in Ionic or in the rare instances when it is found in Attic prose.
- παρά⁺ᴳ is said to be used "wenn angezeigt werden soll, dass die Handlung aus der unmittelbaren Nähe, aus den Mitteln, dem Vermögen jemandes herrühre in materieller oder geistiger Hinsicht" (*ibid.* 510). A few examples from Plato and Xenophon are listed, as well as one each from Lysias and Isocrates. Such a description is so vague it is hard to see what would be excluded from it. It is difficult to imagine a situation in which an agent could act without using the mental or physical resources at his disposal.
- παρά⁺ᴰ is treated more usefully, as its connection with verbs of judging is noted, with examples given from Isaeus, Lycurgus, Demosthenes, Xenophon, and Isocrates (*ibid.* 511). To explain how παρά⁺ᴰ differs from ὑπό, they usefully refer to the spatial sense of the

---

[3] For Ionicisms in tragedy, see Hoffmann–Debrunner (1969: 108).

preposition: "durch παρά⁺ᴰ wird nicht ausgedrückt, dass die Handlung von einem vollgezogen wird, sondern nur, dass sie bei ihm, innerhalb seiner Sphäre vor sich geht."

- πρός again receives vague treatment. KG merely say that πρός is used of the agent in the sense "seitens . . . bei Begriffen des Empfangens, Intransitiven und Passiven, schon bei Hom., häufig bei Hdt., auch bei den Attikern nicht selten" (*ibid.* 516), citing examples with passive verbs from Homer, Herodotus, Xenophon, and Plato. They do not mention that it occurs with many of the same types of verbs that παρά⁺ᴰ does: while παρά⁺ᴰ is found with (i) ἀξιόω and νομίζω, (ii) παιδεύω, and (iii) ἀγαπάω, πρός occurs with (i) ὁμολογέω and ἀδοξέω, (ii) διδάσκω, and (iii) ἀτιμάζω. Furthermore, they do not observe that there is what approaches complementary distribution between the authors which use παρά⁺ᴰ and those that use πρός.

While KG have thus assembled a useful collection of examples, their analysis generally does not proceed beyond noting that a particular preposition is favored by a particular author, e.g. ἀπό in Thucydides. When they do attempt to find a general description characteristic of the individual prepositions, the result is usually too ill-defined to be useful.

Schwyzer's lengthy article on agent expression in Greek (1943) is the most comprehensive treatment of this issue to date. But while he provides useful lists of PACs with non-standard agent markers, his analysis of these examples is again too cursory to do justice to the complexity of the problem. The article as a whole deals with several different topics, including the Indo-European origin of the passive as well as the pragmatic motivation for agent expression in the first place, and it is only the second section, which considers non-standard agent markers, that concerns us here (*ibid.* 13–43).

Schwyzer's general approach with the prepositional agent markers is to introduce each preposition in a brief paragraph and then to list all the examples of its use as an agent marker that he has collected. There is virtually no further discussion of the distinguishing characteristics of each preposition. The three prepositions that he examines first are ἐκ, πρός, and παρά, all with the genitive. (1) ἐκ, according to Schwyzer, "bezeichnet auch beim Passiv den Ausgangspunkt, Ursprung, und zwar den unmittelbaren . . . wie den nur mittelbaren . . . ; nicht immer ist aber die Unterschied scharf. . . . Im Griechischen ist . . . dieser Gebrauch von ἐξ von Homer (schon hier ohne Beschränkung auf besonders naheliegende Verbalbegriffe) bis in die Koine lebendig" (*ibid.* 19). Two criticisms may be made: first, he fails to connect his vague description of ἐκ as a preposition denoting origin or source with the actual examples that follow; second, even though he later groups the examples from Herodotus according to the semantics of the verb, he simply states that there is no limitation of ἐκ to verbs of a particular meaning. He does not note whether the seemingly disparate verbs that occur with ἐκ also occur with ὑπό or with other non-standard agent markers. (2) πρός gets even less attention; he merely states that its use as an agent marker only lasts till about 400, frequently in high Attic poetry and Herodotus (*ibid.* 22). (3) παρά$^{+G}$ is described as parallel to πρός in its use with the passive, though more common in prose, less common in poetry. As with ἐκ, he fails to explain its frequent occurrence with particular verbs: "Wenn auch in den Beispielen einzelne Verba häufiger als andere auftreten, besteht keine Beschränkung auf Verba bestimmter Bedeutung" (*ibid.* 24). He also summarily dismisses παρά$^{+D}$ as only mistakenly considered an agent construction, even though the closest parallels to the PACs with πρός are found with παρά$^{+D}$, not παρά$^{+G}$. After a lengthy discussion of the origin of the construction with ὑπό$^{+G}$, he then turns to ἀπό, which, limited primarily to Thucydides, he rightly recognizes as chiefly marking indirect agents and, with λέγω, agents that act in opposition to one another (*ibid.* 41).

The article's greatest shortcoming is in failing to distinguish the conditions which trigger the use of ἐκ, παρά, and πρός. Schwyzer simply dismisses them as features of an elevated register, and ascribes their use in poetry to an attempt to avoid the banal ὑπό:

Es geht nicht an, den Gebrauch von ἐξ, πρός, παρά zur Einführung des persönlichen Agens beim Passiv schlechthin als poetisch zu bezeichnen. Aber weil ἐξ, πρός, παρά gegenüber dem allgemeinen ὑπό besondere Schattierungen aufweisen, gelten sie, wenn diese zurücktreten, wenigstens als gehoben und werden deshalb von der Poesie, teilweise in bewußter Vermeidung des banalen ὑπό, bevorzugt. (*ibid.* 27)

Because ἐκ and πρός are found chiefly in tragedy and early prose (especially Herodotus), there is good reason to see them as belonging to a high register. But παρά is found as an agent marker in many prose authors: Plato, Xenophon, Lysias, Demosthenes, Polybius, Plutarch – and only marginally in Herodotus and Thucydides. Since it occurs particularly frequently with certain verbs, notably πέμπω and δίδωμι, it also appears to be linguistically motivated rather than a free stylistic variant. Furthermore, its use continues into the period of the Roman Empire in texts not prone to Atticism, including papyri. This distribution suggests that it is not the high-register agent marker Schwyzer would make it out to be.

The most important recent contribution to our understanding of agent marking in Greek comes in a series of studies by Luraghi, culminating in a recent book devoted to the semantic roles expressed by Ancient Greek prepositions. We may start our survey of her work by looking at two early articles on cause and instrument expressions in Ancient Greek, in which she examined the role of διά, both with the genitive and with the accusative.[4] The key point relevant to the current study is that διά with either case always marks a participant that does not control the action of the verb. Accordingly, nouns introduced by this preposition are not agents.

In her 1989 article, Luraghi discusses the use of διά$^{+G}$. Using the framework of Functional Grammar, she describes it as marking either the instrument or the intermediary according as its object is inanimate or animate. In either case, an agent, who controls the action of the verb, uses the instrument or intermediary to carry out the action. Although she recognizes the essential similarity of the two roles, Luraghi further argues that they differ insofar as, in the case of an instrument, the agent still performs the action, whereas in the case of an intermediary, it is the intermediary that does so (1989: 300). Additionally, she explains why the two roles are marked differently – the instrument with the dative, the intermediary with διά$^{+G}$ – by noting that, with an animate noun, the dative would most naturally be interpreted as marking the beneficiary (*ibid.* 301). She also points to a passage from the *Theaetetus* (184b–d) to show that διά$^{+G}$ is also used with inanimate instruments in cases where the dative would be ambiguous (*ibid.* 302–6). Her work thus provides a parallel for two themes that recur in the present study: first, that

---

[4] She returns to this preposition more briefly in 2000: 285–7 and 2003: 174–81.

animacy affects the choice of preposition; second, that a preposition may be chosen in order to clarify a construction.

Then, in a 1994 article, Luraghi turned to the use of διά with the accusative. As with διά⁺ᴳ, the object of the preposition does not control the action of the verb, and is therefore not an agent. With the accusative, however, διά marks cause: that is, the situation which triggers the action of the verb, whether that action is controlled by an agent or not. Again, just as with the instrument, animate nouns receive special treatment. Whereas inanimate causes may be marked by the dative, ὑπό⁺ᴳ, or διά⁺ᴬ, only the last of these may be used with animate causes because the first two are used for beneficiaries and agents respectively (1994: 234–6). Generally speaking, the animate noun by its very nature can play more roles in a sentence than an inanimate object; thus, it must have more specific means of marking these roles.

Later, she approached the problem of agent expressions in Greek directly in a 2000 article on this topic, most of the results of which are echoed in her 2003 monograph. Her main purpose in this article is to illustrate how the spatial meanings of different prepositions can give rise to agent expressions by various metaphorical routes: ἐκ, πρός, and παρά become agent markers because of the metaphor that the agent is the source of the action; ὑπό, both with the dative and with the genitive, becomes one because the location of the patient underneath an entity suggests that it is under the control of the entity, and therefore that that entity is an agent; διά is again interpreted as in the earlier articles as not encoding enough volition-ality to mark a true agent. Moving beyond these broad statements, she also makes some valuable observations about more detailed factors that condition the use of these agent markers, mostly stem-ming from applications of the theory of transitivity put forth by Hopper and Thompson (1980): in short, she explains the presence of many of the passages where ἐκ and πρός mark the agent with reference to the low transitivity of these constructions as against those with ὑπό. First, she points out that, in Homer and Herodotus, both of these prepositions are typically found with verbs marked by relatively low affectedness of the patient (2000: 279–80, 284); second, that πρός in Herodotus is found with nominalized verb forms (*ibid.* 283–4).

While these are all constructive insights, one wishes that Luraghi had occasionally treated the material in greater detail. For example, following Schwyzer, she notes the particularly frequent use of ἀπό in Thucydides and remarks that verbs of higher transitivity are only found with ὑπό (*ibid.* 285; cf. 2003: 128–9). But she does not go on to examine all these constructions individually, a task which, carried out below (pp. 134–40), not only confirms that the factors that account for the use of ἀπό are more complicated than the picture she presents, but also reveals a connection between Thucydides' use of ἀπό with πράσσω and his preference for the dative of agent with this verb, even outside the perfect system. Furthermore, she again rightly notes that the Thucydidean use of ἀπό cannot be the direct ancestor of the Modern Greek use of this preposition as an agent marker, because this use is found extremely rarely in Koine (2000: 285 n. 10). However, she fails to see that what can be observed after the fifth century is the gradual replacement of ὑπό by παρά$^{+G}$ as an agent marker. Quite the contrary, she states of παρά$^{+G}$ that "its occurrences with passive verbs are limited" (*ibid.* 285). That this is not so will be seen in this chapter particularly in the study of agent markers in Demosthenes and, in Chapter 6, in the evidence provided by papyri. Additionally, after noting that, in Herodotus, πρός occurs frequently with nominalizations such as δουλοσύνη (2000: 284; 2003: 292 n. 5), it would have been useful to go beyond looking at such lexical nominalizations to examine whether the same effect could be seen in agent marking with substantivized participles.

But the most general shortcoming in the article is that, in explaining nearly all non-standard agent markers with reference to the low transitivity of the construction, she fails to make finer distinctions that require the introduction of other criteria. Her observation of the fact that, in Herodotus, πρός occurs with verbs of speech and mental activity, while insightful, is too brief to include all the relevant data (2000: 284, 2003: 292). Her claim, for instance, that this use of πρός is most common with verbs of saying is inaccurate: πρός occurs more frequently with verbs of knowing, and it is ἐκ that is more common with verbs of saying.[5] She does note that

---

[5] See the table below on p. 129.

ἐκ occurs with these verbs as well, but she does not go so far as to compare the PACs of λέγω with ἐκ against those with πρός to see what contrastive features might have occasioned the use of one preposition rather than the other. A more exhaustive study of PACs in authors later than Herodotus and Thucydides, moreover, would have revealed that the use of παρά with the genitive and dative corresponds to that of ἐκ and πρός respectively in Herodotus. In short, Luraghi does a good job of suggesting in broad terms that many of the environments in which non-standard agent markers occur are those in which, owing to low transitivity, the agent falls short of being a prototypical agent. But there is still need for an investigation to account for the particular distribution of these different prepositions.

Recent examinations of multiple means of agent marking in languages other than Greek have tended to focus on the concrete spatial meanings of the prepositions as a means of explaining their use in agent constructions. In a 1988 article, "Spatial metaphor in German causative constructions," King provides an account of the use of *von*, *durch*, and *mit* in German passive constructions. The causative of the article's title refers to a distinction drawn between transitive verbs that imply a change of state of the patient, such as *kill* or *open* (King's causatives), and those that do not, such as *hit*. In particular, he looks at pairs of verbs such as the following:

(1) *schlagen* "beat" : *erschlagen* "beat to death"
     würgen "choke" : *erwürgen* "strangle (to death)"

In such verbs, the addition of the prefix *er-* turns a verb into a causative (King 1988: 572). King shows that native speakers find passive constructions with *durch* as the agent marker acceptable with the causative verbs, but not with the simple verbs. Moreover, these constructions are acceptable even with the simple verbs provided that a predicative adjective is added such that they become causative:

(2) *Hans wurde durch Peter erschlagen.*
     *Hans wurde durch Peter geschlagen.
     Hans wurde durch Peter bewußtlos geschlagen.

King argues that *durch* can only be used in causative constructions because, as a preposition marking path, it must be restricted to constructions in which there is a transition from one "event space" to another (*ibid.* 584).

While this explanation provides a neat link between the agent expressions possible with the paired verbs of (1), it is not entirely clear what verbs would fall into his causative category. To determine whether a verb is causative, he checks for the presence of adjectives describing the state resulting from the verb (*dead, broken, open*). Such adjectives would not occur in connection with a non-causative verb like *hit*. Certainly, it would be strange to speak of *the hit boy*, or *the struck man*.[6] But other verbs, such as *delay*, fall less neatly into one category or the other. One might well speak of a *delayed train*, but probably not of a *delayed child*. Yet one of King's examples of an acceptable usage of *durch* involves precisely this collocation (*ibid.* 562):

(3) *Er wurde durch seinen Lehrer aufgehalten.*

In this sentence, does the child really undergo a change of state from *on time* to *delayed*? If so, is it really a more fundamental change of state than that undergone when a person is *hit*? It seems that King overstates his case when he says that *durch* is never used in non-causative constructions, in which there is only one event space. But, if we leave aside these borderline cases, examples (1) and (2) still make clear that the expression of the agent can be affected by the causativity, or, in more general terms, the Aktionsart of the verb. This use of *durch* as an agent marker in constructions involving a change of state does not have a direct parallel in Greek, as διά$^{+G}$ does not act in the same way: it is used instead to mark the intermediary, that is, an animate entity used by the agent to perform the action.[7] Nor do any of the other prepositions used to express the agent seem to have a comparable force. Instead, while there is no instance of Aktionsart regularly affecting agent marking in Greek, the use of the dative of agent with perfect passives is broadly comparable, for the perfect, as a stative (a category not

---

[6] *Stricken*, of course, exists as an adjective, but has a figurative sense that King might consider causative.

[7] See Luraghi 1989.

too far removed from that of Aktionsart),[8] was in its earlier stages incompatible with the agent marker ὑπό.

The most recent full-length study of multiple agent markers in a language is Müller's monograph on agents in early Welsh and Irish. Like King's article, it generally tries to account for the manifold uses of prepositions by reducing them to the spatial meanings that are thought to underlie the more figurative senses. Much of the work is concerned with the arguments of verbal nouns, which occur frequently in Celtic syntax; thus, it is not directly applicable to Greek. Nevertheless, Müller's concluding analysis of agent markers in Irish does bear some relation to the use of Greek prepositions. Four agent markers of Old Irish all appear to have counterparts in Greek with approximately the same spatial meaning. The most common agent marker in Old Irish is *la*, whose "spatial sense . . . can be paraphrased as 'in the vicinity of'" (1999: 195); that such a preposition should come to be used as an agent marker has a parallel in the English *by*. Müller accounts for the development of the agentive use out of the concrete as follows: "The entity defining an area in which a process takes place is linked with the process in such a way that this entity is seen to provide the cause or condition for that process, or carry the responsibility for the process, provided this entity has the capability to do so" (*ibid.* 195–6). A Greek equivalent may be seen in the use of παρά[+D], in sentences like:

(4) D. 21.41 ἂν γὰρ ταῦθ᾽ οὕτως ἐγνωσμέν᾽ ὑπάρχῃ παρ᾽ ὑμῖν
"for if these matters are determined by you in this way"

A second agent marker in Irish is *ó* "from," which marks the origin or point of departure. Like Greek παρά[+G] (as will be seen below), it is found marking the agent nearly always with verbs of giving and speaking, semantic fields in which the action may be thought to emanate from the agent in a spatial sense (*ibid.* 142).

---

[8] If we hold that the Aktionsart of a verb is primarily determined lexically, while aspect is a function of the inflectional categories of a language, then the stative perfect falls better under the latter heading; nevertheless, both Aktionsart and aspect interact closely with each other. See Bertinetto–Delfitto 2000, especially 190–4.

Third, there is *do* "to," which is found when the agent is what Müller calls "low-energy"; instead of being transferred from the agent to the patient, the energy is to some extent self-directed at the agent (*ibid.* 190). It is, for instance, especially frequent in subordinate verbal noun clauses, which, as they give background information, typically involve less energy transfer than takes place in main clauses.[9] As such, the use of a preposition marking the endpoint of a path is appropriate. This construction is not far removed from the Greek use of the dative of agent with perfects, whose stative aspect implies a relatively low amount of energy transfer. Finally, there is *oc* "at," which, like *la*, was used in contexts where there was overlap between a plural agent and the location at which an event took place:

(5) *ra himráided   ac   feraib Hérend*
    "was debated   by/among   the men of Ireland" (*ibid.* 143)

Müller also gives evidence that the marking of the agent with verbal nouns (usually *do*) is different from that with finite passive forms (usually *la*) (1999: 201–2). This observation provides a parallel for the non-standard agent constructions seen with certain participles in Herodotus that resemble verbal nouns. In short, Müller gives semantic and syntactic reasons for the preference of one agent marker over another. Such explanations will hold true for Greek prose as well.

Motivation for non-standard agent markers: overview

Before examining the non-standard agent markers found in the various major authors of classical Greek prose, I will first set out the two main factors which account for the great majority of cases where a preposition other than ὑπό is used to express the agent.

(1) Most important is the meaning of the verb. While the semantic range of verbs that occur with non-standard agent markers in

---

[9] As an example, Müller cites "'Ficfit fornd iar tiachtain dúin' (they will fight against us when we come back)" (1999: 192). One may compare the connection between foregrounding and high transitivity noted in Hopper–Thompson 1980: 284.

classical Greek is fairly broad, one may arrange them along a scale that places verbs of motion, such as πέμπω, at one end and verbs of thought, such as νομίζω, at the other. Intermediate categories are verbs of giving and showing:

(6) πέμπω → δίδωμι → σημαίνω → νομίζω
     Sending → Giving → Showing → Thinking

Sending-verbs involve the motion of the patient from the agent to the recipient, and are thus well suited to an ablatival agent marker. Giving-verbs similarly mark the transfer of the patient from agent to recipient, though they differ in emphasizing the transfer of ownership rather than the physical motion undergone by the patient. With showing-verbs, as with giving-verbs, there is a third party (that is, an indirect object) that is the recipient of a transfer; the difference is that it is not the transfer of a concrete object, but rather of the *awareness* of either an object (*I showed him my car*) or an idea (*I showed him that I knew how to drive*). One general difference, then, between showing- and giving-verbs is that the agent does not relinquish his hold on the patient in the case of the showing-verbs. To move on to the final class, if the showing-verbs involve the transfer of an idea from agent to recipient, the thinking-verbs simply tell of the formulation of an idea without the element of transfer. The link between these two groups is provided by verbs of speaking, which, like showing-verbs, describe the transfer of an idea (one generally speaks to someone else), but, like thinking-verbs, throw more emphasis on the formulation of the idea. In general, verbs that are closer to the first end of this scale are more likely to mark the agent with an ablatival preposition, such as ἐκ or παρά$^{+G}$, while verbs closer to the second end are more likely to use a locatival preposition, such as πρός or παρά$^{+D}$. One further point should also be introduced here. Some verbs usually have ὑπό as the agent marker, but occasionally have a non-standard agent marker. In such cases, the non-standard marker signals that what might potentially be considered an agent is probably best interpreted according to the local sense of the preposition, be it source or location. Other verbs usually use a non-standard agent marker; when they use ὑπό, it is because the status of the agent needs to be clarified. This need generally arises when, compared to the patient, the agent is relatively low in the animacy hierarchy.[10]

(2) Less commonly, the syntax of the verb plays a role. For just as the perfect passive uses constructions different from those employed with the present or aorist passive, so too passive participles may avoid the usual agent marker ὑπό+G. While the perfect passive is distinguished from its present and aorist counterparts by being a stative passive, the passive found in participles differs from that of the finite moods in that the verb is not fully verbal, but rather shows a mixture of nominal and verbal characteristics. The more nominal a participle is, the less applicable a verbal category like voice becomes.[11] In analyzing participles, then, it will be useful to assume the presence of a continuum of nominalization. At one end lie participles at their most verbal, especially in periphrases with εἶναι or in indirect discourse after a verb of knowing; at the other are the most nominalized participles: those that, substantivized, function as the syntactic equivalent of nouns, generally with a definite article, as in (7):

(7) Hdt. 3.137.3   κῶς δὲ ὑμῖν τὰ ποιεύμενα ἕξει καλῶς, ἢν ἀπέλησθε ἡμέας;
"And how will what is being done [= these affairs] be good for you, if you deprive us of him?"

While the many nuances of participial use would no doubt make impossible a precise ranking of participles according to how nominalized they are, it is still reasonable to separate out at least the endpoints of this scale.

Herodotus

Both of these proposed motivations for non-standard agent markers play a role in the agent constructions found in Herodotus. Their

---

[10] For the animacy hierarchy, see Chapter 3.

[11] As examples of voice lost through nominalization, one might consider the ambiguity of the PIE *-tó- suffix with respect to voice: though usually passive, it can also be active, cf. L. potus, Skt gatá- (see Bernert 1943, Hofmann–Szantyr 1965: 290, Szemerényi 1996: 323), or the double meaning of Spanish participles like aburrido or cansado, which, with estar, mean "bored" or "tired," but with ser, "boring" or "tiring."

importance may be illustrated first by examining the PACs found with ποιέω and λέγω, the two verbs whose agents are most frequently marked by ἐκ, itself the most common prepositional agent marker in Herodotus after ὑπό. (PACs with perfect passive verbs and -τέος verbals are omitted from consideration in the following section because their default construction with the dative of agent introduces an additional variable that would obscure the evidence for the passive verbs with which ὑπό is the default agent marker.)

Consider ποιέω first, which occurs in thirteen PACs in Herodotus, most frequently with ἐκ (9×), but also with ὑπό (3×) and πρός (1×). In examples (8) to (13), ἐκ marks the agent of a present participle:

(8) Hdt. 1.191.5   (οἱ Βαβυλώνιοι ἔμαθον) τὸ ἐκ τοῦ Κύρου
ποιεύμενον
"(the Babylonians learned) what was being done by Cyrus"

(9) Hdt. 2.172.4   μαθὼν δὲ ὁ Ἄμασις τὸ ἐκ τῶν ἀστῶν
ποιεύμενον
"and Amasis, after learning what was being done by the citizens"

(10) Hdt. 3.14.8   οἳ τὸ ποιεύμενον πᾶν ἐξ ἐκείνου ἐπ᾽ ἑκάστῃ
ἐξόδῳ Καμβύσῃ ἐσήμαινον
"who told Cambyses all that was being done by him [Psammenitus] at each procession"

(11) Hdt. 5.12.3   οὔτε γὰρ Περσικὰ ἦν οὔτε Λύδια τὰ
ποιεύμενα ἐκ τῆς γυναικός
"for what was being done by the woman was neither Persian nor Lydian"

(12) Hdt. 5.23.1   μαθὼν ὁ Μεγάβαζος τὸ ποιεύμενον ἐκ τοῦ
Ἱστιαίου
"when Megabazus learned what was being done by Histiaeus"

(13) Hdt. 9.66.1   τοῖσι πρήγμασι τοῖσι ἐκ Μαρδονίου
ποιευμένοισι
"with the pursuits that were being conducted by Mardonius"

In (14) to (16), it marks the agent of an aorist participle:

(14) Hdt. 1.10.2   μαθοῦσα δὲ τὸ ποιηθὲν ἐκ τοῦ ἀνδρός
                    "and when she realized what had been done
                    by her husband"

(15) Hdt. 2.151.3   οἱ δὲ [ἐν] φρενὶ λαβόντες τό τε ποιηθὲν ἐκ
                    Ψαμμητίχου καὶ τὸ χρηστήριον
                    "and those who considered both what had
                    been done by Psammetichus and the oracle"

(16) Hdt. 6.22.1   τὸ μὲν ἐς τοὺς Μήδους ἐκ τῶν στρατηγῶν
                    τῶν σφετέρων ποιηθὲν οὐδαμῶς ἤρεσκε
                    "what had been done with regard to the
                    Medes by their generals did not please [some
                    of the Samians] at all"

In (17) and (18), ὑπό marks the agent of a participle, present and
aorist respectively; in (19), it marks the agent of a finite verb:

(17) Hdt. 8.80.1   ἴσθι γὰρ ἐξ ἐμέο τάδε ποιεύμενα ὑπὸ Μήδων
                    "know then that these things were done by
                    the Medes at my prompting"

(18) Hdt. 3.115.2   τοῦτο μὲν γὰρ ὁ Ἠριδανὸς αὐτὸ κατηγορέει
                    τὸ οὔνομα ὡς ἔστι Ἑλληνικὸν καὶ οὐ
                    βάρβαρον, ὑπὸ ποιητέω δέ τινος ποιηθέν
                    "for the word 'Eridanus' itself indicates that
                    the name is Greek and not barbarian, and
                    made up by some poet"

(19) Hdt. 8.13.1   ἐποιέετό τε πᾶν ὑπὸ τοῦ θεοῦ ὅκως ἂν
                    ἐξισωθείη τῷ Ἑλληνικῷ τὸ Περσικόν
                    "and everything was being done by God so
                    that the Persian army might be reduced to
                    the same size as the Greek army"

Finally, in (20), the agent of a present participle is marked by πρός:

(20) Hdt. 7.209.2   ἐθέλων μαθεῖν τὸ ποιεύμενον πρὸς τῶν
                    Λακεδαιμονίων
                    "wanting to learn what was being done by the
                    Lacedaemonians"

How are these different constructions to be explained? At first
glance, the numerical predominance of ἐκ might suggest that the

117

best approach would be to assume that it was the default agent marker with this verb, and that the constructions with ὑπό and πρός are the anomalies to be explained. Yet the three examples with ὑπό do not apparently share anything in common. Perhaps one might account for the use of ὑπό in (17) as due to the desire to avoid a potentially ambiguous repetition of ἐκ, or that in (18) as motivated by the different sense of the verb; but that still leaves (19) unexplained. Indeed, with a divine agent carrying out the action, this is precisely the semantic context in which, on the basis of the examples from epic, we would be most likely to expect ἐκ.[12]

If, however, we take ὑπό to be the default preposition, and look for a conditioning factor that would explain the constructions with ἐκ, we meet with more success: all the PACs with ἐκ except (13) involve a participle that, preceded by the definite article, is acting as a nominal constituent. Example (13) does not fit quite so neatly into this pattern, for the participial phrase functions instead as an adjective modifying τοῖσι πρήγμασι. Nevertheless, the participle is still determined by a definite article, which cannot be said of passages (17) and (18), where ὑπό marks the agent of a participle. In first of these examples, the participle functions as the subordinate verb in an indirect statement; in the second, it is loosely appended to the rest of the sentence with δέ. As for example (20), in which πρός marks the agent, it too resembles the constructions with ἐκ, further evidence that nominalized participles preceded by definite articles have abnormal agent marking.

That it is the nominalization of such participles that motivates their anomalous agent marking is suggested not only by this distribution, but also by the behavior of verbal nouns like ἐντολή. If nominalization triggers non-standard agent markers, then we would expect nouns like these to construe more frequently with ἐκ or πρός than with ὑπό to express agency. This is in fact is the case: indeed, ὑπό[+G] is never used with nouns to indicate the agent.[13]

---

[12] For the examples from epic, see (75), (76), and (92) in Chapter 2. Nor is this use limited to epic: Plato occasionally marks divine agents with ἐκ. See examples (174) and (183) below.

[13] I have personally checked all examples of ὑπό in the first two books. Powell 1938 separates out adnominal PAC usages in the case of ἐκ and πρός, and has none to offer under ὑπό.

The prepositions ἐκ and πρός, on the other hand, are used in this way. To match exactly the distribution of these prepositions with the passive of ποιέω, ἐκ would have to be the more common. While this is not so, πρός being the more frequent, ἐκ is still found with a wider variety of nouns.[14] Many of the non-standard agent markers in Herodotus can thus be explained as triggered when the verb is a participle that has been nominalized to some extent. In such cases, the favored agent marker is ἐκ.

The verb λέγω also occurs in a significant number of PACs with non-standard agent markers, both ἐκ (5×) and πρός (4×); in contrast to ποιέω, however, it is most often ὑπό that marks its agent (27×). With ἐκ we find the following examples:

(21) Hdt. 5.32.1   ὑπερθέντι τὰ ἐκ τοῦ Ἀρισταγόρεω λεγόμενα
"relaying what was being suggested by Aristagoras"

(22) Hdt. 7.149.2   πρὸς τὰ ῥηθέντα ἐκ τῆς βουλῆς ἀμείψασθαι τοισίδε
"they replied to what was said by the council with the following"

(23) Hdt. 7.175.1   ἐβουλεύοντο πρὸς τὰ λεχθέντα ἐξ Ἀλεξάνδρου
"they took counsel with regard to what had been said by Alexander"

(24) Hdt. 7.237.2   τοῖσί τε λεγομένοισι πρότερον ἐκ τούτου σταθμώμενος
"judging in part by what has been advised by him in the past"

(25) Hdt. 8.119.1   ταῦτα οὕτως εἰρέθη ἐκ τοῦ κυβερνήτεω
"this was said in this way by the captain"

With πρός, the following:

---

[14] πρός: (with δουλοσύνη) 3.19.3, 6.45.1, 6.106.2, 7.154.2, 9.27.2, (θάνατος) 1.159.1, (φόνος) 7.158.2. ἐκ: (ἐντολαί) 3.16.7, (συμφορή) 3.64.3, (εὐεργεσίη) 5.11.1, (εὐνοίη) 8.140β.1, (παραίνεσις) 9.44.1. On the basis of so few examples, it is difficult to see a clear difference between the nouns that construe with πρός and those that construe with ἐκ, but it may be significant that the nouns found with πρός all refer to the acts of subjugation and killing that are associated with ὑπό[+D] in Homer.

(26) Hdt. 1.47.2   ὅ τι μέν νυν τὰ λοιπὰ τῶν χρηστηρίων
ἐθέσπισε, οὐ λέγεται πρὸς οὐδαμῶν
"what the rest of the oracles foretold is not
said by anyone"

(27) Hdt. 7.60.1   οὐ γὰρ λέγεται πρὸς οὐδαμῶν ἀνθρώπων
"for it is not said by any men"

(28) Hdt. 9.81.2   οὐ λέγεται πρὸς οὐδαμῶν
"it is not said by anyone"

(29) Hdt. 7.153.4   ὁ δὲ λέγεται πρὸς τῆς Σικελίης τῶν
οἰκητόρων τὰ ὑπεναντία τούτων πεφυκέναι
"but he is said by the inhabitants of Sicily to
have been the opposite of this"

With ὑπό, the following eight PACs are found with participles:

(30) Hdt. 2.47.2   ἔστι μὲν λόγος περὶ αὐτοῦ ὑπ' Αἰγυπτίων
λεγόμενος
"there is a story told about this by the
Egyptians"

(31) Hdt. 2.123.1   τοῖσι μὲν νυν ὑπ' Αἰγυπτίων λεγομένοισι
χράσθω
"let him make use of what is said by the
Egyptians"

(32) Hdt. 2.123.1   ὅτι τὰ λεγόμενα ὑπ' ἑκάστων ἀκοῇ γράφω
"that I write what is said by each person I
talk to"

(33) Hdt. 4.77.1   καίτοι τινὰ ἤδη ἤκουσα λόγον ἄλλον ὑπὸ
Πελοποννησίων λεγόμενον
"but I have heard another account told by the
Peloponnesians"

(34) Hdt. 6.53.1   τάδε δὲ κατὰ τὰ λεγόμενα ὑπ' Ἑλλήνων ἐγὼ
γράφω
"but I write the following according to what
is said by the Greeks"

(35) Hdt. 7.142.2   τούς . . . ἔσφαλλε τὰ δύο τὰ τελευταῖα
ῥηθέντα ὑπὸ τῆς Πυθίης
"the two last lines said by the Pythia baffled
them"

(36) Hdt. 7.167.1 & emsp; ἔστι δὲ ὑπ' αὐτῶν Καρχηδονίων ὅδε λόγος
λεγόμενος
"and the following account is told by the
Carthaginians themselves"

(37) Hdt. 8.135.3   τὰ λεγόμενα ὑπὸ τοῦ προφήτεω γράφειν ἐς
αὐτήν
"to write on it what was said by the prophet"

The remaining nineteen PACs with ὑπό, all with the finite form
λέγεται, are too numerous and uniform in character to cite in full;
the following may be considered representative:[15]

(38) Hdt. 1.87.1   ἐνθαῦτα λέγεται ὑπὸ Λυδῶν Κροῖσον . . .
ἐπιβώσασθαι τὸν Ἀπόλλωνα
"then it is said by the Lydians that Croesus
called upon Apollo"

(39) Hdt. 1.183.3   τὰ δὲ λέγεται ὑπὸ Χαλδαίων, ταῦτα λέγω
"but I shall report what is said by the
Chaldaeans"

(40) Hdt. 1.191.6   ὡς λέγεται ὑπὸ τῶν ταύτη οἰκημένων
"as is said by those who live there"

These PACs with λέγω show that the use of non-standard agent
markers can be motivated by far more complicated factors than
those at work with ποιέω. First, if we attempt once again to attribute
the use of ἐκ to the participial nature of the PACs in question, we
meet with only partial success. Four of the five examples, (21) to
(24), conform to the pattern seen with ποιέω: here too we see ἐκ
used with nominalized participles. There are, however, two reasons why the nominalization of the participles cannot be primarily responsible for the use of ἐκ: first, example (25) is then left
unexplained; second, five of the eight participial PACs with ὑπό,
(31), (32), (34), (35), and (37), also involve such nominalized participles. A far more consistent contrast is that ἐκ always marks a
singular agent, while ὑπό nearly always marks a plural agent: it

---

[15] The others are found at 2.145.4, 2.156.2, 3.14.11, 3.26.3, 3.87.1, 3.105.1, 4.7.2, 4.45.3,
4.90.1, 5.87.1, 6.74.2, 7.12.1, 7.165.1, 8.135.1, 8.138.3, and 9.120.1.

does so in all nineteen examples with λέγεται, and in six of the eight examples with participles. In other words, if Herodotus wanted to say that a given story was told by a particular group or nationality of people, he invariably used ὑπό to mark the agent, never ἐκ; but if he wanted to mark the words spoken by an *individual*, he used ἐκ to mark the agent five out of seven times. Furthermore, in the two exceptional cases, when Herodotus uses ὑπό with a singular agent, the agent is not just any individual, as when he uses ἐκ, but rather an oracle. That the nature of the agent could influence the preposition used to mark it can also be seen from the four PACs with πρός: three times, the agent is οὐδαμῶν. Now οὐδαμῶν occurs as an agent six times in Herodotus, five times with πρός, and only once with ὑπό.[16] If we take together the relative frequency of πρὸς οὐδαμῶν compared to ὑπ' οὐδαμῶν and the correlation of the use of ἐκ and ὑπό to the number of the agent, it seems clear that the nature of the agent could affect how that agent is marked with a passive verb.

But why should this be the case? To answer this question, it will be necessary to look at the other passive verbs that construe with non-standard agent markers. For it will be seen that these verbs fall into broad semantic categories, according as they construe with ἐκ or πρός.[17] Verbs from the ablatival end of the cline introduced on p. 114 prefer to construe with ἐκ. They generally describe discrete actions, such as doing, ordering, and giving. By contrast, πρός is found with verbs at the locatival end, indicating mental attitudes, such as calling, (dis)honoring, and knowing or considering. This distinction in turn will shed light on the reason why λέγω should construe with different agent markers depending on the nature of the agent.

Consider first two verbs that tend to mark the agent with πρός: γινώσκω and νομίζω. The verb γινώσκω occurs in only three PACs in Herodotus:

---

[16] Besides the three listed under (26) to (28), PACs with πρὸς οὐδαμῶν are found at 4.45.1 and 4.45.4 (examples (42) and (43) below) with γινωσκομένη and γινώσκεται respectively. The PAC with ὑπὸ οὐδαμῶν occurs at 4.123.2, with νέμεται.

[17] The perfect passives of such verbs do take the dative where it is expected according to the conditions stated in Chapter 3. For example, five of the ten PACs with νομίζω are datives with perfect or pluperfect indicatives.

(41) Hdt. 2.34.1   ὁ μὲν δὴ Ἴστρος . . . πρὸς πολλῶν γινώσκεται
"the Danube is known by many"

(42) Hdt. 4.45.1   ἡ δὲ Εὐρώπη πρὸς οὐδαμῶν φανερή ἐστι
γινωσκομένη . . . εἰ περίρρυτός ἐστι
"but it is not known clearly by anyone whether
Europe is encircled by water"

(43) Hdt. 4.45.4   ἡ δὲ δὴ Εὐρώπη οὔτε εἰ περίρρυτός ἐστι
γινώσκεται πρὸς οὐδαμῶν ἀνθρώπων
"but neither is it known by any men whether
Europe is encircled by water"

Because the agent in the latter two examples is οὐδαμῶν, the motivation for πρός might have more to do with the agent than with the verb, as in examples (26) to (28), with λέγω. Still, the first sentence suggests that the phenomenon is independent of a particular agent and that the common factor linking these constructions, as well as those with λέγω, might be the nature of the verb.

This is also suggested by the PACs found with νομίζω. Excluding examples with perfect passives, it occurs in four PACs, three with πρός, and one with the dative of agent – and none with ὑπό:

(44) Hdt. 7.2.3   νομιζόμενον εἴη πρὸς πάντων ἀνθρώπων
τὸν πρεσβύτατον τὴν ἀρχὴν ἔχειν
"that it is held as custom by all men that the
oldest son should rule"

(45) Hdt. 7.10.2   ὁ δὲ δὴ ἀπεὼν τοῦ λόγου τάδε ἐν αὐτοῖσι
ἀδικέεται, διαβληθείς τε ὑπὸ τοῦ ἑτέρου καὶ
νομισθεὶς πρὸς τοῦ ἑτέρου κακὸς εἶναι
"but the one who is absent from the
conversation is wronged in such affairs in
that he is both slandered by the one and
thought by the other to be bad"

(46) Hdt. 7.151.1   ἢ νομιζοίατο πρὸς αὐτοῦ εἶναι πολέμιοι
"or whether they were considered by him to
be enemies"

(47) Hdt. 3.16.4   οὕτω δὴ οὐδετέροισι νομιζόμενα ἐνετέλλετο
ποιέειν ὁ Καμβύσης
"thus Cambyses ordered them to do what
was considered customary by neither people"

The use of the dative of agent with the participle νομιζόμενα in (47) is not surprising; it looks little different from a dative of possession. Compare the following passage where a similar dative occurs with the related adjective νόμιμα:

(48) Hdt. 2.79.1   τοῖσι ἄλλα τε ἐπάξιά ἐστι νόμιμα
"and they have other noteworthy customs"

More illustrative are the examples with πρός, especially (45), in which πρός occurs in parallel with ὑπό, and the difference between the two PACs is not one of the agent – in both cases, τοῦ ἑτέρου – but solely one of the verb, with διαβληθεὶς ὑπό paired with νομισθεὶς πρός.

If not the agent, what is it, then, that all the PACs with πρός have in common, considering together those with λέγω, γινώσκω, and νομίζω? First, all three of these verbs refer to acts which involve the framing of a thought: in more syntactic terms, these are all verbs that can be followed by indirect discourse. Second, in every case, the verb describes a durative action. In the examples with γινώσκω, the knowledge in question, or the lack thereof, is not suddenly acquired, but rather is a standing feature. So too in the examples with νομίζω, the verb describes a particular view or custom that is held, not just at one time, but for a period of time.[18] As for the PACs in which πρός occurs with λέγω, it is true that they are no more durative than those in which ὑπό is found; still, compared to those with ἐκ, which refer to specific acts of speaking, they do describe what are essentially lasting states during which a particular subject is *not* said.

To highlight further the semantic similarity between γινώσκω, νομίζω, and λέγω (when it construes with πρός), it will be well to contrast them with two more verbs that avoid marking the

---

[18] Example (45) might seem to contradict this, but, while the aoristic aspect does throw emphasis on the particular point at which the view begins to be held, the wider context of the passage also needs to be considered. It occurs in a general discussion on how, when one says something slanderous to another, wrong is done both by the slanderer and by the one who believes the slander because the victim of the slander, being absent (ἀπεὼν τοῦ λόγου), is unable to defend himself. If the act of slander is viewed as consisting of a conversation (the aforementioned λόγος) and the act of believing the slander, while having its origin in the conversation, continues afterwards, it is reasonable to suggest that νομισθείς here is more durative than διαβληθείς.

agent with ὑπό, but which prefer ἐκ or παρά to πρός: δίδωμι and πέμπω. Consider first δίδωμι, which is found in only four PACs in Herodotus, three with ἐκ, one with πρός:

(49) Hdt. 6.58.1 ταῦτα μὲν ζῶσι τοῖσι βασιλεῦσι δέδοται ἐκ τοῦ κοινοῦ τῶν Σπαρτιητέων
"these prerogatives are given by the Spartan state to the kings while they are alive"

(50) Hdt. 8.114.1 χρηστήριον ἐληλύθεε . . . Ξέρξην αἰτέειν δίκας τοῦ Λεωνίδεω φόνου καὶ τὸ διδόμενον ἐξ ἐκείνου δέκεσθαι
"and an oracle had come that they should ask Xerxes for compensation for the murder of Leonidas and should accept that which was given by him"

(51) Hdt. 8.136.1 τῷ δὴ ἐκ βασιλέος τῆς Φρυγίης ἐδόθη Ἀλάβανδα πόλις μεγάλη νέμεσθαι
"the large Phrygian city of Alabanda was given to him by the king to administer"

(52) Hdt. 4.35.2 τὴν δὲ Ἄργην τε καὶ τὴν Ὦπιν ἅμα αὐτοῖσι τοῖσι θεοῖσι ἀπικέσθαι λέγουσι καί σφι τιμὰς ἄλλας δεδόσθαι πρὸς σφέων
"but they say that Arge and Opis came at the same time as the gods, and that they have been given other honors by them"

On the basis of the relative frequency of the two agent markers, it is reasonable to take ἐκ as a default agent marker with δίδωμι and to seek to account for the exceptional usage of πρός in passage (52). Now, in (52), it is τιμαί that are given, rather than the rights conferred on Spartan kings, compensation for a murder, or a city. While it is true that there is similarity between the giving of τιμαί and the bestowing of rights on the Spartan kings, nevertheless the presence of the word τιμαί itself was probably the decisive factor in singling out this PAC from the others. For δίδωμι τιμάς, taken together, can be understood as approximately equivalent to τιμάω, and τιμάω is a verb that denotes a particular mental attitude towards the object, and whose passive, like that of νομίζω, construes five times with πρός – and never with ἐκ:

(53) Hdt. 2.75.4   καὶ τὴν ἶβιν διὰ τοῦτο τὸ ἔργον τετιμῆσθαι
λέγουσι Ἀράβιοι μεγάλως πρὸς Αἰγυπτίων
"and the Arabians say that, because of this
service, the ibis is honored greatly by the
Egyptians"

(54) Hdt. 5.20.4   ὡς παντελέως μάθητε τιμώμενοι πρὸς ἡμέων
"so that you may learn perfectly that you are
honored by us"

(55) Hdt. 6.52.7   τὸ παιδίον τὸ τιμώμενον πρὸς τῆς
γεινᾱμένης
"the child that was treated more favorably by
his mother"

(56) Hdt. 8.124.2   οὐκ ἐτιμήθη πρὸς τῶν ἐν Σαλαμῖνι
ναυμαχησάντων
"he was not honored by those who fought at
Salamis"

(57) Hdt. 8.125.2   οὔτ' ἂν ἐγὼ ἐὼν Βελβινίτης ἐτιμήθην οὕτω
πρὸς Σπαρτιητέων
"I would not, if I were from Belbina, have
been honored thus by the Spartans"

Because πρός so frequently marks the agent of τιμάω, this usage
will have been transferred to the phrase τιμὰς δεδόσθαι. Giving is
typically a concrete, punctual act, and so we would expect the
passive of δίδωμι to be marked other than by πρός: the usual
construction of δίδωμι with ἐκ confirms this. But when it is honors
that are given, the verb's semantics are closer to those of the verbs
that construe with πρός, thus causing the use of the anomalous
agent marker.

The verb πέμπω falls into a slightly different category. There are
several PACs of πέμπω with ὑπό, and, consequently, one would
not argue that anything other than ὑπό is the default construction.[19]
Nevertheless, of the three PACs with παρά in Herodotus, one is
with πέμπω, one with ἀντιπέμπω:[20]

---

[19] PACs of πέμπω with ὑπό are found at 3.127.3, 6.106.1, 7.137.3, 9.90.1. The first is a
present participle, the latter three are all aorist participles, none strongly nominalized.

[20] The other is with the perfect of λέγω at 7.103.2.

(58) Hdt. 7.106.2 τὰ δῶρα πέμπεται παρὰ τοῦ βασιλεύοντος
αἰεὶ ἐν Πέρσῃσι
"gifts are sent by whoever is ruler of the
Persians at the time"

(59) Hdt. 6.4.2 τὰ δὲ ἀμοιβαῖα τὰ παρὰ τῶν Περσέων
ἀντιπεμπόμενα
"and the reply sent in exchange by the
Persians"

In the case of νομίζω and the other verbs above, a marked absence
of ὑπό from the verbs' PACs suggests that the verb itself was a
factor in determining the agent marker. So too with πέμπω, the verb
seems to select for παρά, though only occasionally, as opposed to
the broader avoidance of ὑπό exhibited by the other verbs. Now
ablatival prepositions as agent markers would be expected of a
sending-verb like πέμπω; nor is παρά the only one found with
πέμπω. The prepositions ἀπό and ἐκ are also used with the passive
of πέμπω:

(60) Hdt. 5.85.1 Ἀθηναῖοι μέν νυν λέγουσι μετὰ τὴν
ἀπαίτησιν ἀποσταλῆναι τριήρεϊ μιῇ τῶν
ἀστῶν [τούτους] οἳ πεμφθέντες (v. l. ἀπο-)
ἀπὸ τοῦ κοινοῦ καὶ ἀπικόμενοι ἐς Αἴγιναν . . .
"the Athenians say that, after this request,
some of their citizens were sent in one
trireme, who, sent by _or_ from the state and
arriving at Aegina . . ."

(61) Hdt. 7.18.3 σὺ δὲ σήμηνον μὲν Πέρσῃσι τὰ ἐκ τοῦ θεοῦ
πεμπόμενα
"tell the Persians the dreams that are being
sent to you by _or_ from God"

(62) Hdt. 7.230.1 ἄγγελον πεμφθέντα ἐκ τοῦ στρατοπέδου
"a messenger sent by _or_ from the camp"

(63) Hdt. 9.89.3 πεμφθεὶς κατά τι πρῆγμα ἐκ τοῦ
στρατοπέδου
"sent on some business by _or_ from the
camp"

Now, of these examples, only (61) is designated as a PAC by Powell, as in the others the local usage of the prepositions seems to predominate. In the end, this interpretation is the more plausible, as, on the one hand, one would prefer not to label (60) as the sole PAC with ἀπό when it can easily be classified as yet another local usage, and, on the other, στρατόπεδον would seem to indicate the camp as a place rather than as an encamped army with the ability to act as a collective agent. Nevertheless, it should be noted that active counterparts of these constructions do exist:[21]

(64) Hdt. 5.109.3   ἡμέας [δὲ] ἀπέπεμψε τὸ κοινὸν τῶν Ἰώνων
                              "the Ionian state sent us"

(65) Hdt. 9.117.1   πρὶν ... τὸ Ἀθηναίων κοινόν σφεας
                              μεταπέμψηται
                              "until the Athenian state sent for them"

(66) Hdt. 8.84.2   ὥστε καὶ ἅπαν ἀκοῦσαι τὸ τῶν Ἑλλήνων
                              στρατόπεδον
                              "such that the entire Greek camp heard"

(67) Hdt. 9.28.1   Λακεδαιμονίων δὲ ἀνέβωσε ἅπαν τὸ
                              στρατόπεδον Ἀθηναίους ἀξιονικοτέρους
                              εἶναι
                              "and the whole camp of the Lacedaemonians
                              cried out that the Athenians were more
                              deserving"

In short, it can be seen that the verbs γινώσκω and νομίζω construe regularly with πρός rather than with ὑπό, that δίδωμι construes with ἐκ, and that there seems to be a link between πέμπω and the agentive use of ablatival prepositions, especially παρά. So far, these snapshots of the agent markers of individual verbs support the initial proposal that verbs involving more motion of the patient away from the agent are likely to have ablatival agent markers, while those involving less motion are likely to construe with locatival prepositions. As a final stage in the argument, it

---

[21] Examples (66) and (67) are admittedly weaker as transformations of (62) and (63), as the verb is different. Still, the point holds good that στρατόπεδον can stand as an agent.

remains to tabulate by verb all the PACs in Herodotus with ἐκ and πρός, the two most common agent markers in Herodotus after ὑπό and the dative:[22]

	ἐκ	πρός
Frequency (all nine books)	45×	31×
Verbs of doing[a]	18× (40%)	1× (3%)
ordering[b]	9× (20%)	0× (0%)
giving[c]	6× (13%)	1× (3%)
saying[d]	7× (16%)	4× (13%)
calling[e]	0× (0%)	4× (13%)
(dis)honoring[f]	0× (0%)	6× (19%)
knowing, considering[g]	0× (0%)	9× (29%)
(other)	5× (11%)	6× (19%)

[a] ἐγείρω, ἐπιτελέω, ἐργάζομαι, μηχανάομαι, ποιέω, πρήσσω, ὑπάρχω
[b] ἀπαγορεύω, ἐντέλλω, ἐπιστέλλω, (προσ)τάσσω
[c] (παρα-, προ-)δίδωμι, δωρέω
[d] (προ)λέγω
[e] καλέω
[f] ἀτιμάζω, τιμάω
[g] ἀξιόω, γινώσκω, δοξόομαι, μακαρίζω, νομίζω

A trend does emerge. Verbs that take ἐκ, though wide in semantic range, tend to denote concrete, telic acts that roughly fall into two categories: first, there are verbs of giving and ordering, where the patient (either a gift or an instruction) is transferred from the agent to a recipient; second, there are verbs of doing. Verbs that take πρός, on the other hand, such as those of calling,[23] (dis)honoring, knowing, and considering, are more likely to describe an atelic

---

[22] Because of rounding, percentages do not always add up to 100 per cent.
[23] Of the four instances of a verb of calling (καλέω in all four), the verb is used three times to indicate a name by which an object is called (2.57.1, 3.115.1, 7.62.1). As καλέω is synonymous with "say" in this case, we might expect it to construe both with ἐκ and with πρός, much as λέγω does. But because it does not refer to particular instances of calling but rather to names that were in long-standing use, the choice of πρός in preference to ἐκ is understandable. Furthermore, in the fourth instance, καλέω is synonymous with "invite." As the act of inviting involves motion towards, not away from, the patient, πρός again fits better than ἐκ would (6.57.3).

mental attitude or process; thus, there is no transfer of the patient. Finally, a verb like λέγω that can construe with either preposition is able to do so because it can refer either to a particular statement by a single individual – in which case ἐκ naturally marks the agent, as the action is comparatively punctual – or to a general saying mentioned repeatedly (or, with the negative πρὸς οὐδαμῶν, continually *not* said), in which case πρός is used, as the verb here approaches γινώσκω in sense. This distribution demonstrates that a link between the semantics of the verb and its non-standard agent markers does exist. Admittedly, the data are not perfect, in that the verbs classified as "other" do not suggest a neat semantic division. Those that construe with ἐκ (ἀναδείκνυμι, καταλύω, κρατύνω, πέμπω, προοφείλω) generally involve some transfer of the patient, but those that take πρός (αἰτέω, ἀπαιρέω, ἑσσόομαι, περιυβρίζω, πλήσσω, ὠφελέω) are certainly not all verbs of mental processes.[24] Still, such verbs make up a small enough percentage of the anomalous PAC usages that it is reasonable to consider them as exceptions in light of the much greater number of examples which support the semantic division.

Thucydides

As is appropriate for an author with so distinctive a style, the prepositions found marking the agent in Thucydides are quite different from those found in other authors.[25] While he shares with Herodotus a propensity for ἐκ, he alone of the classical authors uses ἀπό to mark the agent, thus independently anticipating a change that was to occur in the vernacular over a thousand years later.[26]

Already in Herodotus, we have seen ἐκ used frequently to mark the agent of passive verbs. It is no surprise then that there are four places where ἐκ is used to mark the agent of the passive verb

---

[24] The most egregious exceptions are 3.65.3 δείσας δὲ μὴ ἀπαιρεθέω τὴν ἀρχὴν πρὸς τοῦ ἀδελφεοῦ and 6.38.2 πληγέντα τὴν κεφαλὴν πελέκεϊ ἐν τῷ πρυτανηίῳ πρὸς ἀνδρὸς αὐτομόλου μὲν τῷ λόγῳ, πολεμίου δὲ καὶ ὑποθερμοτέρου τῷ ἔργῳ.

[25] For a general description of the peculiarities of Thucydides' style, see Schmid 1948: 181–204.

[26] There is, to be sure, one PAC with ἀπό in Xenophon, but, in the classical period, only in Thucydides does ἀπό occur often enough as an agent marker for it to be considered a feature of the particular style of an author.

in Thucydides, and a fifth in which it is used with the suppletive passive ξύγκεινται.[27] Because this is far fewer, however, than the number of PACs with ἐκ in Herodotus, the reasons for its use remain less clear. Still, two factors seem to be jointly responsible: first, ἐκ is used when its non-agentive use as an ablatival preposition marking source is also applicable in the context of the PAC; second, in three of the four examples, the verb in the construction is associated elsewhere with non-standard agent marking.

The examples are as follows, starting with the PAC in which the verb is not one that appears to trigger non-standard agent marking elsewhere in Thucydides:

(68) Th. 3.69.1   αἱ δὲ τεσσαράκοντα νῆες . . . ἔκ τε τῶν
Ἀθηναίων ἐπιδιωχθεῖσαι καὶ πρὸς τῇ Κρήτῃ
χειμασθεῖσαι καὶ ἀπ᾽ αὐτῆς σποράδες πρὸς τὴν
Πελοπόννησον κατηνέχθησαν
"and the forty ships were pursued by the
Athenians, were struck by a storm off Crete, and
returned thence, scattered, to the Peloponnese"

Although the use of an ablatival preposition may seem appropriate with a verb of motion like διώκω, in the other six instances where διώκω or a compound thereof occurs in a PAC, the agent is always marked by ὑπό, for example:[28]

(69) Th. 1.137.4   πάρειμι διωκόμενος ὑπὸ τῶν Ἑλλήνων διὰ
τὴν σὴν φιλίαν
"I am here now, pursued by the Greeks
because of my friendship with you"

There is not much to distinguish (68) from (69) and the other examples with ὑπό. The best explanation for the use of ἐκ probably has to do with the other prepositions found in (68): we find out not only that the ships were chased by the Athenians but also that they were struck by a storm near Crete and then went on to the

---

[27] Classen–Steup (1914: 133) and Schwyzer (1943: 22) are in agreement on identifying these PACs.
[28] The other examples are at 1.136.2, 1.136.4, 3.4.2, 7.23.2, and 8.20.1. That the first two of these should occur with the same verb in such close proximity to (69), all with ὑπό, makes it hard to argue that deliberate *variatio* is responsible for the sporadic use of ἐκ.

Peloponnese. Since Thucydides continues after the PAC to describe the subsequent locations visited by the Peloponnesian ships, the use of ἐκ as an agent marker could be due to his conceiving these events primarily in spatial terms. Such geographical specifications are not present in the PACs with ὑπό of διώκω and its compounds.[29]

The other three PACs with ἐκ all involve verbs that occur with non-standard agent markers elsewhere. First, there is the following example with ὁμολογέω:

(70) Th. 2.49.1   ὡς ὡμολογεῖτο ἐκ πάντων
"as was agreed by all"

While this verb does construe with ὑπό in its only other occurrence in a passive construction in Thucydides (4.62.2), it is found frequently with non-standard agent markers in other classical authors, as will be seen below.[30] Its use here in Thucydides should simply be seen as part of this general trend in Attic prose.

The second example occurs with the verb ἐλασσόω:

(71) Th. 5.104.1   τῇ μὲν τύχῃ ἐκ τοῦ θείου μὴ ἐλασσώσεσθαι
"not to be defeated by the gods as far as our fortune is concerned"

Although Schwyzer and Classen-Steup agree in labeling this passage a PAC, ἐκ might not in fact be marking the agent here, as it is not clear that this construction is equivalent to τὸ θεῖον μὴ ἐλασσώσειν ἡμᾶς. Instead, considering the dubious agentive credentials of τὸ θεῖον, the prepositional phrase is closer to marking the source of the action.[31] If this is to be taken as a PAC, the use of ἐκ

---

[29] The PAC at 8.20.1 might seem to be an exception, but καταδιώκω is not the only verb in the construction (καταδιωχθεῖσαι τότε καὶ ἐφορμούμεναι ἴσῳ ἀριθμῷ ὑπὸ Ἀθηναίων). Not only would the presence of ἐφορμούμεναι potentially have deterred Thucydides from using ἐκ, but the idea of ablatival motion away from a pursuer that would have motivated the use of ἐκ in (68) is also absent here, as the ships are at this point blockaded, rather than in open flight.

[30] Some editors (e.g. Stuart Jones' OCT, Rusten) punctuate between ὡμολογεῖτο and ἐκ πάντων, but that requires the prepositional phrase to be understood, rather awkwardly, with the following μάλιστα. The occurrence of ἐκ πάντων in particular as an agent expression with ὁμολογέω in other authors (X. An. 2.6.1, P. Smp. 196a, D. 27.16) further confirms that it should be understood with ὁμολογέω here too.

[31] It does occur as an agent at 5.105.2 (also in the Melian Dialogue), but the verb is the weakly transitive ἄρχω. At any rate, "the divine" is certainly a less definite agent than e.g. a personal name.

should be ascribed to the fact that the agent here could be viewed as a source.[32] Furthermore, there is a parallel in Thucydides for ἐλασσοῦσθαι occurring with a non-standard agent marker:

(72) Th. 8.89.3   οὐκ ἀπὸ τῶν ὁμοίων ἐλασσούμενος
"on the grounds that he was not defeated by his equals"

Whether or not we accept (71) as a PAC in the strict sense, the combined occurrence of (71) and (72) suggests that ἐλασσόω is a verb that itself can be associated with non-standard agent marking.

The final example of a PAC with ἐκ in Thucydides is the following:

(73) Th. 1.20.2   ὑποτοπήσαντες δέ τι . . . ἐκ τῶν ξυνειδότων
σφίσιν Ἱππίᾳ μεμηνῦσθαι
"suspecting that some warning had been given to Hippias by their fellow conspirators"

There are two other PACs with μηνύω in Thucydides, one with ὑπό, one with ἀπό:

(74) Th. 4.89.1   μηνυθέντος τοῦ ἐπιβουλεύματος ὑπὸ
Νικομάχου
"as the plot was revealed by Nicomachus"
(75) Th. 6.28.1   μηνύεται οὖν ἀπὸ μετοίκων τέ τινων καὶ
ἀκολούθων
"so it was revealed by some resident aliens and attendants"

In speaking of this example, Schwyzer ascribes the use of ἀπό to the fact that this sentence expresses "indirekte Denunziation" (1943: 41). Perhaps this is so, but there is no decisive contextual evidence for the assumption that the μέτοικοι and ἀκόλουθοι of (75) are any less direct in their informing than the treacherous conspirators of (73) or Nicomachus in (74). Instead, the clearest distinction can be drawn between the single named informer in (74), marked by ὑπό, and the multiple unnamed informers in (73)

---

[32] Divine agents were not infrequently treated in this way: see note 12 and the examples cited there.

and (75), marked by ἐκ and ἀπό. The best explanation for the non-standard agent markers here, then, is that the unspecified informers are viewed almost as an inanimate source of information: their individual participation in the act of informing is downplayed.

As can be seen from the examples above, these constructions with ἐκ do not share any features that could account in all cases for the use of a preposition other than ὑπό. Instead, a couple of factors seem to have triggered the use of ἐκ. In (68), Thucydides probably used ἐκ to emphasize the concrete spatial relation of the agent to the action of the verb. Similarly in (71) and (73), the non-agentive use of ἐκ to denote source explains its use to mark agents that are only marginally to be considered as the animate entities responsible for the action of the verb; in other words, the objects of the preposition in these two examples are not prototypical agents. An additional factor in these examples may be the verbs themselves, which in both cases construe with ἀπό as well. Finally, the verb certainly seems to have triggered the use of ἐκ in (70), as the particular collocation of ὁμολογέω with ἐκ occurs in other authors as well.

Because ἀπό occurs as an agent marker at least fourteen times in Thucydides, it is easier to determine the reasons for its use than it is for ἐκ.[33] Schwyzer's article goes far in singling out the factors that favor ἀπό as an agent marker (1943: 41). First, he notes that it is used particularly to denote an indirect agent ("vom im Hintergrunde stehenden Drahtzieher"), especially with πράσσω, though also, as seen in (75) above, with μηνύω. Second, he finds the local sense of the preposition still present in its use with προσάγω and λέγω, with the latter of which it is used only when opposing arguments are being presented. Third, he says that in a final two cases, with ἐπιτάσσω and ἐλασσόω, it has become hardly different from ὑπό. This analysis is generally correct and useful, but does not provide a direct contrast with the instances where these verbs are found with the standard agent marker ὑπό. Such an investigation is worthwhile, for it reveals that, of λέγω and πράσσω, the two most common verbs to construe with ἀπό, λέγω, in which the local

---

[33] Twelve instances are given in Schwyzer; I found one additional example (6.45.1) from Books 6 and 7; the final example (5.82.4) comes from Classen's commentary. A related use of ἀπό also appears fairly frequently in Herodotus, where it occurs with γίνομαι to denote the person in whom the subject had its source.

sense of ἀπό predominates, is found several times with ὑπό, while πράσσω, where Schwyzer sees indirect agency, does not construe with ὑπό, but only with an anomalous dative of agent.

As Schwyzer points out, ἀπό, when marking the agent of λέγω, retains a local sense, as all these constructions involve the expression of contrasting opinions:

(76) Th. 3.36.6   ἄλλαι τε γνῶμαι ἀφ' ἑκάστων ἐλέγοντο
"and different opinions were voiced by both sides"

(77) Th. 3.82.7   τά τε ἀπὸ τῶν ἐναντίων καλῶς λεγόμενα
"and what was said by the opposition that was sensible"

(78) Th. 5.82.4   ῥηθέντων πολλῶν ἀφ' ἑκατέρων
"after much was said by both sides"

(79) Th. 6.32.3   ἐλέχθησαν τοιοίδε λόγοι ἀπό τε ἄλλων, τῶν μὲν πιστευόντων τὰ περὶ τῆς στρατείας τῆς τῶν Ἀθηναίων, τῶν δὲ τὰ ἐναντία λεγόντων, καὶ Ἑρμοκράτης . . .
"speeches such as the following were made, both by others – some who believed the reports concerning the Athenian expedition, some who thought the opposite – and Hermocrates [also spoke]"

While λέγω is not found frequently with ὑπό, it does occur four times, and in no case is the idea of opposition present:[34]

(80) Th. 8.94.1   τὸ πάλαι λεγόμενον ὑπὸ Θηραμένους καὶ τῶν μετ' αὐτοῦ
"that which had been said for a while by Theramenes and those with him"

Clearly, ἀπό is used in distinction to ὑπό in those cases where the picture is that of opposing forces approaching an issue from two different directions, thus rendering an ablatival preposition suitable

---

[34] The other examples are found at 2.48.2, 3.16.2, and 8.50.1.

for marking the agent.[35] Consider also the one time that ἀπό marks the agent of προσάγω:

(81) Th. 4.115.2 μηχανῆς μελλούσης προσάξεσθαι αὐτοῖς ἀπὸ τῶν ἐναντίων
"as a siege engine was about to be led against them by their enemies"

This may be contrasted with the one instance where προσάγω is found with ὑπό:

(82) Th. 3.63.2 εἴ τι καὶ ἄκοντες προσήγεσθε ὑπ᾽ Ἀθηναίων
"if you were really being led on unwillingly by the Athenians"

In (81), a siege engine is led against the besieged *from* the camp of the enemy; in (82), however, the Thebans speak of the Plataeans being led on *by* the Athenians. In this latter example, προσάγω has a different, figurative sense – one far less suited to expression of the agent by ἀπό.

In contrast to its use with λέγω, ἀπό marks indirect agency when found with πράσσω. This cannot be demonstrated, however, by comparing PACs with ἀπό against those with ὑπό, as Thucydides never uses ὑπό with the passive of πράσσω. Instead, he employs the dative of agent, even when the verb is not a perfect passive. We may thus set examples (83) to (85) against examples (86) to (88):[36]

(83) Th. 2.101.5 ἐπειδὴ αὐτῷ οὐδὲν ἐπράσσετο ὧν ἕνεκα ἐσέβαλε
"since none of the reasons for his invasion had been accomplished by him"

It is Sitalces himself who invades, but fails to accomplish any of his reasons for doing so.

---

[35] That this distinction should be maintained makes it quite unlikely that the presence of ἀπό in the text of Thucydides should be attributed to the error of a copyist, as is suggested by Jannaris (1897: 370).

[36] While the agent in examples (83) to (85) is in every case some form of αὐτός, this is probably not significant. There are examples with verbs other than πράσσω where the dative of agent with a non-perfect verb is not pronominal: 2.7.2 = (89), 2.35.3, 2.41.4.

(84) Th. 3.85.3 καὶ ὡς οὐδὲν αὐτοῖς ἐπράσσετο
"and as nothing was done by them"

The Corcyraean exiles send envoys to Sparta and Corinth, but these men do not themselves accomplish anything.

(85) Th. 4.121.2 καί τι αὐτῷ καὶ ἐπράσσετο ἐς τὰς πόλεις
ταύτας προδοσίας πέρι
"and something was also worked out by him
with these towns concerning their betrayal"

Brasidas himself was negotiating with these towns with a view to their betrayal. Now the examples with ἀπό:

(86) Th. 4.76.2 τῷ γὰρ Ἱπποκράτει καὶ ἐκείνῳ τὰ Βοιώτια
πράγματα ἀπό τινων ἀνδρῶν ἐν ταῖς πόλεσιν
ἐπράσσετο
"for these Boeotian affairs were conducted with
Hippocrates and Demosthenes by some men in
the cities"

Certain unnamed men are responsible for secret dealings in Boeotia, but at this point it is Hippocrates and Demosthenes who are more directly involved in the action: the latter's arrival in Naupactus, mentioned in the previous sentence, forms the first part of the plan to cause the Boeotians trouble. The comitative dative that is used in reference to Hippocrates and Demosthenes is not far removed from the datives of agent seen in (83) to (85).

(87) Th. 6.61.1 καὶ τὰ μυστικά, ὧν ἐπαίτιος ἦν, μετὰ τοῦ
αὐτοῦ λόγου καὶ τῆς ξυνωμοσίας ἐπὶ τῷ δήμῳ
ἀπ᾽ ἐκείνου ἐδόκει πραχθῆναι
"and the profanation of the mysteries, for which
Alcibiades was blamed, seemed to have been
directed by him for the same reason and as part
of the same plot against the people [as the
mutilation of the Herms]"

Alcibiades is only supposed to have instigated the blasphemous celebrations of the mysteries and not personally have carried them all out. At 8.48.7, he is again marked by ἀπό as an indirect agent with πράσσω. As a final example of this construction, we have the following:

(88) Th. 8.68.4   ὥστε ἀπ᾽ ἀνδρῶν πολλῶν καὶ ξυνετῶν
πραχθὲν τὸ ἔργον . . . προυχώρησεν
"such that the work, carried out by many
intelligent men, advanced"

In this case, the agent could be either direct or indirect.

The contexts suggest that the agents in (86) to (88) are indeed more removed from the action than those in (83) to (85). Furthermore, it is linguistically natural for the more direct agent to be expressed with the dative, the case that also marks the instrument, as the instrument is closer to the action than is the agent: it is, in effect, the extreme instance of the direct agent.[37] Thus, it appears that, for πράσσω, on the one hand, the use of the neutral agent marker ὑπό is superseded by a contrastive agent marking whereby the dative marks direct agents, and ἀπό indirect agents. For λέγω, on the other, ἀπό serves a different purpose: the agent can be expressed by ὑπό, and ἀπό is a marked variant that emphasizes the local notion of arguments coming from opposing sides.

As the other verbs that construe with ἀπό are less common, it is more difficult to fit them into one of these two categories. (i) προσάγω, as seen in example (81), coincides with λέγω in its local use of ἀπό.[38] (ii) ἐπιτάσσω should fall into line with πράσσω, as it too is found with a dative of agent, but not with ὑπό. Example (89), however, does not clearly indicate more direct agency than (90). On the one hand, in (89), the Spartans directly order those who had chosen their side to build more ships:

---

[37] Cf. King on the use of German *mit* (1988: 578).

[38] Rusten also notes a passage where it arguably occurs with the dative of agent (1989: 220), which might suggest that the use of ἀπό as an agent marker could be to denote an indirect agent: εἴ πως σφίσιν ἄνευ δαπάνης καὶ πολιορκίας προσαχθείη (2.77.2). Nevertheless, there are other explanations for the dative σφίσιν than that it is an agent, and the parallel between (81) and the PACs of λέγω with ἀπό is a close one.

(89) Th. 2.7.2   καὶ Λακεδαιμονίοις μὲν . . . τοῖς τἀκείνων
ἑλομένοις ναῦς ἐπετάχθη ποιεῖσθαι[39]
"and those who had taken their side were ordered
by the Lacedaemonians to build ships"

On the other, so too in (90), the ὅμοιοι do not appear to place a
demand on their neighbors any less directly than the Spartans in
(89):

(90) Th. 1.141.1   ἥ τε μεγίστη καὶ ἡ ἐλαχίστη δικαίωσις
ἀπὸ τῶν ὁμοίων πρὸ δίκης τοῖς πέλας
ἐπιτασσομένη
"both the greatest and the smallest claim
demanded by equals of their neighbors before
it is submitted to arbitration"

In this case, it is probably relevant that the agent, τῶν ὁμοίων, is
the same as in (72). The use of a non-standard agent marker in
both cases may have been motivated by a desire to downplay the
agent, in (72) because the ὅμοιοι are viewed simply as a source of
competition, in (90) because they are treated scornfully, as people
at whose hands it would be shameful to suffer mistreatment. (iii)
ἐλασσόω is found once with ἀπό, once with ἐκ, in examples (71)
and (72). As with ἐπιτάσσω, the use of non-standard agent markers
with ἐλασσόω may be attributed to the agents' not being prototypically agentive. (iv) μηνύω, like ἐλασσόω, is also found with ἐκ and
ἀπό in (73) and (75) respectively. Both times, the prepositions'
local use to denote source comes to the fore. (v) ἀγγέλλω likewise
is found with ἀπό:

(91) Th. 6.45.1   ἀπὸ τῶν κατασκόπων σαφῆ ἠγγέλλετο
"clear reports were brought by the scouts"

One may compare (91) to the examples with μηνύω and again
ascribe a local sense to ἀπό.

---

[39] As a reminder that what seems potentially ambiguous to us might have been acceptable
to the ancient Greeks, it is salutary to note that Thucydides is not adverse to using the
dative of agent for Λακεδαιμονίοις even though another dative, τοῖς . . . ἑλομένοις, is
already present as the indirect object of the verb.

We may summarize the motivation for non-standard agent marking in Thucydides as follows. There are not enough instances where ἐκ is used as an agent marker for any pattern as clear as that in Herodotus to emerge. Nevertheless, it may be remarked that some verbs that have a general affinity for non-standard agent marking construe with ἐκ in Thucydides: μηνύω (73) and ἐλασσόω (71) both construe with ἀπό as well elsewhere in Thucydides; ὁμολογέω (70) has non-standard agent marking in several other authors, as seen below. In the case of (71) and (73), it is also probable that ἐκ was used to indicate that what might potentially have been an agent is actually better interpreted as merely the source of the action; such an interpretation could also explain the use of ἐκ in (68), where the concrete spatial sense of the preposition is present. The more plentiful data for ἀπό allow more positive conclusions to be reached, at least regarding its use with λέγω and πράσσω. With λέγω (examples (76) to (79)), ἀπό shows a local sense of opposition not present in passive constructions with ὑπό, but with πράσσω (examples (86) to (88)), ἀπό indicates indirect agency, as it is contrasted not with ὑπό, but with an instrumental-dative of agent, the extreme endpoint of the direct agent. In both cases, the agentive use of ἀπό may be derived from its local use to denote source: when marking opposition, ἀπό conveys the visual metaphor of arguments coming *from* facing sides; when marking indirect agency, the indirect agent is ultimately the source of the action, if somewhat removed from the action itself. The other verbs found with ἀπό do not occur frequently enough to say for certain whether they align more closely with λέγω or πράσσω. Still, the preposition probably conveys a spatial nuance with προσάγω (81), μηνύω (75), and ἀγγέλλω (91). With ἐπιτάσσω (90) and ἐλασσόω (72), the use of ἀπό is perhaps best explained as triggered because the object of the preposition is not actually a true agent; at any rate, ἀπό here does not have a local sense and does not express indirect agency.

Xenophon

Xenophon shows more variety than either Herodotus or Thucydides in the number of different prepositions used to express the agent: ἀπό, ἐκ, παρά (governing both the genitive and the dative), and πρός are all found, though παρά⁺ᴳ is the most common. All of them, moreover, occur with verbs belonging to particular semantic spheres, in contrast to Thucydides, where the verbs that take ἀπό or ἐκ do not fall into clearly defined categories. In the following section, I will first show how the cline introduced on p. 114 is linked to the verbs that have non-standard agent marking in Xenophon. After that, I will look in more detail at the PACs of individual verbs.

The cline in question consists of four categories of verbs arranged in a progression from sending-verbs, where the patient moves away from the agent, through giving- and showing-verbs, to thinking-verbs, where there is no ablatival motion on the part of the patient. These may now be used to classify the verbs found in Xenophon with non-standard agent markers. First, there are the sending-verbs. These are not particularly common with non-standard agent markers in Xenophon, though πέμπω does occur with παρά⁺ᴳ:

(92) X. *Cyr.* 8.2.4 τὰ πεμπόμενα παρὰ βασιλέως
"that which is sent by the king"

(93) X. *HG* 1.1.23 παρὰ δὲ Ἱπποκράτους τοῦ Μινδάρου
ἐπιστολέως εἰς Λακεδαίμονα γράμματα
πεμφθέντα ἑάλωσαν εἰς Ἀθήνας
"a letter sent to Lacedaemon by Hippocrates,
Mindarus' second in command, was captured
and taken to Athens"

(94) X. *An.* 2.1.17 Φαλῖνός ποτε πεμφθεὶς παρὰ βασιλέως
"Phalinus, sent once by the king"

One then passes on to the giving-verbs. Most typical is δίδωμι, which occurs with ἀπό, ἐκ, and παρά in Xenophon:

(95) X. *HG* 7.1.5 ἔτι δὲ καὶ ἀπὸ τῶν θεῶν δέδοται ὑμῖν
εὐτυχεῖν ἐν τούτῳ
"in addition, it has been given to you by the
gods to fare well in this matter"

(96) X. *HG* 3.1.6 ἐκείνῳ δ' αὕτη ἡ χώρα δῶρον ἐκ βασιλέως
ἐδόθη

"and this land was given to him as a gift by
the king"

(97) X. *An.* 1.1.6   καὶ γὰρ ἦσαν αἱ Ἰωνικαὶ πόλεις
Τισσαφέρνους τὸ ἀρχαῖον ἐκ βασιλέως
δεδομέναι
"and in fact the cities of Ionia belonged to
Tissaphernes initially, given to him by the
king"

(98) X. *An.* 2.3.25   διαπεπραγμένος ἥκοι παρὰ βασιλέως
δοθῆναι αὐτῷ σῴζειν τοὺς Ἕλληνας
"he had come after seeing to it that it was
granted to him by the king to keep the
Greeks safe"

(99) X. *Eq.* 5.8   δέδοται δὲ παρὰ θεῶν καὶ ἀγλαΐας ἕνεκεν
ἵππῳ χαίτη
"and the mane has been given to the horse by
the gods also for the sake of ornament"

By contrast, δίδωμι only occurs once with ὑπό:

(100) X. *An.* 7.7.1   αἱ δὲ κῶμαι αὗται ἦσαν δεδομέναι ὑπὸ
Σεύθου Μηδοσάδῃ
"and these villages had been given by
Seuthes to Medosades"

In this category, one may also include the following construction
with συλλέγω:

(101) X. *Cyr.* 6.1.30   ἦσαν δὲ αὐτῷ καὶ κάμηλοι πολλαὶ παρά
τε τῶν φίλων συνειλεγμέναι καὶ <αἱ>
αἰχμάλωτοι πᾶσαι συνηθροισμέναι
"and he also had many camels all collected
together, both gathered for him by friends
and those that had been captured"

Although συλλέγω is not a prototypical verb of giving, it falls into
this semantic sphere of verbs in this instance because the camels
(the patient) are gathered together and given to Cyrus (αὐτῷ).
Additionally, constructions of ὠφελέω with ἀπό may be placed

here, as there is a transfer of benefit to a recipient. Example (102) is typical:

(102) X. *Oec.* 1.15 τῷ δυναμένῳ ἀπὸ τῶν ἐχθρῶν ὠφελεῖσθαι
"to one who is able to be benefited by his enemies *or* benefit from his enemies"[40]

While the preposition in these constructions is only very marginally an agent marker, these examples act as a bridge to the constructions with showing-verbs, as the benefit conferred need not be tangible. More typical of the showing-verbs are two passages with σημαίνω and one with ἐπιδείκνυμι:

(103) X. *Mem.* 1.3.4 εἰ δέ τι δόξειεν αὐτῷ σημαίνεσθαι παρὰ τῶν θεῶν
"if anything seemed to be shown to him by the gods"

(104) X. *Cyr.* 1.6.2 τὰ παρὰ τῶν θεῶν σημαινόμενα
"the signs given by the gods"

(105) X. *Cyr.* 5.5.20 τοῦτ᾽ αὖ παρὰ σοῦ, ἔφη, ἐπιδεικνύσθω
"'let this in turn be shown by you,' he said"

Quite similar to the showing-verbs are the verbs of teaching:

(106) X. *Cyn.* 13.4 κράτιστον μέν ἐστι παρὰ τῆς αὑτοῦ φύσεως τὸ ἀγαθὸν διδάσκεσθαι, δεύτερον δὲ παρὰ τῶν ἀληθῶς ἀγαθόν τι ἐπισταμένων μᾶλλον ἢ ὑπὸ τῶν ἐξαπατᾶν τέχνην ἐχόντων
"it is best to be taught what is good by one's own nature, and second best by those who truly understand something good, rather than by those who are skilled at deceiving"

(107) X. *Cyr.* 1.2.15 οἳ δ᾽ ἂν παιδευθῶσι παρὰ τοῖς δημοσίοις διδασκάλοις
"and those who are taught by public teachers"

---

[40] For the alternative translations, see the discussion on pp. 147–9.

Verbs of speech act as a link between the showing-verbs and thinking-verbs:

(108) X. *Cyr.* 6.1.42 τὰ παρὰ σοῦ λεγόμενα
"that which is said by you"

A good bridge between verbs of speech and the thinking-verbs is provided by ἐπονομάζω. While ostensibly a speaking-verb, it is in the following passage very close to describing an opinion held by those who know Ischomachus: to be *called* good is under most circumstances to be *considered* good:

(109) X. *Oec.* 6.17 ἐπεὶ οὖν τὸν Ἰσχόμαχον ἤκουον πρὸς
πάντων καὶ ἀνδρῶν καὶ γυναικῶν καὶ
ξένων καὶ ἀστῶν καλόν τε κἀγαθὸν
ἐπονομαζόμενον
"so, when I heard that Ischomachus was
called fine and good by all, both men and
women, foreigners and citizens"

Likewise, ὁμολογέω stands in between the speaking-verbs and thinking-verbs. It is found with ἐκ, παρά$^{+G}$, παρά$^{+D}$, and πρός as agent markers but never occurs with ὑπό:

(110) X. *An.* 2.6.1 ὁμολογουμένως ἐκ πάντων τῶν ἐμπείρως
αὐτοῦ ἐχόντων δόξας
"as agreed by all who had an opinion of
him from first-hand experience"

(111) X. *An.* 1.9.1 ὡς παρὰ πάντων ὁμολογεῖται τῶν
Κύρου δοκούντων ἐν πείρᾳ γενέσθαι
"as it is agreed by all who appear to have
had experience with Cyrus"

(112) X. *Cyr.* 1.3.18 ἀλλ' οὐ ταὐτά, ἔφη, ὦ παῖ, παρὰ τῷ
πάππῳ καὶ ἐν Πέρσαις δίκαια
ὁμολογεῖται.
"but the same things, my child, are not
agreed to be just by your grandfather and
among the Persians"

(113) X. *An.* 1.9.20 ὁμολογεῖται πρὸς πάντων κράτιστος δὴ
γενέσθαι θεραπεύειν

"it is agreed by all that he was excellent at
helping out [his friends]"

Finally, there are two thinking-verbs which construe with non-standard agents, νομίζω and ἀδοξέω:

(114) X. *An.* I.2.27   δῶρα ἃ νομίζεται παρὰ βασιλεῖ τίμια
                 "gifts which are considered honorable by
                 the king"

(115) X. *Oec.* 4.2   καὶ εἰκότως μέντοι πάνυ ἀδοξοῦνται πρὸς
                 τῶν πόλεων
                 "and yet it is reasonable that they are held
                 in complete disdain by our cities"

Now that these examples of non-standard agent constructions in Xenophon have been set out according to the semantics of the verb, it remains to connect the prepositions used as agent markers with the four semantic categories of verbs introduced above. To do so, it will be useful to summarize the data presented above by listing the non-standard agent markers found with each verb according as the verb belongs to one of these categories. I use the following abbreviations: A. for ἀπό, E. for ἐκ, P. for παρά$^{+G}$, Pd. for παρά$^{+D}$, and Pr. for πρός.

Sending-verbs	Giving-verbs	Showing- and Speaking-verbs	Thinking-verbs
πέμπω (P.)	δίδωμι (A.E.P.)	σημαίνω (P.)	νομίζω (Pd.)
	συλλέγω (P.)	ἐπιδείκνυμι (P.)	ἀδοξέω (Pr.)
	ὠφελέω (A.)[a]	διδάσκω (P.)	
		παιδεύω (Pd.)	
		λέγω (P.)	
		ἐπονομάζω (Pr.)	
		ὁμολογέω (E.P.Pd.Pr.)	

[a] Although the constructions of ὠφελέω with ἀπό are only marginal PACs at best, I have included them in this table because it is worth noting that it is an ablatival preposition with which it construes when it comes closest to having a non-standard agent marker.

From this chart, two observations may be made: first, that παρά⁺ᴳ, though the most common non-standard agent marker, does not occur with the thinking-verbs; second, that both πρός and παρά⁺ᴰ only occur with verbs in the rightmost two columns. Furthermore, in the third column, they are found more with the speaking- than with the showing-verbs, and are thus closer to the fourth than the second column. These patterns may be connected with the non-agentive uses of the prepositions in question. Because παρά⁺ᴳ most commonly denotes motion away from a person, it makes sense that it should tend towards the left-hand side of the chart, where the verbs describe the transfer of the patient from one sphere to another. Such is also the case with the limited use of ἀπό and ἐκ. Non-agentive παρά⁺ᴰ, however, does not involve ablatival motion, and it is thus used more naturally with verbs where the patient does not undergo such transfer.⁴¹ At first, it might seem odd that πρός⁺ᴳ would fall into line with παρά⁺ᴰ: as a preposition with the genitive, it might also be expected to indicate movement away from its object, as does παρά⁺ᴳ. In fact, πρός⁺ᴳ was rare in a local sense in prose, and when it does occur, it means "on the side of, facing" or "in the presence of": the only two places given in LSJ where it means "from" in a spatial sense come from Homer and Sophocles.⁴² Considering that it does not have ablatival force, it is not surprising that its use as an agent marker is comparable to that of παρά⁺ᴰ.

At this point, I will examine several of these verbs in greater detail in order to establish whether these verbs do not construe with ὑπό at all, like πράσσω in Thucydides, or whether ὑπό does occur, but under conditions clearly differentiated from those which favor the non-standard prepositions.

(i) δίδωμι, as seen in examples (95) to (100) above, is found with four different agent markers in six passages, including just one with ὑπό. Probably, the use of ὑπό in (100) is due to the agent's being the proper noun Σεύθης rather than the βασιλεύς or θεοί of the other five examples. In this respect, these passages may be compared to

---

⁴¹ Cf. the use of *with* in *Antony and Cleopatra* 1.1.58 "Is Caesar with Antonius prized so slight?"

⁴² As an indication of the absence of ablatival force, one may compare Hdt. 1.124.3, where it is contrasted with ἀπό: οὗτοι ἀποστάντες ἀπ' ἐκείνου καὶ γενόμενοι πρὸς σέο.

the Thucydidean examples where ἀπό indicates the remoter agent. The gods and the king are seen as distanced from the action in question, as if acting through intermediaries. Such a scenario also makes clear the link between the use of these prepositions to mark an indirect agent and their use to mark source: if the agent is remote enough, then it may be seen as disconnected from the act itself, and therefore as a source rather than as an agent. Ablatival prepositions are chosen (rather than παρά$^{+D}$ or πρός) because giving-verbs belong clearly to the left-hand side of the cline described above.

(ii) ὠφελέω, like δίδωμι, is a giving-verb that involves the transfer of benefit from the agent to the patient. At first glance, constructions such as that in example (102) resemble those with δίδωμι, with an ablatival preposition as the agent marker of choice.[43] Two differences must be pointed out, however. First is that, unlike δίδωμι, which only construes once with ὑπό, ὠφελέω is found three times with ὑπό:

(116) X. *Mem.* 2.9.8   ὑπὸ Κρίτωνος ὠφελούμενος
                       "benefited by Crito"

(117) X. *Mem.* 2.10.3   ὠφελούμενος ὑπὸ σοῦ μὴ ἀντωφελοίη σε
                       "[if], benefited by you, he did not benefit
                       you in return"

(118) X. *Hier.* 10.4   ὑπ' αὐτῶν ὠφελούμενοι
                       "benefited by them"

Second, the object of the active verb is not that which is given, but the person to whom it is given. Accordingly, the subject of the passive verb is not itself transferred, but instead the beneficiary of the transfer. There is thus potential for confusion between the use of the passive of ὠφελέω construed with an agent ("be benefited by") and the intransitive middle of ὠφελέω – usually homophonous – construed with an object marked by an ablatival preposition

---

[43] I omit from consideration the constructions at *Oec.* 2.8 (ὡς παρὰ σοῦ ὠφελησόμενοι) and X. *Mem.* 1.6.14 (παρ' ὧν ἂν ἡγῶμαι ὠφελήσεσθαί τι αὐτοὺς εἰς ἀρετήν) because the morphology of the verbs argues against interpreting them as passives. While the future middle of this verb could be used as a passive (see Kühner–Gerth 1898: 116), these particular examples should be regarded as middles, for they not only lack the standard agent marker ὑπό, but also have the less clearly passive of the two future mediopassive stems.

("benefit from"). The conceptual difference between the two would be that, in the first case, the object of the preposition would have actively worked for the benefit of the subject of the verb, while in the second case, it would have merely been a source of benefit. Typically, the object of the preposition in these latter cases is inanimate, as in:

(119) X. *Oec.* 5.6   ὠφελούμενοι δὲ καὶ οἱ ἵπποι καὶ αἱ κύνες ἀπὸ
τῆς γεωργίας ἀντωφελοῦσι τὸν χῶρον
"and the horses and dogs, benefited by *or*
benefiting from agriculture, benefit the land
in turn"

But the boundary between the two becomes blurred in cases like (102), cited above. In this passage (*Oec.* 1.7–15), Socrates and Critobulus are discussing the meaning of χρήματα. At Socrates' prompting, Critobulus proposes that χρήματα refers to whatever is beneficial. Socrates then tests this tentative definition by asking whether various ὠφέλιμα qualify as χρήματα or not. He asks whether one ὠφελεῖται ἀπό (either "benefits from" or "is benefited by") various objects, both inanimate, such as pipes or money, and animate, such as flocks, friends, and enemies. Now the use of ὠφελεῖσθαι ἀπό with inanimate objects is naturally taken as middle: one does not expect the pipes actively to work for their owner. Similarly, the point of (102) is to suggest that one may derive benefit even from enemies, in which case the subject is benefited in spite of, not through the volitional agency of, the object of ἀπό. More ambiguous is (120):

(120) X. *Oec.* 1.14   οἱ δὲ φίλοι, ἄν τις ἐπίστηται αὐτοῖς
χρῆσθαι ὥστε ὠφελεῖσθαι ἀπ᾽ αὐτῶν . . .
"and friends, if one knows how to use them
so as to be benefited by them *or* benefit
from them"

On the one hand, it appears as though αὐτῶν in this case could be an agent: friends may reasonably be expected to benefit each other actively. Even so, given the context of this passage – both the wider parallelism with inanimate objects like money and the

148

rather calculating view of friendship suggested by ἄν τις ἐπίστηται αὐτοῖς χρῆσθαι – it is better not to take this as an example of a passive construction.

In conclusion, the constructions of ὠφελέω with ἀπό demonstrate how a preposition can come to rival ὑπό as an agent marker. At first glance, ἀπό appears to compete with ὑπό, in that both prepositions mark the source of some benefit. But while ὑπό introduces a source that actively contributes to that benefit – in other words, an agent – ἀπό marks a source that does not control the benefit and is therefore not an agent: it is used with objects that are merely exploited by the subject of the verb. Even when those objects are people, they are still treated on a par with inanimate entities.

(iii) ὁμολογέω does not occur in Xenophon in any agent constructions other than the four given at (110) to (113) above, in each of which it occurs with a different prepositional construction, counting παρά$^{+G}$ and παρά$^{+D}$ separately. The first instance, with ἐκ, stands out as the verbal form in question is an adverb formed from the present participle; whether this accounts for the expression of the agent is impossible to say, but this collocation does occur in Plato as well (*Smp.* 196a). One may be more optimistic about explaining the use of παρά$^{+D}$ in example (112). First, the collocation δίκαια ὁμολογεῖται is semantically similar to νομίζεται, and as this verb quite regularly takes παρά$^{+D}$, it is not surprising that this expression should as well. Furthermore, the phrase παρὰ τῷ πάππῳ is in parallel with the expression ἐν Πέρσαις. Accordingly, to match the local preposition ἐν, Xenophon uses παρά$^{+D}$ because its local sense, "*chez*," is appropriate for its object, πάππῳ. There is also no obvious difference between the use of παρά$^{+G}$ and πρός in (111) and (113). The most that can be said is that ὁμολογέω is a verb that avoids expression with ὑπό, but is not limited with respect to the non-standard agent markers it takes because it occupies a middle point on the cline from sending- to thinking-verbs.

(iv) νομίζεται occurs quite regularly with παρά$^{+D}$. In addition to (114), the following examples are also found:

(121) X. *Mem.* 1.6.13   παρ᾽ ἡμῖν νομίζεται τὴν ὥραν καὶ τὴν
σοφίαν ὁμοίως μὲν καλόν, ὁμοίως δὲ
αἰσχρὸν διατίθεσθαι εἶναι
"youthful beauty and wisdom are
considered by us to be good or shameful
in the same respects"

(122) X. *Mem.* 2.3.15   παρὰ πᾶσιν ἀνθρώποις τἀναντία
νομίζεται
"the opposite view is held by all men"

(123) X. *Mem.* 4.4.19   παρὰ πᾶσιν ἀνθρώποις πρῶτον
νομίζεται θεοὺς σέβειν
"it is held by all men that the most
important custom is to honor the gods"

(124) X. *Ages.* 4.6   νομίζεται παρ᾽ ἡμῖν τῷ ἄρχοντι κάλλιον
εἶναι τὴν στρατιὰν ἢ ἑαυτὸν πλουτίζειν
"it is thought by us that it is better for the
ruler to enrich his army rather than
himself"

These examples are not matched by any with ὑπό. There is, however, one case where ἐν is used similarly:

(125) X. *Cyr.* 1.3.18   οὗτος μὲν γὰρ τῶν ἐν Μήδοις πάντων
ἑαυτὸν δεσπότην πεποίηκεν, ἐν Πέρσαις
δὲ τὸ ἴσον ἔχειν δίκαιον νομίζεται.
"for he has made himself ruler of all the
Medes, but among *or* by the Persians
equality is considered just"

This passage follows immediately after one cited above at (112),
in which ὁμολογεῖται is construed with παρά⁺ᴰ and ἐν. Likewise,
the use of ἐν with νομίζεται here highlights the semantic closeness
of these two prepositions in constructions with passive verbs. But
should they be considered agent markers? On the one hand, it
is tempting to reject them as local prepositions masquerading as
agent markers, especially ἐν, which, considering its overwhelming
frequency as a local preposition, is best viewed as such even here.
On the other, it is also noteworthy that νομίζεται does not occur
with ὑπό. As there is no reason to explain why the passive of this

verb should fail to construe with an agent altogether,[44] it becomes more plausible to see at least παρά$^{+D}$ as standing in for ὑπό.

(v) σημαίνω occurs in only three PACs in Xenophon. Two with παρά$^{+G}$ are cited above as (103) and (104). The third, with ὑπό, follows after the passage from the *Memorabilia*:

(126) X. *Mem.* 1.3.4   οἵτινες παρὰ τὰ ὑπὸ τῶν θεῶν
σημαινόμενα ποιοῦσί τι
"who do something counter to what is
indicated by the gods"

As Schwyzer points out, the use of ὑπό here prevents the double use of παρά (1943: 25). Because this solitary use of ὑπό may be explained thus, σημαίνω may be another verb that generally selects against ὑπό. With only two other PACs, however, one cannot tell for sure.

(vi) πέμπω provides another example of a verb that construes both with ὑπό and with παρά$^{+G}$. The passages with παρά were given as examples (92) to (94); those with ὑπό are as follows:

(127) X. *Cyr.* 5.3.12   ἀγγέλους πεμπομένους ὑπ᾽ ἐμοῦ
"messengers sent by me"
(128) X. *Cyr.* 6.3.15   ὑπ᾽ ἐμοῦ πεμφθείς
"sent by me"
(129) X. *HG* 1.6.5   ὑπὸ τῆς πόλεως ἐπὶ τὰς ναῦς πεμφθείς
"sent by the city to command the ships"
(130) X. *HG* 3.4.13   πεμφθέντες ὑπὸ Φαρναβάζου
"sent by Pharnabazus"

Now if πέμπω is to construe with a non-standard agent marker, we expect it, as a sending-verb, to occur with παρά$^{+G}$, as indeed it does. Is there any difference, then, between the occasions when it takes παρά and those when it takes ὑπό? Most probably, as with δίδωμι, the nature of the agent plays a role. Both times the agent is the first-person pronoun, ὑπό is found; both times the agent is the king, παρά is found. When the person speaking is referring to himself, he is more likely to see himself as the direct agent of

---

44 There are, for instance, active constructions that seem to be the counterpart to the passives with παρά$^{+D}$. Compare e.g. *HG* 3.5.8 (δίκαιον εἶναι νομίζομεν βοηθεῖν ὑμᾶς τῇ πόλει ὑμῶν) with (124).

the action and thus use ὑπό. But when the author, as a third party, is describing the action of a king, he may instead view the king not so much as a personal agent as an institution that is merely the source of the action. Therefore, in the latter two cases, παρά draws attention away from any personal involvement of the king's.

(vii) διδάσκω most frequently construes with ὑπό:

(131) X. *HG* 5.4.14   διδασκόμενοι ὑπὸ τῶν μετὰ τὰς ἐν Θήβαις σφαγὰς ἐκπεπτωκότων
"informed by those who were exiled after the massacres in Thebes"

(132) X. *HG* 5.4.31   διδαχθεὶς ὑπό του
"told by someone else"

(133) X. *HG* 5.4.44   ἐδιδάχθησαν ὑπὸ τῶν φευγόντων
"they were taught by the exiles"

(134) X. *Oec.* 3.11   διδασκομένη ὑπὸ τοῦ ἀνδρός
"taught by her husband"

Indeed, even in (106) above, the one passage where διδάσκω occurs with a non-standard agent marker, it occurs twice with παρά$^{+G}$, then once with ὑπό. This distribution suggests that ὑπό is the more usual preposition, with παρά being a marked variant. An examination of the agents in (106) shows why παρά is found here in place of ὑπό. Different sources of knowledge about the good are compared: first, one may learn from one's own nature; second, from those who have some understanding of the good; one must avoid being taught, however, by those who only have the skill of deception. Just as ἀπό is used with ὠφελέω when the source of the benefit does not actively set about the benefiting, so too παρά$^{+G}$ is used here with διδάσκω because the source of knowledge, ἡ αὐτοῦ φύσις, merely serves as a general guiding principle, rather than as an engaged teacher. This relation to the act of teaching may be contrasted with the allusion to the sophists at the end of the sentence. However misguided they may be, the sophists actively seek to instruct their pupils; to express their role in teaching, then, Xenophon uses the standard agent preposition ὑπό. Finally, παρά is also used in the intermediate case, of acquiring knowledge of the good from those who themselves understand it. The choice of παρά over ὑπό here may result from pessimism in Socratic circles about the ability of people to teach virtue actively.[45] To summarize, διδάσκω falls into line with ὠφελέω and πέμπω in that its non-standard agent constructions can be described with the most economy by taking the constructions with ὑπό to represent a default; constructions with παρά would then indicate that what might potentially be considered an agent does not exercise enough control over the action to warrant the use of ὑπό.

From the data collected from Xenophon, two important results stand out. The first is that, when a non-standard agent marker occurs with a passive verb, the semantics of the verb in question affect which preposition is chosen. One may classify verbs, as set out on p. 114, along a cline ranging from sending-verbs at one end, through giving-verbs and showing-verbs, to thinking-verbs at the other. Verbs in the first couple of categories tend to construe with ablatival prepositions, especially παρά$^{+G}$, while verbs in the last category take locatival prepositions, like παρά$^{+D}$ or πρός^{+G}. The second result is that the non-standard agent markers are frequently used when what appears to be an agent does not actually control the action and is thus not a true agent. True, there are a couple of verbs that never take ὑπό, namely ὁμολογέω and νομίζω, and in these cases the agents do still appear to control the action. With σημαίνω, too, the use of ὑπό seems to have been triggered by special circumstances in a verb that otherwise favored παρά$^{+G}$. In the other verbs singled out for special examination, however, ὑπό retains its status as the default agent marker, and other prepositions are introduced only when the object of the preposition is not in fact an agent. This phenomenon may be seen especially clearly in the case of ὠφελέω and διδάσκω. After the passive of these verbs, a noun introduced by ὑπό is a true agent, actively benefiting or teaching the patient; a noun introduced by ἀπό or παρά$^{+G}$, however, is simply a source of benefit or learning.

Lysias

The text of Lysias does not provide many examples of passive verbs with non-standard agent markers. This paucity is primarily due to

---

[45] Cf. Pl. *Men.* 89e: ΜΕΝ. ἀλλ' ἀρετῆς διδάσκαλοι οὐ δοκοῦσί σοι εἶναι; ΣΟ. πολλάκις γοῦν ζητῶν εἴ τινες εἶεν αὐτῆς διδάσκαλοι, πάντα ποιῶν οὐ δύναμαι εὑρεῖν.

the small size of the corpus: only a sixth the size of Xenophon's works, a tenth the size of Plato's. Even so, there are enough to show that the collocation of particular non-standard agent markers with particular verbs resembles that found in Xenophon.

Once again, ὁμολογέω is found with παρά$^{+G}$:

(135) Lys. 30.12 τοῦτο δὲ παρὰ πάντων ὁμολογεῖται
"and this is agreed by all"

There is only one other place in Lysias where the passive of ὁμολογέω occurs with an agent. Here too it is construed with a non-standard agent marker, this time a dative of agent – non-standard here because the verb is an aorist. We shall see parallels of this usage in Plato:

(136) Lys. 23.15 πρὶν τοίνυν ταῦτα ὁμολογηθῆναι αὐτῷ
"now, before this was agreed by him"

Although this evidence from Lysias is scanty, it still adds to the impression that ὁμολογέω is anomalous in its agent constructions.

There is only one instance in Lysias where παρά$^{+D}$ is found in an agent construction.[46] It occurs with γιγνώσκω, a verb semantically similar to νομίζω, the verb found most often with παρά$^{+D}$ in Xenophon:

(137) Lys. 1.2 καὶ ταῦτα οὐκ ἂν εἴη μόνον παρ' ὑμῖν οὕτως
ἐγνωσμένα, ἀλλ' ἐν ἁπάσῃ τῇ Ἑλλάδι
"and these matters would be recognized thus
not only by you, but in all of Greece"

While the parallelism with the spatial expression ἐν ἁπάσῃ τῇ Ἑλλάδι suggests that the local sense of παρά$^{+D}$ predominates here, the object of the preposition, the second-person plural pronoun, is the agent in the sentence that precedes, rendering it difficult to reject an agentive interpretation of this phrase. As for νομίζεται,

---

[46] The only other use of παρά$^{+D}$ that could potentially be considered agentive comes from Lys. 3.29 τῷ γὰρ ἂν δόξειε πιστὸν ὡς ἐγὼ προνοηθεὶς καὶ ἐπιβουλεύων ἦλθον ἐπὶ τὴν Σίμωνος οἰκίαν μεθ' ἡμέραν, μετὰ τοῦ μειρακίου, τοσούτων ἀνθρώπων παρ' αὐτῷ συνειλεγμένων. The speaker places an emphasis on the improbability of his physically confronting an opponent with so many friends gathered around him; accordingly, the local sense of παρά$^{+D}$ predominates here.

because it does not occur with an agent in any of the speeches, it cannot be determined whether Lysias, like Xenophon, would have avoided expressing its agent with ὑπό.

The preposition ἐκ is found in some marginal agentive constructions with ὠφελέω. As in the examples from Xenophon, the object of the preposition does not initiate the action:

(138) Lys. 21.18   πολλὰς ἀρχὰς ἄρξας ἐκ τῶν ὑμετέρων
                 ὠφέλημαι
                 "having served in many offices, I have been
                 benefited by *or* have benefited from your
                 possessions"

(139) Lys. 22.20   καὶ οὕτω μεγάλα ἐξ αὐτῆς ὠφελοῦνται
                 "and they are benefited by *or* draw benefit
                 from this [business] to such an extent"

(140) Lys. 27.7   ὑμᾶς ἐξαπατήσαντας ἐκ τῶν ὑμετέρων
                 ὠφελεῖσθαι
                 "by deceiving you to be benefited by *or* to
                 benefit from your possessions"

In all these sentences, the object of ἐκ is merely an inanimate source of benefit, and thus not a true agent. In this connection, one may also note one instance of ἀπό marking the inanimate source of benefit:

(141) Lys. 18.20   οὐκ ἐλάττω ἀπ᾽ αὐτῶν ὑμεῖς ὠφεληθήσεσθε ἢ
                 ἡμεῖς οἱ κεκτημένοι
                 "no less will you be benefited by the property
                 than we who have acquired it"

By contrast, there is one case where ἐκ is used when its object may reasonably be considered a true agent:

(142) Lys. 16.18   τὰ μὲν γὰρ τοιαῦτα ἐπιτηδεύματα οὔτε τοὺς
                 ἰδιώτας οὔτε τὸ κοινὸν τῆς πόλεως βλάπτει,
                 ἐκ δὲ τῶν κινδυνεύειν ἐθελόντων πρὸς τοὺς
                 πολεμίους ἅπαντες ὑμεῖς ὠφελεῖσθε
                 "for such practices harm neither private
                 citizens nor the city as a whole, but you all are
                 benefited by those who are willing to face
                 danger against the enemy"

The speaker remarks that the Athenians benefit from those who are willing to risk their lives against the enemy. There are two reasons to consider these volunteers to be a true agent of ὠφελέω. First, it is unlikely that people would face their enemies willingly except out of some active desire to help the community. Second, the sentence as a whole notes that while the practices of the aristocracy do not harm the city, their willingness to fight helps it. The volunteers are thus parallel to the ἐπιτηδεύματα of the first half of the sentence, which, though inanimate, are still agentive enough to be the subject of the active verb βλάπτω. On both these grounds, then, ἐκ should here be considered a true agent marker. As in Xenophon, ὑπό is also found with ὠφελέω, if only once:

(143) Lys. 9.14   ἔχω δὲ καὶ τοιαῦτα εἰπεῖν, ἐξ ὧν ὠφελοίμην ἂν
               πολὺ δικαιότερον ὑπὸ τῶν ἀντιδίκων ἢ κακῶς
               πάσχοιμι
               "and I can also say such things, as a result of
               which it would be much more just for me to be
               benefited by my opponents than to be treated ill
               by them"

There are two main reasons why ὑπό would be the preferred preposition here. First, ἐκ is already present in the sense "as a result of," and its repeated use might cause confusion. Furthermore, the passive of ὠφελέω is parallel with the active of πάσχω, here acting as a passive to ποιέω. Because πάσχω does not have the same tendency to construe with ἐκ, it might have provided additional impetus for the use of ὑπό.

There remain a couple of agent constructions that do not match any found in Xenophon. The first is:

(144) Lys. 5.1   τὰ παρὰ τῶν ἄλλων εἰρημένα
              "that which has been said by the others"

Judging on the basis of Lysias' language alone, there is no obvious explanation for the use of παρά here. In a comparable passage, ὑπό is used twice in succession:

(145) Lys. 12.77   πάντα γὰρ τὰ ὑπ' ἐμοῦ εἰρημένα ἐν τῇ βουλῇ
                ἀπολογούμενος ἔλεγεν . . . τοῖς εἰρημένοις
                τρόποις ὑπ' ἐμοῦ

> "for, during his defense before the council, he
> said everything that has been said by me . . . in
> the manner that has been mentioned by me"

Furthermore, the other two PACs with λέγω, both with the aorist,
also have ὑπό as the agent marker:

(146) Lys. 2.54 τὰ ὑπὸ πολλῶν κινδυνευθέντα ὑφ᾽ ἑνὸς ῥηθῆναι
"for that which was risked by many to be
recounted by one"

(147) Lys. 32.18 πολλῶν καὶ δεινῶν ὑπὸ τῆς γυναικὸς
ῥηθέντων
"after many terrible things were said by the
woman"

If λέγω is not used with non-standard agent markers elsewhere
in Lysias, then the explanation for (144) must be sought in other
authors. Most likely is that it should be compared to the passages
in Thucydides, examples (76) to (79) above, where ἀπό is used
with λέγω when opposing opinions are presented, for the opening
of Lysias 5 does introduce a contrast between what has been said
by others and what will be said by the speaker.

The final example of a non-standard agent marker in Lysias is
the following:

(148) Lys. 9.20 τούτων μὲν οὖν ἀδικούντων μετρίως
ἠγανάκτουν, ἡγούμενος τετάχθαι τοὺς μὲν
ἐχθροὺς κακῶς ποιεῖν, τοὺς δὲ φίλους εὖ· παρ᾽
ὑμῶν δὲ τοῦ δικαίου στερηθεὶς πολὺ ἂν μᾶλλον
λυπηθείην.
"so long as these men were treating me
unjustly, I was moderately annoyed, feeling that
it is established that one treats one's enemies
badly, and one's friends well; but if deprived of
justice by you, I would be much more upset"

Because the passive of στερέω is not found in any other agent
constructions, one cannot say whether the use of παρά here is due
to the verb itself or to the particular context of the example. It is

probable, however, that the explanation given for (144) is at work here as well, as there is again a contrast. On the one hand, the speaker accepts that it is natural to be wronged by his enemies; on the other, he would not think it right to be deprived of justice by the jury.

Of the other four verbs whose passive constructions in Xenophon I singled out for study, two do not occur in PACs in Lysias (σημαίνω, πέμπω).⁴⁷ The other two, δίδωμι and διδάσκω, just have a single agent construction with ὑπό each (Frag. 24.1.4 (Budé) / 120.78 (Teubner) and 2.19 respectively).

In short, because the surviving corpus of the speeches of Lysias is so limited, one cannot say much about his use of non-standard agent markers with passive verbs. Still, it is possible to detect traces of the same conditions for non-standard agent markers in Lysias that obtained in Xenophon and Thucydides as well. As in Xenophon, ὁμολογέω has abnormal agent markers, being construed once with παρά⁺ᴳ, once with the dative (when the verb is not a perfect passive). Furthermore, παρά⁺ᴰ occurs in Xenophon primarily with thinking-verbs; so too in Lysias, the one time it may be considered an agent marker, it occurs with γιγνώσκω. Finally, ὠφελέω is construed with ablatival prepositions in both authors, though ἐκ predominates in Lysias, as against ἀπό in Xenophon. In both authors, these non-standard prepositions are chiefly found when the object of the preposition does not actively carry out the benefit in question, although Lysias does use ἐκ once with what appears to be a true agent. The similarities between Lysias and Thucydides are more tenuous. But the two remaining PACs with non-standard agent markers in Lysias both involve the presence of παρά⁺ᴳ in contexts that call to mind the Thucydidean use of ἀπό with λέγω in situations where opposing arguments are being presented. On the whole, the evidence provided by Lysias is slight, but it still lends additional support for the explanations of non-standard agent marking put forward so far.

⁴⁷ The passives of μεταπέμπω and ὑποπέμπω do occur with agents, but μεταπέμπω has substantially different semantics from πέμπω, and little can be inferred from the solitary use of ὑπό as an agent marker with ὑποπέμπω (1.15).

Plato

The dialogues of Plato provide some forty examples of non-standard agent constructions. Generally speaking, the non-standard agent markers in Plato occur with the same verbs that avoid constructions with ὑπό in Xenophon and Lysias, including ὁμολογέω and δίδωμι. Once again, I will look at all these verbs in turn to determine whether they are more common with ὑπό or with other prepositions. I will begin by looking at verbs that construe with the ablatival prepositions ἐκ and παρά⁺ᴳ, and will then proceed to those found with the locatival prepositions παρά⁺ᴰ and πρός.

As in other authors, πέμπω and its compounds are found with non-standard agent markers. They are not very common in Plato, occurring in only three PACs, each with a different agent marker:

(149) Pl. *Mx.* 236d   προπεμφθέντες κοινῇ μὲν ὑπὸ τῆς
     πόλεως, ἰδίᾳ δὲ ὑπὸ τῶν οἰκείων
     "escorted publicly by the city, and
     privately by their relatives"

(150) Pl. *Phdr.* 245b   ὡς οὐκ ἐπ' ὠφελίᾳ ὁ ἔρως τῷ ἐρῶντι καὶ
     τῷ ἐρωμένῳ ἐκ θεῶν ἐπιπέμπεται
     "that it is not to their advantage that love
     is sent by the gods to the lover and the
     beloved"

(151) Pl. *Ep.* 347a   ὅθεν οὐδ' ἂν ὁ θυρωρὸς ἤθελέν με ἀφεῖναι
     μὴ πεμφθείσης αὐτῷ τινος ἐντολῆς παρὰ
     Διονυσίου
     "from which place the gatekeeper would
     not have been willing to release me unless
     some command was sent to him by
     Dionysius"

Because each of these PACs involves a different compound of πέμπω, no firm conclusions about the motivating factors for each agent expression may be reached. In (149), προπέμπω, "escort," is probably the furthest removed from the meaning of the simple verb πέμπω. This fact may explain the retention of the usual agent marker ὑπό, although it is also possible that ὑπό was motivated by the agent, πόλεως, which, because it is low on the animacy hierarchy, might require more explicit agent marking.⁴⁸ With a noun denoting a physical place as well as a political institution, there would have been more reason to construe παρά⁺ᴳ as ablatival. In (150), the use of ἐκ may be attributed either to a general tendency of πέμπω not to construe with ὑπό or to the fact that, in this passage, the gods' role as agents is not emphasized; see the discussion on (173) below. Example (151), the only PAC with the simple verb πέμπω in Plato, resembles constructions (92) through (94) in Xenophon. One cannot conclude anything certain on the basis of this one passage, but it does support the view that πέμπω had a proclivity for construction with παρά⁺ᴳ.

The verb ὁμολογέω is very frequent in the works of Plato; furthermore, when it occurs in PACs, the agent marker is almost never ὑπό. Because the means of marking the agent is strongly correlated to the nature of the agent, it will be useful to present the connection between these factors in a table. As the dative of agent is one of the preferred means of marking the agent, I will give two tables, one for the constructions where the verb is not a perfect (and the dative of agent is not expected), one for those where it is a perfect (and the dative of agent *is* expected).

(i) Non-perfect verbs:

dative (14×)	παρά⁺ᴳ (12×)	ὑπό (3×)	ἐκ (1×)
• ἡμῖν (9×)	• πάντων (2×)	• ἐκείνου	• πάντων
• σοι	• πολλῶν (2×)	• τῶν πολλῶν	
• οἷς	• βελτιόνων	ἀνθρώπων	
• αὐτῷ	• χειρόνων	• σοῦ	
• ὑμῖν	• τούτων		
• νῷν	• σοῦ (3×)		
	• ἐμοῦ		
	• ἡμῶν		

From this chart, it is clear that the two most common means of expressing the agent with ὁμολογέω are the dative of agent and

---

⁴⁸ For more discussion of the interaction of the animacy hierarchy with prepositional agent markers, see the section on δίδωμι below.

παρά$^{+G}$. For the most part, if the agent is a pronoun, the dative is used: all fourteen datives of agent are pronouns. Furthermore, the nine times that the agent is non-pronominal, a prepositional construction is used. There is overlap, however, in that eight of the pronominal agents are construed with a preposition rather than with the dative. Two questions must then be considered: what triggers this use of prepositions with pronouns, and what differences can be detected among the use of the various prepositions?

To start with the first question, two of the prepositional PACs with pronominal agents result from the neighboring presence of non-pronominal agents that would not have been marked by the dative:

(152) Pl. *Grg.* 475d ἄλλο τι οὖν ὑπὸ μὲν τῶν πολλῶν
ἀνθρώπων καὶ ὑπὸ σοῦ ὡμολογεῖτο
ἡμῖν^{49} ἐν τῷ ἔμπροσθεν χρόνῳ αἴσχιον
εἶναι τὸ ἀδικεῖν τοῦ ἀδικεῖσθαι;
"Isn't it the case that it was earlier agreed
(with us) by many people and by you that
to do wrong is more shameful than to be
wronged?"

(153) Pl. *Smp.* 202c καὶ πῶς ἄν . . . ὁμολογοῖτο μέγας θεὸς
εἶναι παρὰ τούτων
"And how could it be agreed by these men
that he is a great god?"

The construction in (153) will have been influenced by that in (154):

(154) Pl. *Smp.* 202b ὁμολογεῖταί γε παρὰ πάντων μέγας
θεὸς εἶναι
"but it is agreed by everyone that he is a
great god"

---

49 The use of the ethic dative ἡμῖν in juxtaposition with the indisputable agent marker ὑπό could give rise to the suspicion that apparently agentive occurrences of ἡμῖν in other places may also be no more than ethic datives. While this possibility cannot be ruled out, there are enough cases where the dative of agent is used with ὁμολογέω with pronouns not open to this interpretation to require the recognition of datives of agent with this verb. This being the case, it is likely that some, if not all, of the instances of ἡμῖν tabulated may be considered agents.

In a further four instances, a prepositional agent marker is probably preferred because the agent is emphasized, either by καί or by γε:

(155) Pl. *R.* 499d χαλεπὰ δὲ καὶ παρ᾽ ἡμῶν ὁμολογεῖται
"but that it is difficult is agreed by us, too"

(156) Pl. *Grg.* 470b τοῦτο μὲν δή, ὡς ἔοικε, καὶ παρὰ σοῦ καὶ παρ᾽ ἐμοῦ ὁμολογεῖται
"this, then, as it seems, is agreed both by you and by me"

(157) Pl. *Tht.* 171b ἐξ ἁπάντων ἄρα ἀπὸ Πρωταγόρου ἀρξαμένων ἀμφισβητήσεται, μᾶλλον δὲ ὑπό γε ἐκείνου ὁμολογήσεται
"so, starting from Protagoras, it will be disputed by all – or rather, it will be agreed by him at least"

When the dative is used, the agent is never strengthened in this way. Contrast with the above:

(158) Pl. *R.* 478a καὶ δῆλον ὅτι ἕτερον ἐπιστήμης δόξα ὁμολογεῖται ἡμῖν
"and clearly it is agreed by us that opinion is different from knowledge"

In the final two examples of pronominal agents introduced by prepositions, the reason why the preposition was selected instead of the dative of agent is obscure:

(159) Pl. *Chrm.* 173e οὗτοι γὰρ ἐπιστημόνως ζῶντες οὐχ ὁμολογοῦνται παρὰ σοῦ εὐδαίμονες εἶναι
"for those who live in a knowledgeable way are not agreed by you to be happy"

(160) Pl. *Prt.* 360c δι᾽ ὃ δὲ δειλοί εἰσιν, δειλία ὁμολογεῖται παρὰ σοῦ;
"but the reason why they are cowards – that is agreed by you to be cowardice?"

There is little to distinguish between these two passages and the following:

(161) Pl. *Grg.* 497e   οἶμαι γάρ σοι οὐδὲ ταύτῃ ὁμολογεῖσθαι
"for I think that it is not agreed by you in this way either"

Considering that the prepositional construction seems to be more emphatic in other cases, the agents in (159) and (160) are also presumably highlighted by the use of the preposition.

What, then, is the difference between ὑπό, παρά, and ἐκ in these agent constructions? As παρά is by far the most common, the best approach is to look for conditions that triggered the use of the other two. The easiest to account for is ἐκ:

(162) Pl. *Smp.* 196a   ὃ δὴ διαφερόντως ἐκ πάντων
ὁμολογουμένως Ἔρως ἔχει
"which Love has to an exceptional extent, as is agreed by all"

This construction may be compared to X. *An.* 2.6.1, quoted above under (110), where ἐκ πάντων is again found with ὁμολογουμένως: this particular collocation simply seems to have been idiomatic.[50] By contrast, the use of ὑπό was motivated by a need to clarify the role of the agent. In (152), the agent might need particular highlighting because of the competing presence of ἡμῖν; in (157), the agentive nature of ἐκείνου needs to be emphasized both in opposition to the ablatival prepositions that precede and also in light of the context as a whole, discussed below as example (167).

In tenses other than the perfect, then, when the passive of ὁμολογέω construes with an agent, a pronominal agent is marked with the dative of agent, a nominal agent with παρά$^{+G}$. Pronouns too, however, can be marked by παρά when the pronoun is parallel with a noun, or when the agent is emphasized, as by καί or γε. In two places, ὑπό is used instead of παρά because the role of the agent needs to be clarified.

---

[50] The Thucydidean PAC of ὁμολογέω with ἐκ is not dissimilar (example (70) above).

(ii) Perfect verbs:

dative	παρά$^{+G}$	ὑπό	ἐκ
• ἡμῖν (21×) • ἐμοὶ καὶ Ἀγάθωνι • ἐμοί τε καὶ σοί • σοί	none	• ἐμοῦ	none

PACs in Plato with the perfect passive of ὁμολογέω are no different from those of other verbs. All but one are with the dative of agent, including one with a noun as the agent, a relative rarity:

(163) Pl. *Smp.* 201d   ἐκ τῶν ὡμολογημένων ἐμοὶ καὶ Ἀγάθωνι
"from that which has been agreed by me
and Agathon"

Use of the dative of agent here is no doubt motivated by the conjunction of the noun with ἐμοί. In one place, however, the agent is expressed by ὑπό:

(164) Pl. *Chrm.* 164c   ἐκ τῶν ἔμπροσθεν ὑπ᾽ ἐμοῦ
ὡμολογημένων
"from that which has earlier been agreed
by me"

It is difficult to explain why ὑπό should have been chosen over the dative of agent here, especially comparing (164) with (163).

While some of the agent markers used with ὁμολογέω in Plato thus remain obscure, a clearer pattern emerges than was seen in the works of Xenophon, who used ἐκ, παρά$^{+G}$, παρά$^{+D}$, and πρός once each. In Plato, it is παρά$^{+G}$ that predominates as the agent marker with nouns; while it is also found sometimes with pronouns, here it is the dative of agent that is preferred. In the four PACs in Xenophon, (110) through (113), the agent was always nominal, so it cannot be determined whether this conditioning factor applied there as well. It is noticeable, however, that of the two PACs in

Lysias, the agent is marked by παρά⁺ᴳ with πάντων (135), and by the dative with the pronoun αὐτῷ (136).

In Plato, there are four places where the passive of ἀμφισβητέω, the antonym of ὁμολογέω, occurs with what could be considered an agent expression. As each one involves a different agent marker, it is as difficult to determine the criteria that distinguish between these constructions as it was for ὁμολογέω in Xenophon. First, there is one straightforward instance of the dative of agent, probably analogous to its use with ὁμολογέω:[51]

(165) Pl. *Lg.* 638d   ἀμφισβητεῖται δ᾽ αὖ καὶ τοῦτο ἡμῖν
               "and in turn this too is disputed by us"

Second, it is found once with παρά⁺ᴰ:

(166) Pl. *Phlb.* 20a   εἴ πῃ καθ᾽ ἕτερόν τινα τρόπον οἷός τ᾽ εἶ καὶ
               βούλει δηλῶσαί πως ἄλλως τὰ νῦν
               ἀμφισβητούμενα παρ᾽ ἡμῖν
               "if perhaps in some other way you are able
               and willing to demonstrate differently what
               is now being disputed by us"

While not comparable to PACs with ὁμολογέω in Plato, the use of παρά⁺ᴰ with ὁμολογέω in Xenophon provides a possible model.

The final two PACs come in close proximity to one another. Furthermore, as might be expected considering Socrates' fondness for contrasting one idea with its opposite, ὁμολογέω occurs as well, also in a PAC. Accordingly, it is worth quoting this passage in its full context, inasmuch as the agent expressions of the two verbs can shed light on each other:

(167) Pl. *Tht.* 171b   Σω: Ὁ δέ γ᾽ αὖ ὁμολογεῖ καὶ ταύτην ἀληθῆ
               τὴν δόξαν ἐξ ὧν γέγραφεν.
               Θεο: Φαίνεται.

---

[51] Possibly, one might detect another dative of agent at *Lg.* 714b: τὸ γὰρ δίκαιον καὶ ἄδικον οἷ χρὴ βλέπειν, πάλιν ἡμῖν ἀμφισβητούμενον ἐλήλυθεν. It seems better, however, to take ἡμῖν in conjunction with πάλιν and ἐλήλυθεν as meaning "has come back to us," with the participle simply meaning "as a point of contention."

Σω: Ἐξ ἁπάντων ἄρα ἀπὸ Πρωταγόρου
ἀρξαμένων ἀμφισβητήσεται, μᾶλλον δὲ
ὑπό γε ἐκείνου ὁμολογήσεται, ὅταν τῷ
τἀναντία λέγοντι συγχωρῇ ἀληθῆ αὐτὸν
δοξάζειν, τότε καὶ ὁ Πρωταγόρας αὐτὸς
συγχωρήσεται μήτε κύνα μήτε τὸν
ἐπιτυχόντα ἄνθρωπον μέτρον εἶναι μηδὲ
περὶ ἑνὸς οὗ ἂν μὴ μάθῃ. οὐχ οὕτως;
Θεο: Οὕτως.
Σω: Οὐκοῦν ἐπειδὴ ἀμφισβητεῖται ὑπὸ
πάντων, οὐδενὶ ἂν εἴη ἡ Πρωταγόρου
Ἀλήθεια ἀληθής . . .

"Socrates: But [Protagoras] agrees that this
opinion too [i.e., that of his opponents] is
true, to judge from what he wrote.
Theodorus: It seems so.
S: So, starting from Protagoras, it will be
disputed from all sides [*or* by all] – or
rather, it will be agreed by him at least,
when he concedes to one who opposes him
that his opinion must be true – then even
Protagoras himself will concede that
neither a dog nor any random man is the
measure of even one thing which he has
not learned. Isn't it so?
T: So it is.
S: So, since it is disputed by all,
Protagoras' work *Truth* is true for no one."

In this passage, Socrates is arguing against Protagoras' relativist
dictum that man is the measure of all things. The main counter-
argument that he is making here is the following: if Protagoras
says that whatever a man believes to be true is true, then anyone believing the contrary of Protagoras' belief must in fact be
correct in Protagoras' own view. Protagoras must thus contradict himself. Now, in this excerpt, there are three potential PACs,
italicized in the text above. The second and third constructions
are indisputably PACs, but there is some question regarding the

first. Nineteenth-century commentators differentiated it from a true agent. Wohlrab (1891: 140) quotes Stallbaum: "Non haec praepositio causam efficientem, quam vocant, in eiusmodi locis significat, sed potius originem et quasi locum, unde quid veniat, ut respondeat nostro: *von seiten*," with references to the passages of Thucydides and Xenophon cited above at (70) and (110). Campbell agrees, translating: "'On all hands, then, including Protagoras', we find it disputed, or rather on his part it is admitted'" (1883: 108). But, as he renders the indisputably agentive ὑπό γε ἐκείνου, with the non-agentive "on his part," he makes no clear distinction between the two usages. Such is the case with many subsequent translators, either rendering both ἐξ ἁπάντων and ὑπό γε ἐκείνου as agentive (Kennedy (1894: 152–3), Jowett (1953: 270), Burnyeat (1990: 298)) or as non-agentive (Diès: "de tous côtés donc, à commencer par Protagoras, il y aura contestation; ou, plutôt, de sa part à lui, il y aura adhésion" (1924: 201)). Waterfield's translation does seem to distinguish between the two, but as it is quite free, it is hard to be sure: "from all sides, Protagoras' doctrine entails that it is arguable – or rather, that he will admit" (1987: 64).

In light of the context, it seems best to accept Campbell's position that ἐξ ἁπάντων is not an agent expression. First, as Campbell points out, in the preceding sentence, the clause ἐξ ὧν γέγραφεν gives an example of ἐξ used in the sense "in light of," "considering." As this meaning would still be in the reader's mind on reaching ἐξ ἁπάντων, it seems likely that, in the second occurrence as well, the preposition would be interpreted broadly as marking source. Second, in the following passage, ὑπό is used to mark the agent of ὁμολογέω, a verb that does not normally construe with ὑπό. If Plato thought a clear agent expression was important enough here to use ὑπό even with ὁμολογέω, then one would expect him to use it with ἀμφισβητέω as well – especially considering that he uses ὑπό with ἀμφισβητέω itself a few lines further down. Accordingly, it seems best to count only three agent expressions with ἀμφισβητέω: one each with the dative of agent, παρά$^{+D}$, and ὑπό.

As in the other authors discussed so far, ὠφελέω is associated with non-standard agent markers. In Plato, however, there is a sharper delineation between the use of ὑπό when one is benefited by a person and ἀπό when one is benefited by an object. The eight times that ὑπό is used with ὠφελεῖσθαι, the agent is always a human or a god; the seven times that ἀπό is used, the would-be agent is always inanimate.[52] There is also one occurrence of ἐκ, used of financial benefit from the public treasury (*R.* 343e). While παρά[+G] is found once, it is in the spurious *Amatores*, and, considering the frequency of ὑπό and ἀπό with this verb in the genuine works, its use with the passive of ὠφελέω may be rejected as non-Platonic. Because there is such a clear distinction between the use of ὑπό with animate agents and ἀπό with inanimates that could not actively benefit one, it is best to see the PACs of ὠφελέω in Plato as limited to those with the standard agent marker ὑπό.

In Plato, σημαίνω does not occur in any PACs.[53] Consequently, no support is added to or taken away from the view that it has a tendency to construe with παρά[+G], as suggested by data from the works of Xenophon.

The verb διδάσκω is relatively rare in the passive.[54] Still, together with its compound ἀναδιδάσκω, it furnishes two PACs in Plato, one with ὑπό, one with παρά[+G]:

(168) Pl. *La.* 189a   γηράσκων γὰρ πολλὰ διδάσκεσθαι
       ἐθέλω ὑπὸ χρηστῶν μόνον
       "for, as I grow old, I want to be taught
       many things – but only by good men"
(169) Pl. *Hi.Ma.* 301d   νῦν δὲ παρὰ σοῦ ἤδη ἀνεδιδάχθημεν
       ὅτι ...
       "but now we have been taught by you
       that ..."

Because there are only these two PACs, one from the *Hippias Major*, a dialogue that might be spurious, we cannot say whether

---

[52] The PACs with ὑπό occur at *Ap.* 25d, *Phdr.* 232d, *Thg.* 127d, *Grg.* 512a (with ἀπό as a variant reading) and 525b, *Hp. Ma.* 285a, *R.* 347d and 380b; those with ἀπό at *Euthphr.* 15a, *Euthd.* 280c, *Hp. Ma.* 304e, *R.* 346c (twice), 346d, and 401c.

[53] There is one PAC with κατασημαίνω: τὰς δ'ἐπισκήψεις τὰς ἀρχὰς φυλάττειν κατασεσημασμένας ὑπ'ἀμφοῖν (*Lg.* 937b). However, the specific concrete sense of the compound verb here ("seal up") is quite different from that evident in the PACs with σημαίνω in Xenophon. This construction thus has no bearing on the question of which agent marker would be expected with σημαίνω.

[54] One may compare Latin, in which the passive of *doceo* is usually replaced by *disco* (Menge–Burkard–Schauer 2000: 172).

Plato preferred ὑπό or παρά to express the agent of διδάσκω. Still, even if Plato did not write (169), the presence of παρά⁺ᴳ indicates that its use with διδάσκω was not just a stylistic feature limited to Xenophon.

Another verb that frequently takes non-standard agent markers is δίδωμι. In Plato, it occurs in eleven PACs, six times with ὑπό, four times with παρά⁺ᴳ, and once with ἐκ. As the conditioning factors are quite complicated, it will be necessary to line up those contrasting examples that occur in similar environments so as to determine what differences, if any, exist between them. By comparing only those PACs with like agents, we may eliminate one variable from consideration. Thus, I will first consider PACs with gods as agents, then those with pronouns as agents, and finally the remainder.

Five of the eleven PACs of δίδωμι have gods as agents, and all three agent markers are represented:

(170) Pl. *Ap.* 31a ὅτι δ᾽ ἐγὼ τυγχάνω ὢν τοιοῦτος οἷος ὑπὸ τοῦ θεοῦ τῇ πόλει δεδόσθαι
"but that I happen to be such a person as to have been given by God to the city"

(171) Pl. *Ti.* 47d ἡ δὲ ἁρμονία . . . ὑπὸ Μουσῶν δέδοται
"but harmony has been given by the Muses"

(172) Pl. *Ti.* 47e καὶ ῥυθμὸς . . . ὑπὸ τῶν αὐτῶν ἐδόθη
"and rhythm has been given by them as well"

(173) Pl. *Phdr.* 245c ὡς ἐπ᾽ εὐτυχίᾳ τῇ μεγίστῃ παρὰ θεῶν ἡ τοιαύτη μανία δίδοται
"that such a madness is given by the gods for our greatest happiness"

(174) Pl. *Ly.* 204c τοῦτο δέ μοί πως ἐκ θεοῦ δέδοται, ταχὺ οἵῳ τ᾽ εἶναι γνῶναι ἐρῶντά τε καὶ ἐρώμενον
"but this has been given to me by God, that I am quickly able to recognize the lover and the beloved"

While there is no sharp distinction among the uses of the three prepositions, it does seem that in (170) to (172), with ὑπό, the agents are more involved in the action than are the agents in the other two constructions. In (170), for instance, Socrates has just mentioned the possibility of God sending another like him to rouse the Athenians from their philosophical slumber. The god, then, is conceived of as a definite agent, and the act of his giving a beneficial trouble-maker to the Athenians is emphasized. Similarly, the PACs in (171) and (172) come in the middle of Timaeus' speech on the gods' creation of the universe. As the gods have been agents throughout this speech, it is here natural to use a preposition that clearly marks them as such. This may be contrasted with (174), in which Socrates acknowledges a god-given ability to tell when people are in love. The act of the giving is not highlighted; Socrates simply has this gift, and it comes from God. It thus makes sense to use the less agentive preposition ἐκ. Similarly, passage (173) is taken from Socrates' speech on the types of divine madness, and the context underlines the beneficial effects of madness on humans, not the gods' action in bestowing it. This interpretation is supported by the fact that references to the gods in the preceding paragraph also avoid the unambiguous agent marker ὑπό:

(175) Pl. *Phdr.* 245b   τοσαῦτα μέν σοι καὶ ἔτι πλείω ἔχω μανίας
                  γιγνομένης ἀπὸ θεῶν λέγειν καλὰ ἔργα
                  "Such are the fine consequences – and I
                  can tell you even more – of the madness
                  that comes from the gods"

(176) *ibid.*   ὡς οὐκ ἐπ' ὠφελίᾳ ὁ ἔρως ... ἐκ θεῶν
                  ἐπιπέμπεται
                  "that it is not to their advantage that love is
                  sent by the gods"

When gods are the agents, then, ὑπό is used with δίδωμι if the act of giving is contextually important; παρά or ἐκ is found when the emphasis is merely on the beneficiary's having received the gift from the gods.

Three of the PACs of δίδωμι are with personal pronouns, two with παρά, one with ὑπό:

(177) Pl. *Grg.* 499c ἀνάγκη μοι κατὰ τὸν παλαιὸν λόγον τὸ
παρὸν εὖ ποιεῖν καὶ τοῦτο δέχεσθαι τὸ
διδόμενον παρὰ σοῦ
"I must, as the old saying has it, do the
best with what I have and accept this that
is given by you"

(178) Pl. *Criti.* 108a καὶ πρός γε ἔτι τρίτῳ δεδόσθω ταὐτὸν
τοῦτο Ἑρμοκράτει παρ᾽ ἡμῶν
"and, in addition, let this same favor be
given by us to Hermocrates, as the third to
speak"

(179) Pl. *Lg.* 837e τὸ δέ μοι δεδομένον ὑπὸ σφῷν ἴτω
"and let us be done with what has been
granted to me by you two"

In all three cases, the gift in question is some point of argument or
request for sympathy conceded by one speaker to another in the
course of a dialogue. Contextually, then, they are all quite similar. Furthermore, it is plainly not the case with (178) at any rate,
that παρά somehow indicates that its object is not a true agent:
the preceding line has the first-person pronoun as the subject of
the verb (τί δ᾽ οὐ μέλλομεν, ὦ Κριτία, διδόναι;). While there is no
equally clear sign that παρά marks a true agent in (177), the preceding lines do portray Socrates playfully complaining about how
Callicles has been deceiving him. Consequently, it seems right to
view παρά as implying just as much as ὑπό that Callicles conceded a point as an active participant in a discussion, rather than
merely specifying him as the source of the object granted, as with
(173) and (174). In other words, while (174) could be translated
"God-given" (and "which God gave" would seem over-translated),
one could quite easily render (177) "which you have conceded." If
anything distinguishes (179), it is that it comes from the *Laws*, an
unusual work of Plato's, in that, among other anomalies, Socrates
is absent.[55] By contrast, examples (177) and (178) are both spoken by Socrates. While there is no conclusive evidence that Plato's
Socrates particularly favors παρά as an agent marker, the use of

---

[55] For the anomalous stylistic position of the *Laws* in Plato's work, see Müller 1968: 98–130
and Rutherford 1995: 302.

ὑπό rather than παρά in (179) may reflect the stylistic stiltedness of the *Laws* as against the greater conversational liveliness when Socrates is present.[56] Whatever the explanation of its absence in (179), the reason why παρά can mark true agents with pronouns is that pronouns are high enough on the animacy hierarchy that they are easily construed as agents no matter what preposition governs them.

The final three PACs of δίδωμι are with other common nouns, twice with ὑπό, once with παρά:

(180) Pl. *Smp.* 183b τῷ δ' ἐρῶντι πάντα ταῦτα ποιοῦντι χάρις
ἔπεστι, καὶ δέδοται ὑπὸ τοῦ νόμου ἄνευ
ὀνείδους πράττειν
"and grace attends the lover who does all
these things, and it is given by custom for
him to act without reproach"

(181) Pl. *Lg.* 718a δαπάνης τε τῆς διδομένης ὑπὸ τύχης τὸ
μέτριον τοῖς κεκμηκόσιν νέμοντα
"allotting to the dead the proper amount of
the money given by circumstances"

(182) Pl. *Lg.* 907a οἳ τὸ δίκαιον οὐκ ἄν ποτε προδοῖεν ἕνεκα
δώρων παρὰ ἀδίκων ἀνδρῶν ἀνοσίως
διδομένων
"who would never betray what is just
because of bribes given crookedly by unjust
men"

It is immediately apparent that ὑπό is found with the two inanimate (though personified) agents, παρά with the animate ἀνδρῶν. In (182), παρά seems to be used much as in (173) to express that the agent is not important *qua* agent, but is merely the source of the gift. One could imagine the sentence rewritten without the

---

[56] Dickey has shown that terms of address are used differently by Socrates than by other speakers in Plato's dialogues (1996: 119–27), so it would not be surprising if his choice of agent markers should also be idiosyncratic. Indeed, there is some slight evidence that he uses παρά[+G] where other speakers might use ὑπό, e.g. examples (159) and (160), spoken by Socrates, with παρά[+G], but (164), not spoken by him, with ὑπό; also, in (168), Laches uses ὑπό, while in (169), Socrates uses παρά[+G]. But against these we must set the examples where other speakers also use non-standard agent markers, e.g. all three of PACs with δωρέομαι, (183) to (185).

ἀνοσίως διδομένων, and δώρων παρὰ ἀδίκων ἀνδρῶν could still mean quite happily "gifts from unjust men." In (180) and (181) on the other hand, ὑπό is the agent marker even though ὁ νόμος and ἡ τύχη are not agents in the surrounding context. It is true in the case of (180) that the phrase ὡς ὁ νόμος φησὶν ὁ ἐνθάδε follows several lines later, but the overall context is hardly a discussion of, say, the role νόμος plays in determining what sort of behaviors are sanctioned. Indeed, ὑπὸ τοῦ νόμου seems virtually equivalent to κατὰ τὸν νόμον. There is even less reason to take ὑπό in (181) as emphasizing the role of τύχη as agent. In these two examples, since ὑπό is not introduced to highlight the agentive status of the noun, as in (170) and (171), it instead must simply express the agent without any further implications.

This observation may be linked to a discrepancy between the behavior of ὠφελέω and δίδωμι. The passive of ὠφελέω occurs with ὑπό when the agent is human, ἀπό when the would-be agent is inanimate; the passive of δίδωμι generally occurs with παρά when the agent is human, ὑπό when it is an inanimate agent, such as νόμος or τύχη. The resolution of the seeming paradox lies in the differing role played by the inanimate agents with the two verbs. With ὠφελέω, on the one hand, the ambiguity between the middle "benefit from" and the passive "be benefited by" means that there will always be scope for confusion between agent and source, be they animate or inanimate. Hence, ὑπό here is, as usual, the default agent marker, while ἀπό is found with inanimates, which are more likely to be seen as the source rather than the agent of the benefit. On the other hand, with δίδωμι, there is no middle with a meaning analogous to that of ὠφελέω. Now ὑπό is still the agent marker *par excellence*, and the ablatival prepositions still denote source, but the use of a non-standard agent marker, rather than shifting the construction from being passive to middle, potentially does no more than change the nuance of the passive construction. Thus, with δίδωμι, animate agents, especially personal pronouns, are free to be marked by παρά, because with agents so high on the animacy hierarchy, either the straightforward ὑπό or the alternative παρά, with its nuance of ablatival motion, could be interpreted as agentive. Inanimate agents, however, because they are inanimate, need to be marked all the more clearly as such: thus, ὑπό must be used, for παρά would be too easily understood as a preposition marking source.

The verb δωρέομαι, semantically similar to δίδωμι, likewise construes with non-standard agent markers. The three PACs with this verb in Plato are as follows:

(183) Pl. *Ti.* 47b   ἐξ ὧν ἐπορισάμεθα φιλοσοφίας γένος, οὗ μεῖζον ἀγαθὸν οὔτ᾽ ἦλθεν οὔτε ἥξει ποτὲ τῷ θνητῷ γένει δωρηθὲν ἐκ θεῶν

"from which [inquiries into the natural world] we acquired the stock of philosophy; than this no greater good, given by the gods, either has come or will ever come to the human race"

(184) Pl. *Ti.* 47c   φωνῆς τε δὴ καὶ ἀκοῆς πέρι πάλιν ὁ αὐτὸς λόγος, ἐπὶ ταὐτὰ τῶν αὐτῶν ἕνεκα παρὰ θεῶν δεδωρῆσθαι

"the same reasoning applies to sound and hearing, that they have been given by the gods for the same reasons and directed towards the same results"

(185) Pl. *Plt.* 274c   ὅθεν δὴ τὰ πάλαι λεχθέντα παρὰ θεῶν δῶρα ἡμῖν δεδώρηται μετ᾽ ἀναγκαίας διδαχῆς καὶ παιδεύσεως, πῦρ μὲν παρὰ Προμηθέως, τέχναι δὲ παρ᾽ Ἡφαίστου καὶ τῆς συντέχνου, σπέρματα δὲ αὖ καὶ φυτὰ παρ᾽ ἄλλων

"for this reason, the gifts that have been recounted since ancient times have been given to us by the gods together with the necessity of teaching and education: fire by Prometheus, craftsmanship by Hephaestus and his fellow worker, and seeds and plants in turn by others"

Again, we find the ablatival prepositions ἐκ and παρά⁺ᴳ occurring with a giving-verb. In contrast to δίδωμι, however, δωρέω does not occur in any PACs with ὑπό. Moreover, there is a difference in that the agents found with these non-standard markers appear to be just as agentive as those of δίδωμι found with ὑπό. Examples (183) and (184), for instance, both occur in the same passage

as (171), in which the Muses are considered agentive enough for
Plato to construe δίδωμι with ὑπό. Now it is possible to explain
away the occurrence of ἐκ in (183). The gift of philosophy did not
come directly from gods; rather, men acquired it for themselves
(ἐπορισάμεθα) as a result of the natural observations made possible
by the gods' gift of sight to mankind.[57] But the gift given in (184)
is that of sound and hearing, that is, the immediate gifts of the
gods. The situation in (185) is more ambiguous. On the one hand,
the final three phrases with παρά aim more at setting out which
god was responsible for which gift, rather than highlighting the act
of the giving itself. On the other, like (183) and (184), it is taken
from a cosmological passage in which divine agency is considered,
and so the objects of παρά could in fact be fully agentive. On the
whole, there are simply too few occurrences of δωρέομαι to make
any strong statements, but it is worth noting that παρά$^{+G}$ is used
here as one might expect ὑπό to be used.

One verb that Plato construes with παρά$^{+G}$, πληρόω, does not
fit clearly into the cline of verbs set out above. The construction
only occurs once:

(186) Pl. *Smp.* 175e   οἶμαι γάρ με παρὰ σοῦ πολλῆς καὶ καλῆς
σοφίας πληρωθήσεσθαι
"for I think that I will be filled with much
fine wisdom from you [Agathon]"

In this passage, the subject of the verb, Socrates, is to be filled with
wisdom, and the verb thus comes close in sense to ὠφελεῖσθαι. But
this passage should not in fact be considered a PAC: the object of
the preposition is not seen as deliberately controlling the action,
but rather as an involuntary source of the wisdom. That Agathon is
not viewed as actively conferring the wisdom can be seen from the
wider context, in which Socrates is imagining that it would indeed
be wonderful if wisdom could be passed from one to another in as
regular a fashion as water along a strand of wool. While this passage

---

[57] It seems odd that Luraghi, in speaking of this passage, notes that, in contrast to παρά,
"the occurrence of *ek* profiles active involvement of the landmark, rather than simply
spatial origin" (2003: 104). If anything, of the three instances of the passive of δωρέω
with θεῶν as the agent, this passage with ἐκ depicts the least involvement on the part of
the agent.

cannot be included as a PAC, it nevertheless shows, in exhibiting a non-agentive prepositional use that resembles an agentive one, how such a preposition as παρά⁺G could be taken up as an agent marker.

The verb νομίζω does not occur with an agent in any of Plato's genuine dialogues. It is found twice in the *Minos* with παρά⁺D marking the agent (316a, 316b). Although these PACs come from a spurious work, they still add further support to the theory that νομίζεται selected against ὑπό as an agent marker.

There are three passages where δουλόω or καταδουλόω is construed with an agent. In the two passages with καταδουλόω, ὑπό marks the agent both times; δουλόω itself only occurs in one PAC, but with two agents, one marked by ὑπό the other by πρός⁺G:

(187) Pl. *Smp.* 219e   καταδεδουλωμένος τε ὑπὸ τοῦ
                     ἀνθρώπου ὡς οὐδεὶς ὑπ᾽ οὐδενὸς ἄλλου
                     περιῇα
                     "and, enslaved by the man, as no one has
                     ever been by anyone else, I went about"

(188) Pl. *Euthd.* 303c   παντάπασι καταδουλωθεὶς ὑπὸ τῆς
                     σοφίας αὐτοῖν
                     "completely enslaved by the wisdom of
                     these two"

(189) Pl. *Mx.* 244c   διανοουμένη δὲ ἡ πόλις μὴ ἂν ἔτι ἀμῦναι
                     μήτε Ἕλλησι πρὸς ἀλλήλων
                     δουλουμένοις μήτε ὑπὸ βαρβάρων
                     "and the city, deciding on the course of
                     no longer defending Greeks from being
                     enslaved either by each other or by
                     barbarians"

Clearly, the agent expression that requires explanation is πρὸς ἀλλήλων. Because it occurs in parallel with ὑπὸ βαρβάρων, the motivation for πρός must lie in the nature of the agent ἀλλήλων. If the non-standard πρός is used with ἀλλήλων, it seems likely that this noun is somehow less prototypical an agent than βαρβάρων. In support of this interpretation, one may observe that reciprocal actions such as this, in which agents act upon each other, involve less of an energy transfer from agent to patient. The agent, after all, is to some extent a patient as well. Now δουλόω does not fall at all into the continuum of verbs introduced on p. 114. The use of the local preposition πρός^{+G}, however, does make sense insofar as enslavement does not involve the motion of the patient away from the agent, physically or figuratively, as is the case with the verbs that take ablatival prepositions like παρά$^{+G}$.

From this collection of data, it is clear that there is no single means of accounting for all the non-standard agent markers in Plato. In general, one may speak of two broad motivations for their use: first, they are sometimes used in situations in which the would-be agent is not fully agentive; second, they sometimes appear to be the default prepositions used with particular verbs. Several different prepositions belong in the first category. The use of ἀπό with ὠφελέω provides an extreme example, where the object of the preposition is far enough from being an agent that these constructions are best not considered to be PACs. A further usage that fits in here is that of πρὸς ἀλλήλων with δουλόω (189), which must be motivated by the fact that, in a reciprocal action, the verb does not depict a solely unidirectional transfer of energy from agent to patient. More common in this function is ἐκ, which marks less agent than source with ἐπιπέμπω (150), δωρέομαι (183), and δίδωμι (174).[58] It is worth noting that, in all these cases, the agent in question is either θεοῦ or θεῶν. This coincidence recalls the PACs of πέμπω in Xenophon, where παρά$^{+G}$ was preferred when the agent was the king. Both kings and gods are distant figures who would often work through intermediary agents and would thus be less likely to collocate with ὑπό. Possibly, παρά$^{+G}$ also indicates more source than agent with δίδωμι; at any rate, it is true of the PACs where the agent is divine that the god's status as an agent is more pronounced in the surrounding context in those constructions in which ὑπό is used (compare (170) to (172) with (173)).

More often, however, παρά$^{+G}$ marks agents just as engaged in the action as those marked by ὑπό. Indeed, for some verbs it

---

[58] The construction of ἀμφισβητέω with ἐκ (167) would also belong here, except that it is, like the PACs of ὠφελέω with ἀπό, too unagentive to be considered a true PAC.

appears to be the default agent marker. Unfortunately, this tendency is never pronounced enough to be incontrovertibly true, but the combined data from several verbs nevertheless point in this direction. First, ὁμολογέω occurs very frequently in PACs in Plato. Most of these are either with the dative, only found with pronouns, or with παρά+G, found with nouns and pronouns. The split between the dative and παρά+G is presumably based on the animacy hierarchy, and the overwhelming majority of prepositional PACs with παρά+G would then be explained by calling this preposition the default agent marker with nouns. Second, rather than labeling the use of παρά+G with δίδωμι as only quasi-agentive, it might be better to regard this as the default marker, while ὑπό was reserved for occasions when the role of the agent needed to be clarified. While this interpretation certainly works well for the three PACs with common nouns other than gods, any explanation ultimately stumbles on the fact that there is no clear difference between ὑπό and παρά in the PACs with pronouns. Thus, it is impossible to single out either of the two prepositions as a default agent marker with this verb. Finally, there are two other verbs, δωρέομαι and πέμπω, which might have παρά+G as a default agent marker, although a conclusive answer is impossible owing to the paucity of PACs with these verbs. With all these verbs that prefer παρά+G to mark the agent, ὑπό is only used when it is necessary to emphasize the agency of agent, as can be seen in some of the PACs of ὁμολογέω, (157), and δίδωμι, (180) and (181).

Demosthenes

The main trend that will be evident in the works of Demosthenes is that non-standard agent marking has become limited to παρά, either with the genitive or with the dative. Although the split between these two uses remains much as it was in earlier authors, with the genitive found with verbs involving the motion of the patient, the dative with verbs that denote mental activity on the part of the agent, it is perhaps possible that παρά+G is making its way into territory earlier occupied by ὑπό, thus foreshadowing its eventual rise as the agent marker of choice. Again, I will give all the PACs of particular verbs that are prone to non-standard agent marking.[59]

As elsewhere, πέμπω is frequently construed with παρά[+G]. In Demosthenes, there are four PACs of πέμπω with παρά[+G]:

(190) D. 7.1   δεινὸν γὰρ ἂν εἴη, εἰ τὴν ἐπὶ τοῦ βήματος
                   παρρησίαν αἱ παρ᾽ ἐκείνου πεμπόμεναι
                   ἐπιστολαὶ ἀνέλοιεν
                   "for it would be terrible if the letters sent by
                   him should end the freedom of speech of the
                   speaker's platform"

(191) D. 7.18   οἱ πρέσβεις οἱ παρ᾽ ἐκείνου πεμφθέντες
                   "the representatives sent by him"

(192) D. 18.148   εἰ μὲν τοίνυν τοῦτ᾽ ἢ τῶν παρ᾽ ἑαυτοῦ
                   πεμπομένων ἱερομνημόνων ἢ τῶν ἐκείνου
                   συμμάχων εἰσηγοῖτό τις
                   "so if anyone, either of the religious
                   representatives sent by him or of his allies,
                   should introduce this"

(193) D. 32.14   μετὰ ταῦθ᾽ ἧκεν οὗτος ἔχων τὸν παρ᾽ ἡμῶν
                   πεμφθέντα πρεσβευτήν
                   "after this he arrived, together with the
                   representative sent by us"

What stands out about these four PACs with παρά is that they are all of the form: article + prepositional phrase + participle. This regularity contrasts with the four PACs with ὑπό:

(194) D. 18.137   καίτοι ὅστις τῷ ὑπὸ τῶν πολεμίων πεμφθέντι
                   μόνος μόνῳ συνῄει
                   "yet a man who met, one on one, with someone
                   sent by the enemy"

(195) D. 18.244   οὐδαμοῦ πώποθ᾽, ὅποι πρεσβευτὴς ἐπέμφθην
                   ὑφ᾽ ὑμῶν ἐγώ, ἡττηθεὶς ἀπῆλθον τῶν παρὰ
                   Φιλίππου πρέσβεων

---

[59] In all the data that follow, I omit data from speeches labeled as spurious by the TLG unless otherwise specified.

"never, wherever I was sent as a representative
by you, did I return bested by the ambassadors
from Philip"

(196) D. 32.11   οὗτος ὁ πεμφθεὶς ὑφ' ἡμῶν (Ἀριστοφῶν ὄνομ'
αὐτῷ), ὃς καὶ . . .
"this one, sent by us (Aristophon by name),
who also . . ."

(197) D. 45.18   ὁ δὲ πεμφθεὶς ὑπὸ τούτου παρέχειν τοῦτο
"and one [said] that, sent by him, he supplied
this"

Here there is one PAC, (194), of the same form as the PACs with
παρά. However, (195) has a finite verb, and (196) and (197),
while both involving participles with articles, have the prepositional phrase after, rather than before, the participle. To account
for the use of παρά in one particular syntactic context, one may
compare its use in the second half of (195) in the phrase τῶν παρὰ
Φιλίππου πρέσβεων. It here denotes personal source in a context
where a participle of a verb like πεμπομένων could in theory be
understood from the finite verb in the preceding line – but where
that participle is absent from the actual construction. The implication is that the use of παρά does not depend on the presence of a
passive verb; παρά is therefore less particularly an agent marker.
In this context, one is reminded of the PACs in Herodotus where
participles – especially those that, with the definite article, acted as
nouns – construed with non-standard agent markers. When sandwiched between the article and the participle, the agent phrase
looks particularly as if it modifies a noun, not a verb, and is thus
all the more prone to anomalous agent marking. Finally, in (194),
the use of ὑπό in a context conducive to παρά was probably triggered by the fact that the agent, πολέμιοι, is lower on the animacy
hierarchy than the pronominal agents found in all the PACs with
παρά.

Another sending-verb is ἀποστέλλω. Although it does not occur
in any PACs in the genuine speeches of Demosthenes, there is one
in a spurious speech:

(198) D. 56.10   τὰ γράμματα τὰ παρὰ τούτου ἀποσταλέντα
"the letter sent by him"

Note that the syntactic context here is the same as with the PACs of πέμπω with παρά in the genuine speeches.

The giving-verb δίδωμι likewise construes both with παρά and ὑπό. There are four PACs with παρά:

(199) D. 18.202 ὅτι καὶ παρὰ Θηβαίων καὶ παρὰ τῶν ἔτι
τούτων πρότερον ἰσχυρῶν γενομένων
Λακεδαιμονίων καὶ παρὰ τοῦ Περσῶν
βασιλέως μετὰ πολλῆς χάριτος τοῦτ᾽ ἂν
ἀσμένως ἐδόθη τῇ πόλει
"that this would have been gladly granted to the
city with great thanks both by the Thebans and
by the Lacedaemonians who before them had
been powerful and by the king of the Persians"

(200) D. 18.293 ἔμοιγ᾽ εἰ τοῦτο δοθείη παρ᾽ ὑμῶν
"if this were to be granted to me by you"

(201) D. 20.42 δοθείσης ἀτελείας αὐτῷ διὰ ταῦτα παρ᾽ ὑμῶν
"when, because of this, immunity was granted
to him by you"

(202) D. 21.170 τούτοις γὰρ δὴ μέγισται δέδονται δωρειαὶ
παρ᾽ ὑμῶν καὶ ὑπὲρ μεγίστων
"the greatest gifts have been given to them by
you in return for the greatest services"

There are only two with ὑπό, and they are exactly the same:[60]

(203) D. 27.56 οἴεσθ᾽ οὐκ ἂν αὐτὴν λαβεῖν δοθεῖσαν ὑπὸ τοῦ
(= 29.48) πατρός;
"do you think that he would not have taken her
[my mother] as wife, given as she was by my
father?"

In contrast to the PACs with πέμπω, παρά[+G] is not restricted here to just one syntactic context: it is found with indicatives, a participle, and an optative. In this case, it is ὑπό that is the more marginal agent marker. Its use in (203) is probably to be connected with the particular sense that δίδωμι has there: that of bequeathing a

---

[60] Indeed, the whole of 29.47–9 is virtually the same as 27.55–7; thus, these two PACs are best counted as one example rather than two.

wife. Because the patient is animate, it is likely that ὑπό is used for the same reason that it is with the perfect in the same circumstances: with two animate participants as agent and patient, one needs to be more specific about which is which.[61]

The other giving-verb that frequently appears with non-standard agent markers is ὠφελέω. There is only one PAC with ὠφελέω in the genuine speeches of Demosthenes, but as the agent marker is παρά[+G], it fits in with the expected pattern:

(204) D. 21.139 οὓς μὰ τοὺς θεοὺς οὐδὲν ὠφελεῖσθαι νομίζω παρὰ τούτου
"by the gods, I think that they are not at all benefited by him"

We turn now to the showing-verbs. One, διδάσκω, only occurs in one PAC in Demosthenes, with ὑπό:[62]

(205) D. 19.135 οὐ καταφρονεῖ Φίλιππος . . . τῆς πόλεως τῆς ὑμετέρας, οὐδ᾽ ἀχρηστοτέρους ὑμᾶς νομίσας Θηβαίων ἐκείνους εἵλετ᾽ ἀνθ᾽ ὑμῶν ἀλλ᾽ ὑπὸ τούτων ἐδιδάχθη
"Philip does not despise your city, nor did he choose the Thebans instead of you because he thought you were less capable, but rather he was informed by these men here"

Nothing may be inferred from this single PAC. Another showing-verb, σημαίνω, does not occur in any passive constructions.

One verb that construes with παρά[+G], φυλάσσω, does not fit into any of the semantic categories introduced above. It occurs in two PACs, one with παρά[+G], one with ὑπό:

(206) D. 21.3 οὕτω δὲ τούτων ἐχόντων, ὅσα μὲν παρ᾽ ἐμοῦ προσῆκε φυλαχθῆναι, πάντα δικαίως ὑμῖν τετήρηται

---

[61] Furthermore, in this sense, the compound verb ἐκδίδωμι is common (see LSJ s.v. 2a). It also construes with ὑπό, both at 23.143 (genuine) and 40.19 (spurious, and again of a woman given in marriage).

[62] The compound προδιδάσκω is also found at 7.23: ὑπὸ τῶν ἐνθάδε διδασκάλων προδεδιδαγμένος.

> "and, such being the case, every protective
> measure one might rightly expect to be taken
> by me has duly been observed on your behalf"

(207) D. 23.186 ὃς αὐτός ποτε τοὺς ὑμετέρους ἐχθροὺς μισθὸν
λαμβάνων ἐδορυφόρει, τοῦτον ὑφ' ὑμετέρου
ψηφίσματος φανῆναι φυλαττόμενον

> "that one who himself was once a hired
> bodyguard for your enemies should now be
> seen to be protected by your vote"

It is easy to explain why (207) should have ὑπό where (206) has
παρά⁺ᴳ: the agent in (207) is the inanimate ψήφισμα, and, as has
been seen elsewhere, an inanimate agent requires more specific
agent-marking than would an animate agent. Less clear is why
φυλάσσω, which does not indicate motion on the part of the patient,
should have παρά⁺ᴳ as a non-standard agent marker. Probably, the
explanation is connected with the different functions of the patient
of the verb in the two examples. In (206), the patient, ὅσα, refers
to the steps taken in order to ensure the protection indicated by the
verb; if the sentence were rewritten in the active, it would be an
internal accusative. By contrast, in (207), the patient is the *person*
who is being protected. In this case, it would be strange to use
a source preposition to express the agent; but when the patient
refers to the actions of an individual in protecting others, it makes
more sense to see these as emanating from the agent. Accordingly,
Demosthenes uses παρά⁺ᴳ.

Rather more instructive are the PACs of ἀξιόω, as this verb
has several meanings which cross over from the giving-verbs to
the thinking-verbs. On the one hand, it has the concrete sense "to
honor (with an office), to evaluate (at a price)," in which case it is
more like a giving-verb. Sometimes, on the other hand, it has the
more abstract sense "to honor, deem worthy," behaving more like
a thinking-verb. Now there are five places where its passive occurs
with an agent, twice marked by ὑπό, once by παρά⁺ᴳ, and twice
by παρά⁺ᴰ. I have lined them up in order from the most to least
concrete, judged primarily by the nature of the object with which
the patient is honored. In the first instance, a daughter is endowed
with a concrete dowry of two talents by her father:

(208) D. 27.65 δυοῖν ταλάντοιν ὑπὸ τοῦ πατρὸς ἀξιωθεῖσα
"thought worthy of a dowry of two talents by
her father"

Next, we have Glaucetes honored with the specific title of
ambassador:

(209) D. 24.129 πρεσβευτὴς ἀξιωθεὶς εἶναι ὑφ᾽ ὑμῶν
"thought worthy by you to be ambassador"

Following this, there is Iphicrates, who, like Glaucetes, is honored
with what are presumably concrete distinctions, but, in contrast,
these are not specified:

(210) D. 21.62 καὶ δόξης καὶ τιμῶν τετυχηκόθ᾽ ὧν ἐκεῖνος
ἠξίωτο παρ᾽ ὑμῶν
"and who had met with the glory and honors of
which he had been thought worthy by you"

Next, the Athenians are deemed worthy of sacrifice and praise, but
no offices are mentioned:

(211) D. 19.86 ὅτε μὲν τὰ δέοντ᾽ ἐποιεῖτε, θυσιῶν καὶ ἐπαίνων
ἠξιοῦσθε παρ᾽ ὑμῖν αὐτοῖς καὶ παρὰ τοῖς ἄλλοις
"when you were doing what was necessary, you
were thought worthy of sacrificial festivals and
praise, both by yourselves and by others"

The final passage provides the most abstract instance of ἀξιόω,
which, in contrast to all the other examples, does not here construe with a genitive of the honor bestowed, but instead means "be
thought highly of" in an absolute sense.

(212) D. 19.30 καὶ τὰ πράγματ᾽ ἐστὶ φαῦλα ὧν ἡ πόλις
ἀξιοῦται παρὰ τοῖς ἄλλοις
"[this does not mean that] it is also for
insignificant achievements that the city is
thought highly of by others"

Although one might dispute the ranking of the central three PACs,
the endpoints seem well established, with ἀξιόω signifying the
concrete worth of two talents in (208), and the abstract worthiness

of Athens in (212). Now, as explanations for the agent marking with ἀξιόω, one may rule out the nature of the agent: the second-person pronoun occurs with all three agent markers. Furthermore, it is unlikely that the morphosyntax of the verb has had an effect, even if only ὑπό occurs in the only two participial examples, as this pattern does not correlate to those found elsewhere. To explain the agent marking of ἀξιόω, then, it seems best to propose that ὑπό is preferred with the more concrete constructions, παρά$^{+D}$ with those that relate more of a mental stance: again, this holds true at least for the ends of the spectrum, even if the details of the placement of παρά$^{+G}$ cannot be established owing to the paucity of examples.

With γιγνώσκω, we move further into the thinking-verbs. As expected, the non-standard agent marker found here is παρά$^{+D}$. There are two PACs with παρά$^{+D}$, as against five with ὑπό:

(213) D. 21.41   ἂν γὰρ ταῦθ' οὕτως ἐγνωσμέν' ὑπάρχῃ παρ' ὑμῖν
"for if these matters are determined by you in this way"

(214) D. 29.2   τὰ παρ' ὑμῖν γνωσθέντα πραττόμενος αὐτόν
"exacting of him the penalty determined by you"

(215) D. 20.2   καὶ γὰρ εἴρηται τρόπον τινὰ καὶ ὑφ' ὑμῶν ἴσως γιγνώσκεται
"for it has been said to some extent and it is perhaps recognized by you"

(216) D. 24.9   ἄκυρα δὲ τὰ γνωσθένθ' ὑπὸ τῆς βουλῆς καὶ τοῦ δήμου καὶ τοῦ δικαστηρίου καθίστησιν
"he renders invalid what has been determined by the council and the people and the court"

(217) D. 24.90   περὶ τῶν ἐκ τοῦ παρεληλυθότος χρόνου κριθέντων ἐναντία τοῖς ὑφ' ὑμῶν ἐγνωσμένοις προστάττει
"as for the decisions made in earlier times, he prescribes the opposite of what had been determined by you"

(218) D. 27.1   ἀπέχρη γὰρ ἂν τοῖς ὑπ' ἐκείνων γνωσθεῖσιν
ἐμμένειν
"for it would have been sufficient to abide by
what had been determined by them"

(219) D. 30.18   πῶς οὐ φανερὸν ὅτι προστάντες τοῦ
πράγματος τὰ γνωσθένθ' ὑφ' ὑμῶν
ἀποστερῆσαί με ζητοῦσιν;
"Is it not clear that, in managing this business,
they seek to deprive me of that which was
determined by you?"

Unfortunately, there do not appear to be any factors that condition
the use of παρά$^{+D}$ and ὑπό. Consider first factors pertaining to the
verb. One might suspect that one preposition would be associated
with a general sense of γιγνώσκω, "know, recognize," and another
with the specific legal meaning of "judge, determine" (LSJ s.v. II).
In fact, only in (215) does the general sense occur, while the legal
usage occurs with both παρά$^{+D}$ and ὑπό. Nor is agent expression
connected with the morphosyntax of the verb: aorist and perfect
participles both occur with both prepositions in (214) and (218) and
in (213) and (217) respectively. Turning to the nature of the agent,
one again finds no grounds for distinguishing between the PACs
with ὑπό and those with παρά$^{+D}$, as the second-person pronoun
occurs quite readily with both.[63] One must thus suppose that the
co-occurrence of ὑπό and παρά$^{+D}$ is merely free variation, with
the local preposition favored as a non-standard PAC because the
verb in question is a thinking-verb.

A second thinking-verb, νομίζω, behaves similarly erratically.
It occurs in three PACs, two with παρά$^{+D}$, one with ὑπό:[64]

(220) D. 2.3   ὁ μὲν γὰρ ὅσῳ πλείον' ὑπὲρ τὴν ἀξίαν πεποίηκε
τὴν αὑτοῦ, τοσούτῳ θαυμαστότερος παρὰ
πᾶσι νομίζεται
"for the more he has extended his worth beyond
its due, the more wonderful he is considered by
all"

[63] Still, it is probably significant that (216), the one PAC without a high-agentive pronoun
as agent, does have ὑπό as the agent marker.

[64] There is a further PAC in one of the prooemia (2.2), but these are of doubtful authenticity.

(221) D. 29.26 τὸν ἄνθρωπον τοῦτον ἀφεῖναι τὸν πατέρ᾽ ἡνίκ᾽
ἐτελεύτα, καὶ νομίζεσθαι παρ᾽ ἡμῖν τοῦτον
ἐλεύθερον
"that my father freed this man when he was
dying, and that he was considered by us to be
free"

(222) D. 39.33 δεινόν γ᾽ ἂν εἴη, εἰ κατὰ μὲν τῶν ὑπὸ τοῦ
πατρὸς αὐτοῦ νομιζομένων παίδων οἱ περὶ
τῶν γονέων ἰσχύσουσιν νόμοι
"it would be terrible if the laws concerning
parents will apply to children who are
considered by their father as his own"

The use of παρά⁺ᴰ in (220) with πᾶσι is much like PACs seen
with this verb in other authors. But the other two involve a different
sense of νομίζω: that of family members recognizing the status of
another in the household, be it a freedman, as in (221), or a child, as
in (222). Why (221) should be construed with παρά⁺ᴰ, and (222)
with ὑπό is not entirely clear, although it is likely that the nature
of the agent played some role. Most of the PACs of νομίζεται with
παρά⁺ᴰ have involved agents that were plural in number, as in
(220). It may be that πατήρ, as a singular agent and, moreover,
one that is not a pronoun, motivated the use of ὑπό instead of the
παρά⁺ᴰ more regularly found with this verb.

The verb ἐλεέω may be loosely grouped together with the
thinking-verbs, inasmuch as it denotes a mental attitude of the
agent, in this case one of pity. Of the five PACs formed with this
verb in Demosthenes, four have the usual ὑπό as the agent marker:

(223) D. 21.99 ὁρῶν τὰ τοῦδ᾽ οὐκ ἐλεηθένθ᾽ ὑπὸ τούτου
"seeing that this man's children were not pitied
by him"

(224) D. 27.53 ἵνα δοκῶν εἶναι πλούσιος ἧττον ὑφ᾽ ὑμῶν
ἐλεοίμην
"so that, appearing to be rich, I would be pitied
less by you"

(225) D. 28.16 ἀλλὰ τὰ χρήματά με πάντ᾽ ἀπεστερηκὼς μετὰ
τῶν συνεπιτρόπων, ἐλεεῖσθαι νῦν ὑφ᾽ ὑμῶν
ἀξιώσει

> "but although he has, together with his
> co-guardians, deprived me of all my goods, he
> will now ask to be pitied by you"

(226) D. 53.29 ἢ γὰρ ὀρφανοὺς ἢ ἐπικλήρους
κατασκευάσαντες ἀξιώσουσιν ἐλεεῖσθαι ὑφ᾽
ὑμῶν
"for, after producing orphans or heirs, they will
ask to be pitied by you"

One, on the other hand, has παρά⁺ᴰ:

(227) D. 27.57 ἵν᾽ ἧττον ἐλεηθῶ παρ᾽ ὑμῖν
"so that I would be pitied less by you"

Considering the extreme similarity between the contexts of (224) and (227), it is once again necessary to postulate free variation to account for the use of παρά here. That it takes the dative is natural as, like the more prototypical thinking-verbs, ἐλεέω does not involve the transfer of the patient.

Another thinking-verb that alternates between expressing the agent with ὑπό and παρά⁺ᴰ is πιστεύω. In this case, however, it is παρά⁺ᴰ that is the more common agent marker:[65]

(228) D. 22.1 ἐμὲ δ᾽ οὐδ᾽ ἂν ἐδέξατο τῶν ὄντων ἀνθρώπων
οὐδὲ εἷς, εἰ τὰ κατασκευασθένθ᾽ ὑπὸ τούτου παρ᾽
ὑμῖν ἐπιστεύθη
"but not a single living man would welcome me,
if what has been fabricated by this man were
believed by you"

(229) D. 23.4 οὐχὶ τῶν ἐνοχλούντων ὑμᾶς οὐδὲ τῶν
πολιτευομένων καὶ πιστευομένων παρ᾽ ὑμῖν ὤν
"as I am not one of those who trouble you nor
one of those politicians who are believed by
you"

---

[65] I take παρά⁺ᴳ at 19.277 with προλαβόντα rather than πισθευθῆναι, because that interpretation suits the word order better, and παρά⁺ᴳ is commonly found as an adjunct of λαμβάνω and its compounds. As for the spurious speeches, ὑπό also occurs at 52.13, 58.4, and Prooemium 2.16; παρά⁺ᴰ also occurs at 58.44.

(230) D. 28.5   τηλικαύτην δ' ἀνελόντας μαρτυρίαν οὕτως
οἴεσθαι δεῖν εἰκῆ πιστεύεσθαι παρ' ὑμῖν
"and after destroying such important evidence,
to think that they must be believed by you
blindly in this way"

(231) D. 30.38   Ἄφοβον παρεχόμενος μάρτυρα καὶ Τιμοκράτην
... ἀξιώσει πιστεύεσθαι παρ' ὑμῖν
"supplying Aphobus and Timocrates as
witnesses, he will expect to be believed by you"

In contrast, ὑπό is only found once:

(232) D. 19.289   καὶ συνεροῦσί τινες τούτοις τῶν ὑφ' ὑμῶν
πεπιστευμένων
"and some of those who have been believed by
you will support them"

As the agent is the same in all five examples, the motivation for
ὑπό must lie in the verb. Example (232) is distinguished by having
a verb in the perfect; accordingly, this construction is reminiscent
of (164), a passage in Plato in which the only prepositional PAC
with the perfect of ὁμολογέω, there too a participle, has ὑπό as the
agent marker even though other tenses have a strong preference
for παρά+G. Perhaps the same motivating factor triggers the use
of ὑπό in (232) as well.

In Demosthenes, as in all the other authors, ὁμολογέω construes with several different agent markers: five times with ὑπό,
four times with παρά+G, three times with παρά+D, and once
with ἐκ.

(233) D. 16.3   ἀπὸ δὲ τῶν ὁμολογουμένων ὑφ' ἁπάντων
ἄρξομαι
"I shall begin from what is agreed by everyone"

(234) D. 18.251   ὥσθ' ὑπὸ σοῦ γ' ὡμολόγημαι μηδὲν εἶναι τοῦ
Κεφάλου χείρων πολίτης
"and so it has been agreed by you that I am no
worse a citizen than Cephalus"

(235) D. 29.44   ἐπειδὴ τοίνυν ὡμολόγηθ᾽ ὑπ᾽ αὐτοῦ τούτου
τὸν πατέρ᾽ ἡμῶν τελευτῶντα τοσοῦτον
ἀργύριον τούτων ἑκάστῳ δοῦναι . . .
"so, since it had been agreed by this very man
that our father, when he was dying, gave so
much money to each of them"

(236) D. 34.47   τὸ μὲν ὁμολογούμενον ὑπ᾽ αὐτοῦ τούτου
ἄκυρον ποιήσαιτε
"you should not consider authoritative what is
agreed by this very man"

(237) D. 41.24   ὡς ὡμολογεῖτο τότε τὰ σημεῖα τῶν
γραμμάτων ὑπὸ τῆς τούτου γυναικός
"that the seals of the documents were
acknowledged then by his wife"

(238) D. 34.5   σκέψασθε δέ . . . ὅ τι ὁμολογεῖται παρ᾽ αὐτῶν
τούτων
"but consider what is conceded by these very
men"

(239) D. 41.21   ὁμολογουμένων δὲ τῶν σημείων καὶ παρὰ τῆς
τούτου γυναικὸς καὶ παρὰ τῆς ἐμῆς
"as the seals were acknowledged both by his
wife and by mine"

(240) D. 54.32   ἀφεὶς τοὺς καὶ παρ᾽ αὐτῶν τούτων
ὁμολογουμένους τύπτειν ἐμέ
"after dismissing those who were agreed even
by these very men to have struck me"

(241) D. 55.9   τὸ μὲν γὰρ χωρίον ὁμολογεῖται καὶ παρ᾽
αὐτῶν τούτων ἡμέτερον ἴδιον εἶναι
"for the land is agreed even by these very men
to be our private property"

(242) D. 7.18   ὃ παρὰ πᾶσιν ἀνθρώποις ὁμολογεῖται δίκαιον
εἶναι
"which is agreed by all men to be fair"

(243) D. 7.29   ἃ παρὰ πᾶσιν ἀνθρώποις ὁμολογεῖται δίκαια
εἶναι
"what is agreed by all men to be fair"

(244) D. 57.47   φαίνομαι τοίνυν . . . τὸν μὲν ἄλλον χρόνον
ἅπαντα παρὰ πᾶσιν τοῖς νῦν κατηγοροῦσι
πολίτης ὡμολογημένος
"so it is clear that, at every other time, I am
agreed to have been a citizen by all those who
now accuse me"

(245) D. 27.16   πῶς οὐκ ἐκ πάντων ὁμολογουμένου τοῦ
πράγματος εὑρεθήσεται φανερῶς τὴν
προῖκα . . . κεκομισμένος
"how, since the matter is agreed by all, will he
not be found quite clearly to have received the
dowry"

The easiest of the non-standard agent markers to explain are ἐκ and
παρά⁺ᴰ. Both appear elsewhere with the same agent with which
they occur here, πάντες: ἐκ is regularly used with the passive of
ὁμολογέω to mark this agent, and παρά⁺ᴰ occurs with πᾶσιν in
several PACs with νομίζεται, both in Demosthenes (220) and in
Xenophon (121).

Finding a distinction between the PACs with ὑπό and those with
παρά⁺ᴳ, however, is quite difficult. Clearly, the agent is not the
decisive factor: compare (235) and (236) with (238), (240), and
(241), or (237) with (239). Nor is it certain that the syntax of the
verb plays a role. Because the only two PACs with a verb in the
(plu)perfect, (234) and (235), both mark their agents with ὑπό,
a conditioning factor such as was suggested for (232) might be
at work here too. But there is no split between indicative forms
preferring one agent marker and participles another. Furthermore,
a comparison of (236) and (238) or (237) and (239) reveals little
difference in the context that might have selected for one preposition or the other. Yet again, there remains only the conclusion
that, with certain verbs at least, there was free variation in Demosthenes between ὑπό and either παρά⁺ᴳ or παρά⁺ᴰ. Although this
might seem a weak explanation, it is worth noting that παρά⁺ᴳ
later supplanted ὑπό as the standard agent marker. A stage when
there was free variation with certain verbs would be a reasonable

stepping-stone to this later development. One should also ask why it is that an apparent thinking-verb like ὁμολογέω construes so often with παρά[+G] rather than παρά[+D]. Probably, it is because, in several of these passages, the verb conveys the sense that something has been acknowledged or even conceded. When ὁμολογεῖται refers thus to a point of debate being admitted by the speaker's opponents, as in (238), it becomes more like a giving- than a thinking-verb.[66] This nuance of meaning also helps to explain why three of the four agents marked by παρά[+G] are αὐτῶν τούτων: when something is agreed on by your opponents, it is more likely to be a concession, and the verb thus comes closer to being a giving-verb.[67]

In general, the conditions that trigger the various agent markers found in Demosthenes resemble those in other authors. First and foremost, verbs that describe the motion of the patient away from the agent have παρά[+G] as an alternative agent marker, while those that describe mental processes that do not involve such motion have παρά[+D]. This pattern is most clearly seen in the PACs of πέμπω and δίδωμι on the one hand, and γιγνώσκω, νομίζω, πιστεύω, and ἐλεέω on the other. Other verbs, namely ὁμολογέω and ἀξιόω, may take παρά with either the genitive or the dative. With ὁμολογέω, there is some evidence that παρά[+G] is used when the action described is a dynamic transfer of agreement (that is, the concession of a point by the speaker's opponents), while παρά[+D] marks a more static assessment (in (242) and (243) a general agreement about what is fair, in (244) a long-standing point held by the speaker's accusers). The same is perhaps also true of ἀξιόω, but there are too few examples to be certain.

Second, ὑπό is at times used with πέμπω, δίδωμι, and probably φυλάσσω to clarify grammatical relations in cases where the agent is relatively low in the animacy hierarchy compared to the patient. There is also further evidence that participles can trigger unusual agent marking. On the one hand, παρά[+G] with πέμπω occurs

---

[66] As a parallel, one may compare the use of the middle verb ἀνομολογέομαι with παρά[+G] in the sense "get agreement from" (that is, "get someone to agree") in Pl. *Smp.* 199b: ἵνα ἀνομολογησάμενος παρ᾽ αὐτοῦ οὕτως ἤδη λέγω. Such is the meaning given by Dover in his commentary; LSJ does not give any glosses that fit this passage.

[67] That said, one cannot eliminate the need to postulate free variation, because ὑπό is also found in these circumstances.

solely with the prepositional phrase sandwiched between the article and the participial form of the verb, presumably because, in this context, the participle seems strongly nominalized, a condition conducive to non-standard agent marking in Herodotus as well. On the other, ὑπό occurs with the perfect participle of πιστεύω, a verb that elsewhere marks its agent with παρά$^{+D}$; this may be connected to a similar anomaly in the PACs of ὁμολογέω in Plato. Finally, in Demosthenes, there is, for the first time, a strong case to be made for the existence of free variation in the choice of agent marker, particularly in the PACs of γιγνώσκω and ὁμολογέω, in which ὑπό alternates seemingly randomly with παρά$^{+D}$ and παρά$^{+G}$ respectively. This phenomenon may herald the beginning of the slow decline of ὑπό as the standard agent marker in Greek.

Conclusion

In considering non-standard agent markers, two main questions must be addressed. First, what determines which non-standard agent marker is used? Second, what determines why a non-standard agent marker is used in the first place?

(1) For the most part, non-standard agent markers may be grouped into two categories: ablatival prepositions, like ἐκ, παρά$^{+G}$, and occasionally ἀπό; and locatival prepositions, like παρά$^{+D}$ and πρός^{+G}. In Herodotus, the preferred prepositions are ἐκ and πρός^{+G}; in Thucydides, the locatival prepositions are absent, and both ἐκ and ἀπό are found in ablatival capacity; in the other authors, παρά$^{+G}$ and παρά$^{+D}$ are the prepositions of choice. Whether an ablatival or locatival preposition is chosen depends on the semantics of the verb. One may line up verbs on a cline with those that describe motion of the patient away from the agent on one end ("send"), and those that do not describe such motion on the other end ("think"). Not surprisingly, ablatival prepositions are used as agent markers for verbs closer to the first end, whereas locatival prepositions are used for verbs closer to the second end. This rule holds true no matter which preposition is preferred by the author in question. Thus, in Herodotus, verbs of giving and ordering usually mark their agents with ἐκ, while verbs of thinking and knowing mark them with πρός. In Demosthenes, however, verbs

of sending and giving mark their agents with παρά$^{+G}$, verbs of thinking and believing with παρά$^{+D}$.

(2) In examining the circumstances under which non-standard agent markers are preferred to ὑπό, it will be useful to consider two types of verbs: those that normally construe with ὑπό and those that normally construe with a non-standard marker. Generally speaking, verbs of the former category use non-standard agent markers in situations where what might potentially be considered an agent is more accurately described by some other semantic role such as source or location. To give one example, ὠφελέω occurs most frequently with ὑπό; when it occurs with a non-standard preposition, like ἀπό in Plato, the oblique noun is not actively effecting the benefit, and is therefore better described as a source than an agent. Other verbs, however, belonging to the second category, do not have ὑπό as a default agent marker. With these verbs, ὑπό marks the agent when there is a particular need to clarify the role of that agent. One such verb is δίδωμι, which, in Demosthenes, construes more frequently with παρά$^{+G}$ than with ὑπό. The latter preposition does occur, however, when the patient is animate. With a patient relatively high on the animacy hierarchy, it is necessary to delineate more clearly the role of the agent. In Plato, the agent marking found with this verb when the agent is a common noun also exemplifies this phenomenon: with ἄνδρες, παρά is an adequate agent marker, but with νόμος and τύχη, less prototypical agents, ὑπό is used instead.

5

AGENT CONSTRUCTIONS WITH
PREPOSITIONS OTHER THAN ὑπό:
TRAGEDY AND COMEDY

As Schwyzer pointed out in his article on expressions of the agent, the Attic tragedians provide many examples of non-standard agent markers (1943: 20–8). In fact, ὑπό is so rare in comparison to other prepositions, that, were these plays our only source of Ancient Greek, we would not at first glance be able to pinpoint it as the default agent marker. In iambic passages of the *Oresteia*, for instance, ὑπό only occurs in three PACs, as against seven with πρός^{+G}, two with ἐκ, and one with παρά. Does this variety of agent marking mirror that in prose of the period, or is it simply a feature of poetic diction, conditioned by the meter? In order to answer this question, I will look at prepositional PACs in Aeschylus, Sophocles, and Euripides. To impose some uniformity on the data, I will only consider PACs in iambic passages. Because this limitation reduces the number of PACs under consideration, I will extend the study to those constructions where agent expressions occur with intransitive verbs, such as πάσχω or ἀποθνῄσκω, that act as suppletive passives to transitive counterparts like ποιέω and ἀποκτείνω. Such constructions are quite common in tragedy because of the frequent description of suffering in the genre.

In general, the pattern in prose whereby certain agent markers are associated with certain verbs does not hold true in poetry. For example, καταγελάω construes with ὑπό in Aeschylus, while γελάω construes with παρά$^{+G}$ in Sophocles and ἐκ in Euripides (in all authors limited to one example each). Because of the limited size of the corpus, direct comparisons of the sort employed for prose authors are impossible, but the general impression remains one of randomness. Nor can one start with one particular agent marker as a default and explain the others as deviations therefrom: ἐκ and ὑπό are equally common as agent markers in Sophocles, while πρός^{+G} predominates in Aeschylus and Euripides, with ἐκ and ὑπό not far behind. A pattern does emerge, however, when one looks at where in the line each of these prepositions occurs. Almost always, if the agent marker occurs at a point in the line where both ὑπό and another preposition would fit, then ὑπό is used. Conversely, there is only a handful of cases where the otherwise more common πρός is found when ὑπό would also fit the meter. Broadly speaking, the relative infrequency of ὑπό can then be ascribed to its having a metrical shape less convenient for the iambic trimeter. With two short syllables in a row, it must either be elided, occur before a word beginning in a double consonant, or fall at the end of the line in anastrophe; it cannot occur before a word beginning with a single consonant (e.g. the article), or after a syllable that is short by nature. In theory, it could stand for a resolved long syllable, but in practice this only occurs in the comic trimeter.[1] Indeed, it is because resolution of ὑπό is allowed in comedy that Aristophanes can make much greater use of it than did the tragedians. In tragedy, however, the stricter metrical rules made πρός and ἐκ, in particular, more attractive than ὑπό. The following section will examine the PACs in Aeschylus, Sophocles, Euripides, Aristophanes, and Menander in turn, highlighting subtle differences in how they mark the agent. In the case of the tragedians, I will illustrate the impossibility of establishing any semantic or syntactic conditions that would explain the variety of agent markers. To show that their profusion can only be explained by reference to metrical considerations, I will look in detail at where in the line each of the agent markers occurred. Finally, I will show that the agent expressions in comedy are more similar to those in prose.

Aeschylus

In the six plays that may confidently be attributed to Aeschylus, the distribution of agent markers is as follows:[2]

---

[1] West notes that, in tragedy, resolutions usually occur in words of three or more syllables (1987: 26).

[2] Slightly different figures for Aeschylus and Sophocles are given in Moorhouse, who includes PACs in lyric, but excludes those with non-human agents (1982: 129).

	ἐκ	παρά	πρός	ὑπό	total
with morphological passive verbs	3	1	9	7	20
with suppletive passives	1	0	3	0	4
total	4	1	12	7	24

Two of the prepositions used to mark the agent, παρά and ἐκ, are relatively rare. They also occur in contexts reminiscent of those where they occur in prose. In this they differ from πρός, which is found in a far wider range of environments than in any prose text.

The preposition παρά, like ὑπό, consists of two short syllables. As such, it has some of the same metrical restrictions. Unsurprisingly, then, it only occurs in one PAC in Aeschylus:

(1) A. A. 312–13 τοιοίδε τοί μοι λαμπαδηφόρων νόμοι
ἄλλος παρ' ἄλλου διαδοχαῖς πληρούμενοι
"such laws there are for my torch-bearers, one
supplied by another in succession"

This passage raises two points. First, the use of παρά$^{+G}$ with πληρόω has a prose parallel from the *Symposium* (175e). Unlike the PACs with πρός, it is thus limited to a context where there is some general linguistic justification for it. Second, one cannot exclude the possibility that παρά should really be interpreted as true ablatival preposition rather than as an agent marker. Although Schwyzer lists this passage as a PAC, its imagery emphasizes the geographical procession of the beacon-fires, rather than the agency of one fire in lighting the next. These two perspectives are, of course, related, in that it is the inherent ambiguity between "filled from" and "filled by" that makes πληρόω a verb likely to mark its agent with παρά in the first place.

Also fairly rare, though more common than παρά, is the preposition ἐκ. Like παρά, it occurs in environments where it might be expected in prose, although the correlation is not as close. The three proper PACs are as follows:

(2) A. *Supp.* 942–3 τοιάδε δημόπρακτος ἐκ πόλεως μία
ψῆφος κέκρανται

"thus the popular decree has been
determined unanimously by the city"

(3) A. *Ch.* 1006   ὀλοίμην πρόσθεν ἐκ θεῶν ἄπαις
"may I, childless, be killed first by the
gods"

(4) A. *A.* 1290   ὀμώμοται γὰρ ὅρκος ἐκ θεῶν μέγας³
"for a great oath has been sworn by the
gods"

In two of the three passages, the agent is θεῶν. This is again reminiscent of Plato, where ἐκ often introduces gods as agents, for gods
are often removed from the action itself and thus closer to being a
source than an agent (cf. *Phdr.* 245b, *Ly.* 204c, and *Ti.* 47b). While
this holds true for (3), the oath sworn in (4) would presumably have
been sworn by them directly. Even so, perhaps it is not the act of
swearing itself that is important here so much as the divine origin of
the oath; this interpretation may be supported by the perfect tense
of the verb.⁴ In (2), ἐκ could again have been triggered because the
agent, in this case the city, only indirectly causes the action. That
the use of ἐκ is associated with indirect agents like θεῶν is also
suggested by two occurrences in expressions that resemble PACs:

(5) A. *Pers.* 373 οὐ γὰρ τὸ μέλλον ἐκ θεῶν ἠπίστατο
"for he did not understand what was intended
by the gods"

(6) A. *Th.* 23 καλῶς τὰ πλείω πόλεμος ἐκ θεῶν κυρεῖ
"war comes from the gods in a way that for the
most part turns out well"

The verbs, on the other hand, are not as similar to those found with
ἐκ in prose. In (2), the use of κραίνω recalls the frequent collocation
of ἐκ with verbs of doing in Herodotus, but the other two verbs do
not have prose parallels. Still, despite this extension of usage, ἐκ,
like παρά, provides an example of a preposition whose use in
Aeschylus is broadly in line with that found in prose.

³ This line, transposed to *A.* 1284 in the OCT, is rejected by Fraenkel (1950: 600–2). He
does think, however, that the line is "probably Aeschylean."
⁴ One may compare the use of παρά with the perfect passive in Pl. *Ti.* 47c and *Plt.* 274c.

Turning to πρός, however, we find a different picture altogether. Whereas ἐκ and παρά are circumscribed as to the environments in which they appear, πρός collocates freely with all manner of verbs and agents. Indeed, it is more common than ὑπό. Before retreating to meter as a means of explaining its predominance, it will first be necessary to demonstrate that it is not distinguished from ὑπό with respect to either the verbs or agents with which it construes. Consider, first, the verbs found with πρός and ὑπό respectively:

	πρός	ὑπό
speaking	κλῄζω	ὑμνέω
striking	πλήσσω (2×)	παίω
honoring	–	ἀποτιμάω
		καταγελάω
		τιμαλφέω
other	ἀφαιρέω	θάπτω
	ὁράω	πορθέω
	πείθω	
	πιπράσκω	
	πορσύνω	
	τάσσω	

Both πρός and ὑπό are found with verbs of speaking and striking; furthermore, aside from the verbs of honoring, which are the domain of ὑπό, the other verbs occurring with πρός and ὑπό cannot be arranged into any categories in opposition to one another. Even the verbs of honoring cannot be assigned to ὑπό without qualification, for there are two constructions similar to PACs with the adjective ἄτιμος, one with πρός, one with ὑπό:

(7) A. *Eu.* 882–4　ὡς μήποτ᾽ εἴπῃς πρὸς νεωτέρας ἐμοῦ
　　　　　　　θεὸς παλαιὰ καὶ πολισσούχων βροτῶν
　　　　　　　ἄτιμος ἔρρειν τοῦδ᾽ ἀπόξενος πέδου
　　　　　　　"so that you will never say that you, an
　　　　　　　ancient goddess, depart from this plain as an
　　　　　　　exile, dishonored by me, a younger goddess,
　　　　　　　and the men who hold the city"

(8) A. *Th.* 1024 ἄτιμον εἶναι δ' ἐκφορᯎς φίλων ἥπο
"not to be honored by friends with a
funeral"

Furthermore, even if there were an underlying trend in Aeschylus for verbs of honoring to be construed with ἧπό, this would go against the pattern in Herodotus, where these verbs are among those most likely to take πρός. Perhaps more significant is the observation that the suppletive passives occur relatively frequently with πρός but not at all with ἧπό. Below, we will see that Sophocles similarly prefers πρός to ἐκ and παρά (though not ἧπό) in constructions with suppletive passives.

As far as agents are concerned, it is hard to compare those occurring with πρός and ἧπό directly because meter becomes an issue here. Because the preposition need not be next to the verb, there is only minimal metrical interplay between these two elements. The agent, however, will come directly after the preposition, except in cases of anastrophe. Therefore, there is a strong limitation on the types of agents that can construe with ἧπό: any agent with a definite article, for instance, would be excluded. As it happens, ἧπό only occurs in Aeschylus with agents that begin with a vowel, and, in proper PACs, does not occur at all in anastrophe. Once these metrical considerations have been accounted for, there is little to distinguish the agents that occur with the two prepositions:[5]

	πρός	ἧπό
pronouns	το᯾; τίνος;	ἜμἮν α᭨τἮν (2×)
humans	ἄλλων ναυτίλων ἀνδρός τᯞς τεκούσης σοφο᯾ διδασκάλου ἀρσένων	ἐχθρἮν ἀστἮν (2×)
other agents	δίκης θεἮν	οἰωνἮν

[5] In this table, I omit PACs with suppletive passives.

As neither the agent nor the verb can be linked to the choice of πρός or ὑπό as agent marker, meter is left as the most likely criterion by which one or the other preposition was selected. Most of the time, only one of these two prepositions will fit the point in the line where an agent marker is needed. Occasionally, however, the two are metrically interchangeable; in such places, where meter would not have played a role, we may perhaps see more clearly what factors would have favored one preposition over the other. Unfortunately, no single tragedian provides enough such PACs to determine the extent to which the selection of πρός and ὑπό was a matter of individual style. Taken together, however, they do generally suggest that, when either preposition could be used, ὑπό was preferred.

There are three such metrically interchangeable agent markers in Aeschylus, two with ὑπό, one with πρός:

(9) A. A. 1271–2   κἀν τοῖσδε κόσμοις καταγελωμένην
      †μέτα†
      φίλων ὑπ᾽ ἐχθρῶν
      "and mocked in this finery by friends who
      are enemies"

(10) A. Eu. 807   ὑπ᾽ ἀστῶν τῶνδε τιμαλφουμένας
      "honored by these citizens"

(11) A. Supp. 282–3   Κύπριος χαρακτήρ τ᾽ ἐν γυναικείοις
      τύποις
      εἰκὼς πέπληκται τεκτόνων πρὸς ἀρσένων
      "and similar is the Cyprian stamp that
      is struck on female forms by male
      craftsmen"

Naturally, little can be surmised from these examples alone. In light of the data from the other tragedians, however, it will be tempting to take ὑπό as the default preposition, with πρός used under special circumstances. Thus, in these three Aeschylean PACs, it is worth noting that ὑπό is used twice where πρός is metrically possible, while πρός is only found once in the same circumstances, even though πρός is generally the more common agent marker. Still, (11) has no distinctive features that would account for why πρός would be chosen instead of ὑπό, unless the verb was viewed as a stative perfect and thus incompatible with the standard marker ὑπό. Before making any definite pronouncements, however, we must turn to data from the other tragedians.

Prometheus Bound

Because it is uncertain whether Aeschylus wrote the *Prometheus Bound*, I have separated it for consideration apart from the six plays indisputably attributed to him.[6] In fact, the distribution of agent markers in the *Prometheus* is roughly comparable with that in the six other plays, with πρός and ὑπό leading the figures. However, there is a difference in that PACs are considerably more common in the *Prometheus* than in the other plays, with nearly half as many examples as the other six plays put together:

	ἐκ	παρά	πρός	ὑπό	total
with morphological passive verbs	I	I	4	2	8
with suppletive passives	I	0	3	0	4
total	2	I	7	2	12

The two minority prepositions, παρά and ἐκ, are again used as they are in prose and in the other works of Aeschylus. For instance, παρά again occurs with a verb for which there are prose parallels (see X. *Cyn.* 13.4 and Pl. *Hi. Ma.* 301d):

(12) A. *Pr.* 634 τὰ λοιπὰ δ' ἄθλων σοῦ διδαχθήτω πάρα
     "let the remainder of her trials be told to her by you"

Furthermore, the PAC of ἐκ with a suppletive passive again has a god as the agent:

(13) A. *Pr.* 759 ἥτις ἐκ Διὸς πάσχω κακῶς
     "I, who am made to suffer badly by Zeus"

The other PAC with ἐκ, like the one with παρά, involves a verb that construes with ἐκ in prose as well (compare Lys. 16.18):

---

[6] For a discussion of the authenticity of the *Prometheus*, see Griffith 1977.

(14) A. *Pr.* 221–2   τοιάδ' ἐξ ἐμοῦ
ὁ τῶν θεῶν τύραννος ὠφελημένος
"such has the tyrant of the gods been
benefited by me"

As with the other plays in the Aeschylean corpus, πρός is more
common than ὑπό as an agent marker. Again, there is no clear
difference between the verbs or agents that construe with the two
prepositions. In the *Prometheus*, there are five PACs in contexts
where the two prepositions are metrically equivalent:

(15) A. *Pr.* 761–2   Ιω: πρὸς τοῦ τύραννα σκῆπτρα
                  συληθήσεται;
           Πρ: πρὸς αὐτὸς αὐτοῦ κενοφρόνων
                  βουλευμάτων
           "Io: By whom will be he stripped of his
           tyrant's scepter?
           Prometheus: By his own empty-minded
           plans."
(16) A. *Pr.* 948   πρὸς ὧν τ' ἐκεῖνος ἐκπίπτει κράτους
           "by which [marriage] he will be driven out
           of power"
(17) A. *Pr.* 996   πρὸς οὗ χρεών νιν ἐκπεσεῖν τυραννίδος
           "by whom it is fated that he will be driven
           from his tyranny"
(18) A. *Pr.* 306   οἵαις ὑπ' αὐτοῦ πημοναῖσι κάμπτομαι
           "with what pains I am tortured by him"
(19) A. *Pr.* 833–4   ὑφ' ὧν σὺ λαμπρῶς κοὐδὲν αἰνικτηρίως
           προσηγορεύθης ἡ Διὸς κλεινὴ δάμαρ
           "by whom you were addressed gloriously
           and not at all mysteriously as the illustrious
           wife of Zeus"

If we assume that πρός was the default agent marker, then nothing
could explain the use of ὑπό in (18) and (19) when πρός would
serve just as well. If, however, ὑπό was the default agent marker,
one can account for the three anomalous instances of πρός: in the
second line of (15), even though ὑπό would have been metrically
possible before αὐτός, πρός is maintained in order to echo the

preceding line. As for (16) and (17), in both cases the verb is a suppletive passive.[7] It has already been seen in the other plays of Aeschylus, and will further be seen in the works of Sophocles, that these intransitive verbs have a proclivity to construe with πρός. Once again, the evidence is meager, but it does suggest that ὑπό, despite its rarity, was still the preferred agent marker when metrically admissible.

Sophocles

The distribution of agent markers in Sophocles is rather different from that found in either Aeschylus or the *Prometheus Bound*.[8] The most striking difference is the greater frequency of PACs with ἐκ, and indeed a greater number of PACs in total. Also apparent is a strong tendency for suppletive passives to be construed with πρός:

	ἐκ	παρά	πρός	ὑπό	total
with morphological passive verbs	17	5	16	17	55
with suppletive passives	5	0	20	8	33
total	22	5	36	25	88

That ἐκ should be so much more common suggests that its use had spread beyond the contexts in which it appears in prose and in Aeschylus. An examination of the PACs with ἐκ shows that this is indeed the case. In fact, the same appears to be true of the PACs with παρά as well. In general, the impression given by the agent markers in Sophocles is one of interchangeability, with the exception of the tendency of suppletive passives to mark their agent with πρός.

In order to determine the linguistic conditions that led Sophocles to choose one agent marker over another, it is necessary to eliminate meter as a variable. This may best be achieved by singling out those

---

[7] The text is corrupt in (16), but even if the verb Aeschylus wrote was not ἐκπίπτει, the parallel with (17) could still justify the use of πρός.

[8] For a general discussion of prepositional usage in Sophocles, see Moorhouse 1982.

PACs in which more than one agent marker would be metrically possible; I call these metrically open PACs. In Sophocles, these PACs fall into two broad categories: those in which ὑπό is metrically possible, and those where it is not. What this classification highlights is that, when ὑπό was metrically possible, Sophocles used it to the complete exclusion of other agent markers; in contexts where it did not fit the meter, both ἐκ and παρά compete with πρός, with πρός preferred to both of these prepositions by approximately a 2:1 ratio.

First, there are sixteen PACs where both ὑπό and at least one other agent marker are metrically possible. In the following table, I have listed them all according to which prepositions, in addition to ὑπό, would fit at the point in the line where ὑπό occurs. Starred PACs are those occurring with suppletive passives:

ἐκ	παρά	παρά, πρός	ἐκ, παρά, πρός
Aj. 289–90	Aj. 498	Ant. 727	El. 444–5
*OC 391	*Tr. 1077	Tr. 1104	OT 29
OC 1388	Ph. 6	Ph. 1005	*OC 274
	*Ph. 583	OC 1013	OC 850–1
	OC 737–8		

Apart from one possible exception, ὑπό is in all cases preferred to the other potential agent markers. In the one problematic passage, πάρα and ὕπο are variant readings:

(20) S. Ph. 6 ταχθεὶς τόδ' ἔρδειν τῶν ἀνασσόντων ὕπο
(z πάρα)
"assigned this task by those in charge"

Even here, however, ὕπο is no doubt the correct reading. Not only is it to be found in the majority of the manuscripts, but also, if we read ὕπο here, then we are left with the firm rule that ὑπό is always the preferred agent marker if it is metrically admissible. This holds true for morphological and suppletive passives alike.

The situation is considerably more complicated in passages where ὑπό does not fit the meter. Metrically open PACs that do not admit of ὑπό may be divided into two categories: those where either ἐκ or πρός is possible, and those where either παρά or πρός is possible. In contrast to the PACs above, where ὑπό is the clear favorite over all the other agent markers, there is here considerable variation in both categories as to whether πρός or the alternative preposition is used, although πρός is always the more common option. Again, I present the data in a table, with asterisks marking PACs with suppletive passives:

preposition in text	πρός or ἐκ possible	πρός or παρά possible
πρός	Aj. 651–2	Aj. 829
	*Aj. 759	*OT 1237
	Aj. 838	Ant. 205
	*Aj. 1033	*Ant. 679
	El. 70	*Tr. 1132
	El. 790	Ph. 1070–1
	OT 357	
	OT 358	
	*OT 949	
	Ant. 408	
	Ant. 1313	
	Tr. 169–70	
	*Tr. 191	
	*Tr. 1131	
	*Tr. 1160	
	Ph. 383–4	
	*Ph. 1074–5	
	OC 599–600	
alternative preposition	El. 409	Tr. 596
	El. 1411–12	OC 1122
	OT 225	OC 1500
	OT 1382–3	
	Ant. 293–4	
	Ph. 335	
	OC 67	

One conclusion may be drawn immediately from this chart: πρός is always preferred whenever the verb is a suppletive passive. This exclusive use of πρός with suppletive passives largely accounts for the numerical predominance of πρός in the table above. It then remains to determine what conditions selected for πρός or the alternative preposition when the verb was a morphological passive. First, consider the six PACs where either πρός or παρά is possible. Three have πρός:

(21) S. *Aj.* 829   πρὸς ἐχθρῶν του κατοπτευθεὶς πάρος
     "seen earlier by any of my enemies"

(22) S. *Ant.* 205–6[9]   ἐὰν δ' ἄθαπτον καὶ πρὸς οἰωνῶν δέμας
     καὶ πρὸς κυνῶν ἐδεστὸν αἰκισθέν τ' ἰδεῖν
     "and to leave the body unburied, eaten by
     birds and dogs, visibly mutilated"

(23) S. *Ph.* 1070–1   ἦ καὶ πρὸς ὑμῶν ὧδ' ἐρῆμος, ὦ ξένοι,
     λειφθήσομαι δὴ κοὔκ ἐποικτερεῖτέ με;
     "and shall I be left here by you, strangers,
     all alone, and will you not pity me?"

Three have παρά:

(24) S. *Tr.* 596–7   μόνον παρ' ὑμῶν[10] εὖ στεγοίμεθ'· ὡς σκότῳ
     κἂν αἰσχρὰ πράσσῃς, οὔποτ' αἰσχύνῃ πεσῇ
     "only, may we be well concealed by you;
     as in darkness, even if you are doing
     something shameful, you will never fall
     in shame"

(25) S. *OC* 1121–2   ἐπίσταμαι γὰρ τήνδε τὴν ἐς τάσδε μοι
     τέρψιν παρ' ἄλλου μηδενὸς πεφασμένην
     "for I understand that my pleasure at seeing
     my children has not been granted to me by
     anyone else"

(26) S. *OC* 1500   τίς αὖ παρ' ὑμῶν κοινὸς ἠχεῖται[11] κτύπος
     "what noise is this that is now jointly
     echoed by you"

As πρός generally seems to be the preferred preposition, the best place to start is to look for characteristics shared by the PACs with παρά. Certainly in (25) and (26), the preposition, though agentive,

---

[9] It is only the πρός in the first line that could be replaced by παρά.
[10] ὑμῖν Zg, **t** s.l.   [11] ἠγεῖται **zt**.

could also be interpreted as marking source, particularly in (25), where φαίνω almost acts as a giving-verb, inasmuch as to show Oedipus τέρψιν is really to give him pleasure. Similarly, in (26), the noise of the summoning of Theseus may be conceived of as having the chorus and Oedipus as its source. Such an interpretation of παρά would certainly have to be adopted if the (non-passive) variant ἡγεῖται were read. The remaining passage, (24), is more problematic, partly because of the variant παρ᾽ ὑμῖν. The context is as follows: Deianeira is about to give the fatal robe to the herald Lichas to pass on to Heracles; she has told the chorus of her plans, and asks that what she has said be kept secret by the chorus. There is no strong reason for the chorus to have been considered the source of the protection in any physical sense. While nearly any action can, in some sense, be viewed as emanating from the agent, the crucial point is that this is no more the case in (24) than it is with the PACs with πρός. The variant reading with the dative fits with the semantics of the verb better, as Deianeira could be picturing herself as sheltered in the presence of the chorus. However, ὑμῖν has poorer manuscript attestation, and παρά$^{+D}$ has no parallels as an agent marker elsewhere in Sophocles. As there are no conditions, then, that satisfactorily explain the use of παρά here, it appears that choice of agent marker in such circumstances was simply determined by poetic license. If we try the contrary approach of looking for characteristics shared by the PACs with πρός, we meet with even less success. In the end, we must conclude that, when πρός and παρά were both metrically possible agent markers of true passive verbs, πρός is probably the preferred preposition, inasmuch as two of the PACs with παρά appear to have been motivated by that preposition's role of marking source. But the remaining PAC with παρά cannot be explained in this way and must thus be attributed to free variation.

I turn now to the PACs where either πρός or ἐκ would be metrically admissible. These are more numerous than those just discussed, and there is perhaps more reason here for starting from the assumption that πρός was the preferred agent marker, for the PACs with πρός outnumber those with ἐκ by eleven to seven. First, those with πρός:

(27) S. *Aj*. 651–2   ἐθηλύνθην στόμα
πρὸς τῆσδε τῆς γυναικός
"I was softened in my speech by this
woman"

(28) S. *Aj*. 838   πρὸς τῶν Ἀτρειδῶν ὡς διόλλυμαι τάλας
"how I, wretched, am undone by the
Atridae"

(29) S. *El*. 69–70   σοῦ γὰρ ἔρχομαι
δίκη καθαρτὴς πρὸς θεῶν ὡρμημένος
"for I come, with justice, as one who
will purify you, prompted by the
gods"

(30) S. *El*. 789–90   ὅθ' ὧδ' ἔχων
πρὸς τῆσδ' ὑβρίζῃ μητρός
"when, in such a state, you are outraged
by this mother of yours"

(31) S. *OT* 357–8   Οι: πρὸς τοῦ διδαχθείς; οὐ γὰρ ἔκ γε τῆς
τέχνης.
Τε: πρὸς σοῦ· σὺ γάρ μ' ἄκοντα
προύτρέψω λέγειν.
"Oedipus: Informed by whom? For you
did not learn it from your prophetic skill.
Tiresias: By you, for you encouraged me
to speak against my will."

(32) S. *Ant*. 408   πρὸς σοῦ τὰ δείν' ἐκεῖν' ἐπηπειλημένοι
"threatened by you with those horrors"

(33) S. *Ant*. 1312–13 ὡς αἰτίαν γε τῶνδε κἀκείνων ἔχων
πρὸς τῆς θανούσης τῆσδ' ἐπεσκήπτου
μόρων
"you were charged by this dead woman as
the one responsible for this death and
that"

(34) S. *Tr*. 169   τοιαῦτ' ἔφραζε πρὸς θεῶν εἱμαρμένα
"he declared that such events were fated
by the gods"

(35) S. *Ph*. 383–4   τῶν ἐμῶν τητώμενος
πρὸς τοῦ κακίστου κἀκ κακῶν Ὀδυσσέως

"deprived of what is mine by Odysseus,
the most wicked man to have been born to
wicked parents"

(36) S. *OC* 599–600   γῆς ἐμῆς ἀπηλάθην
πρὸς τῶν ἐμαυτοῦ σπερμάτων
"I was driven from my country by my own
children"

Next, those with ἐκ:

(37) S. *El.* 409   ἐκ τοῦ φίλων πεισθεῖσα;
"Persuaded by which of her friends?"

(38) S. *El.* 1411–12   ἀλλ᾽ οὐκ ἐκ σέθεν
ᾠκτίρεθ᾽ οὗτος οὐδ᾽ ὁ γεννήσας πατήρ
"but neither he nor the father who begot
him was pitied by you"

(39) S. *OT* 225   ἀνδρὸς ἐκ τίνος διώλετο
"by what man he was killed"

(40) S. *OT* 1382–3   τὸν ἐκ θεῶν
φανέντ᾽ ἄναγνον καὶ γένους τοῦ Λαΐου
"the one shown by the gods to be unholy
and of Laius' family"

(41) S. *Ant.* 293–4   ἐκ τῶνδε τούτους ἐξεπίσταμαι καλῶς
παρηγμένους μισθοῖσιν
"I understand quite well that the guards
were corrupted by these men with bribes"

(42) S. *Ph.* 335   τοξευτός, ὡς λέγουσιν, ἐκ Φοίβου δαμείς
"shot with an arrow, as they say, defeated
by Phoebus"

(43) S. *OC* 67   ἐκ τοῦ κατ᾽ ἄστυ βασιλέως τάδ᾽ ἄρχεται
"these parts are ruled by the king in the
city"

Unfortunately, despite the larger number of examples, it is even
harder here to see any sort of pattern that might explain the choice
of one preposition over the other. If one looks at the agents, for
instance, it is true that, as in other authors, ἐκ occurs twice with
gods, in (40) and (42). But so too does πρός, in (29) and (34).
Furthermore, both ἐκ and πρός also occur regularly with both

pronouns ((37), (38), (41) against (31), (32)) and nouns denoting humans ((39), (43) against (27), (28), (30), (33), (35), (36)). Nor are the verbs that occur with ἐκ sharply distinguished from those that occur with πρός. Both prepositions occur with a wide range of verbs. While the only exact overlap is that διόλλυμι is found with both prepositions ((28) and (39)), some of the other verbs can be grouped into pairs that fall into approximately the same semantic field: on the one hand, the verbs of threatening and blaming with πρός, (32) and (33), and, on the other, that of persuading with ἐκ, (37), are all essentially verbs of speaking in which the agent tries to affect the emotional state of the listener. Likewise, informing (31), with πρός, and showing (40), with ἐκ, are not dissimilar actions. From these comparisons, it might be tempting to see ἐκ as being used when the patient is somehow more affected by the action; but this idea is confuted by examples like (27) where Ajax is actually softened up (a PAC with πρός with a highly affected patient) and (38) where the patient is pitied (a PAC with ἐκ with a less highly affected patient).

One respect in which the use of the two prepositions does differ slightly is in the placement in the line. Although both prepositions can occur both at the beginning of the line and internally, πρός is used nearly always at the beginning (nine times out of eleven), while ἐκ is used line-initially in only three out of seven PACs. Furthermore, a prepositional phrase with πρός never ends the line, whereas phrases with ἐκ do in (38) and (40). These figures suggest that poetic considerations affected the choice of agent marker not only in that some prepositions were metrically impossible in particular contexts, but also in that they might simply have seemed more stylistically appropriate at a particular point in the line.

In some respects, the data for Sophocles lead to more conclusive results than do those for Aeschylus. First, it is clear that, whenever the meter permitted, Sophocles used ὑπό to mark the agent. Second, in cases where the verb was a suppletive passive, if ὑπό was not metrically admissible, but πρός was, then πρός was clearly favored over the other agent markers. Beyond these two statements, however, little definite can be said. Whenever either (i) ἐκ and πρός or (ii) παρά and πρός fit the meter, both prepositions are found with little to distinguish between the two. The only tendency that may be observed is that πρός occurs more often at the beginning of the line, suggesting that the poet's stylistic judgment still plays some part, even where the two prepositions are metrically equivalent.

Euripides

When turning from Aeschylus and Sophocles to Euripides, the striking difference is that there do not seem to be any PACs at all with παρά$^{+G}$.[12] This fact is particularly interesting because παρά$^{+G}$ is precisely the non-standard agent marker that becomes prevalent in prose over the period from the fifth into the fourth century. In addition, it was also the non-standard agent marker most common in the Ptolemaic papyri.[13] It is hard to escape the conclusion that Euripides avoided this prepositional usage because it was perceived as belonging to a lower register. There is, to be sure, one place where Euripides does use παρά with the dative:

(44) E. *Med.* 1336–7   νυμφευθεῖσα δὲ
παρ' ἀνδρὶ τῷδε καὶ τεκοῦσά μοι τέκνα
"but married by me, your husband, and
having borne me children"

These lines are spoken by Jason just after he has learned that Medea has killed their children. The presence of παρά$^{+D}$ may probably be attributed to a desire on Jason's part to downplay any agency of his own in marrying Medea: best to use a preposition that could also be interpreted as local, an interpretation rendered more likely in light of Euripides' reluctance to mark the agent with παρά with either case.[14]

To return to the agent markers that Euripides does use, I have set out the same statistics as are presented above for the other tragedians, but only for seven of Euripides' plays (*Cyclops, Alcestis, Medea, Suppliant Women, Electra, Heracles,* and *Iphigenia in Tauris*), in other words, a corpus of roughly the same size as that examined for Aeschylus and Sophocles:

[12] Schwyzer lists none, nor were there any in the seven plays I examined.
[13] See Mayser 1934: 484–6, 510. For the later development of παρά$^{+G}$, see Chapter 6.
[14] In the rest of this section on Euripides, παρά stands for παρά$^{+G}$.

	ἐκ	πρός	ὑπό	total
with morphological passive verbs	7	13	9	29
with suppletive passives	4	5	8	17
total	11	18	17	46

Again, I will begin with the metrically open PACs as, by eliminating meter from consideration, they provide the most valuable information as to why Euripides chose one agent marker over another.

The following chart lists the PACs in the seven specified plays of Euripides where ὑπό would fit the meter, grouped according to the other prepositions that would also be metrically possible. Asterisks indicate PACs with suppletive passives, and the preposition found in the text is ὑπό unless otherwise specified.

παρά	παρά, πρός	ἐκ, παρά, πρός
Alc. 942	*Supp.* 336	*Med.* 255–6 (πρός)
*Supp. 402	*Supp.* 1175	*Cyc.* 229
*Supp. 528	*El.* 277	*Cyc.* 230
Supp. 877		
HF 20-1		
*HF 853		

Like Sophocles, Euripides generally prefers to use ὑπό if it is metrically possible, there being only one exception in the seven plays examined. Still, it would be misleading to suggest from the table above that there is somehow an 11:1 preference for ὑπό. First, Euripides does not use παρά as an agent marker, so it is doubtful whether the PACs in the first column should even count as metrically open. The PACs in the middle column do represent places where ὑπό has clearly been preferred to its rival πρός. But all the passages in the last column are problematic: the first because πρός is chosen over ὑπό, the other two because they come from the *Cyclops*, a satyr play, and are metrically unusual. Consider first the PAC with πρός:

(45) E. *Med.* 255–6   ἐγὼ δ' ἔρημος ἄπολις οὖσ' ὑβρίζομαι
πρὸς ἀνδρός, ἐκ γῆς βαρβάρου λελησμένη
"but I, deserted, without a city, am
outraged by my husband after having been
taken as booty from a barbarian land"

As it is not likely that πρός would have been preferred because of
the agent (cf. *HF* 853) or the verb (no exact parallels, but cf. *Supp.*
336 or *HF* 20–21), we are again left with the possibility that the
avoidance of ὑπό was here conditioned by some stylistic criterion.
In fact, aside from the metrically anomalous *Cyclops*, there are
only two places in the entire corpus of Euripides where ὑπό is
the first word in a line of iambic trimeter, Fr. 312.1 (Nauck) and
Fr. *Alexander* 43.97.[15] By contrast, there are seven places in the
Alcestis and *Medea* alone where πρός begins a trimeter.

Now example (45), on the one hand, appears to be a passage
that argues against taking ὑπό as a default agent marker, but it
can alternatively be explained by observing that Euripides avoided
line-initial ὑπό. Passage (46), on the other, at first seems to support
the idea that ὑπό was the default agent marker, but falls through
in the end because of the metrical oddity of the *Cyclops*:

(46) E. *Cyc.* 228–30   Σι: ὤμοι, πυρέσσω συγκεκομμένος τάλας.
Κυ: ὑπὸ τοῦ; τίς ἐς σὸν κρᾶτ' ἐπύκτευσεν,
γέρον;
Σι: ὑπὸ τῶνδε, Κύκλωψ, ὅτι τὰ σ' οὐκ
εἴων φέρειν.
"Silenus: Alas, wretched me – I was
beaten up and now I'm burning.
Cyclops: By whom? Who beat upon your
head, old man?
S: By these men, Cyclops, because I did
not allow them to steal your possessions."

These PACs are metrically quite different from those found elsewhere. While tragedy never allows ὑπό to stand as a resolved
long syllable, such resolution is frequent in Aristophanes and is

---

[15] The fragment from the *Alexander* may be found in Snell 1937: 17.

permitted here in a satyr play as well.[16] Additionally, as noted above, this is the only extant play of Euripides' in which ὑπό ever occurs at the beginning of the line. On these grounds, then, we cannot use these PACs to support the contention that ὑπό was a default agent marker in Euripides – at any rate, not in his tragedies. In the end, only the three PACs of the central column remain as unproblematic PACs where both ὑπό and another preposition were metrically possible agent markers. As ὑπό was selected in all three, it is likely that in Euripides, as in Sophocles, ὑπό was a default agent marker, and that the high frequency of other prepositions was due to their metrical utility.

To examine, in turn, the relative positions of πρός and ἐκ in Euripides' choice of agent markers, I will set out the PACs in which the two prepositions would be metrically equivalent. First, those with ἐκ:

(47) E. *IT* 1076 ὡς ἔκ γ᾽ ἐμοῦ σοι πάντα σιγηθήσεται
"as everything will be kept quiet by me for your sake"

(48) E. *HF* 1329–30 ταῦτ᾽ ἐπωνομασμένα
σέθεν τὸ λοιπὸν ἐκ βροτῶν κεκλήσεται
"from now on, these will be named after you by mortals"

Next, those with πρός:

(49) E. *Med.* 704–5 Μη: ὄλωλα· καὶ πρός γ᾽ ἐξελαύνομαι
χθονός.
Αι: πρὸς τοῦ; τόδ᾽ ἄλλο καινὸν αὖ λέγεις
κακόν.
"Medea: I am ruined, and, what's more, I'm being banished from the land.
Aegeus: By whom? You speak of another new evil."

(50) E. *Supp.* 552–3 πρός τε γὰρ τοῦ δυστυχοῦς,
ὡς εὐτυχήσῃ, τίμιος γεραίρεται

---

[16] For the intermediate position of satyric drama between tragedy and comedy with respect to resolutions, see West 1987: 26.

"for it is held in honor by anyone who is
unfortunate, so that he may gain good
fortune"

(51) E. *El.* 8–10
ἐν δὲ δώμασιν
θνῄσκει γυναικὸς πρὸς Κλυταιμήστρας
δόλῳ
καὶ τοῦ Θυέστου παιδὸς Αἰγίσθου χερί
"and at home he was killed treacherously
by his wife Clytemnestra and by the hand
of Aegisthus son of Thyestes"

As with Sophocles, there is no clear distinction between the environments in which ἐκ and πρός occur. It is true that both the PACs with ἐκ have verbs in the future, while the three with πρός have verbs in the present. But because there is no linguistic motivation for this, and because there are so few examples, this is best ascribed to chance. Possibly, it is significant that the one PAC with a suppletive passive, (51), has πρός; this would parallel the distribution in Sophocles. But as far as the others are concerned, verbs of approximately the same semantic field construe with two different prepositions in (48) and (50). It may not be obvious that "calling" and "honoring" are related, but in other authors, notably Herodotus, they often construe with the same non-standard agent markers.[17] On the whole, it seems most likely that, in Euripides as in Sophocles, ἐκ and πρός were used interchangeably as agent markers whenever ὑπό did not fit the meter.

Finally, we may mention that there is one place in the seven selected plays where ἀπό is used in such a way that it might be identified as an agent marker:

(52) E. *IT* 1369–70
καὶ κῶλ᾽ ἀπ᾽ ἀμφοῖν τοῖν νεανίαιν ἅμα
ἐς πλευρὰ καὶ πρὸς ἦπαρ ἠκοντίζετο
"and limbs were hurled forth [like missiles]
from both young men at the same time into
our sides, towards our livers"

---

[17] As further proof of the semantic similarity of calling and honoring, we may note the etymology of κλέος: that which is heard, or called out, is honored.

216

This passage is reminiscent of two places in Homer where ἀπό is used to denote motion away from the human body in contexts where it might be interpreted as agentive:

(53) *Il.* 23.714–15 τετρίγει δ᾽ ἄρα νῶτα θρασειάων ἀπὸ χειρῶν
ἑλκόμενα στερέως
"and their backs creaked, tugged firmly by bold hands"

(54) *Od.* 4.522–3 πολλὰ δ᾽ ἀπ᾽ αὐτοῦ
δάκρυα θερμὰ χέοντ᾽
"and many hot tears were shed by him"

It is probably best to take ἀπό in (52) as marking source, rather than agent, for two reasons. First, it does not occur elsewhere as an agent marker, and it would thus be uneconomical to posit it as one here. Second, by including a description of where the blows are landing, the context suggests a very visual picture of limbs (that is, kicks) flying out from Orestes and Pylades.

All in all, the PACs in Euripides seem generally similar to those in Sophocles. The preferred agent marker seems to have been ὑπό, and ἐκ and πρός were used more or less indiscriminately when ὑπό did not fit the meter. The main difference is that Euripides does not use παρά⁺ᴳ, presumably because its increasing use in prose had rendered it less appropriate for poetry.

Comedy

All three of the main tragedians show a great amount of variety in agent marking. From their works alone, it would be difficult to extrapolate that ὑπό was the primary agent marker in classical Attic. Comedy, however, provides a much different picture. The plays of Aristophanes use ὑπό almost exclusively to mark the agent. Too little of Menander survives to reach any firm conclusions, but he too appears to have preferred ὑπό. As noted above in the discussion of the two PACs with ὑπό from the satyr play *Cyclops*, comic meter, with its ready admittance of resolution, was better suited for a preposition consisting of two short syllables. Another feature that sets comedy apart from tragedy is that the most common non-standard agent marker is παρά⁺ᴰ, and it is found in the same contexts as in prose. The main agent marker in comedy is clearly ὑπό. Of the twelve prepositional PACs in the *Clouds*, all have ὑπό;[18] of the eleven in the *Acharnians*, all but one have ὑπό (the exception having παρά⁺ᴳ);[19] of the eleven in the *Birds*, all but one have ὑπό (the exception having παρά⁺ᴰ).[20] Less Menander survives, but both of the PACs in the *Dyscolus* are with ὑπό.[21] There are few PACs with other agent markers. In Aristophanes, the most common is παρά⁺ᴰ, which occurs five times:

(55) Ar. *V.* 1049 ὁ δὲ ποιητὴς οὐδὲν χείρων παρὰ τοῖσι
σοφοῖς νενόμισται
"but the poet is considered no worse
by the wise"

(56) Ar. *Lys.* 11–12 ὅτιὴ παρὰ μὲν τοῖς ἀνδράσιν νενομίσμεθα
εἶναι πανοῦργοι
"because we are considered by men to be
roguish"

(57) Ar. *V.* 1089–90 ὥστε παρὰ τοῖς βαρβάροισι πανταχοῦ
καὶ νῦν ἔτι
μηδὲν Ἀττικοῦ καλεῖσθαι σφηκὸς
ἀνδρικώτερον
"and so, by barbarians everywhere, even
now nothing is said to be manlier than an
Attic wasp"

(58) Ar. *Av.* 761 ἀτταγᾶς οὗτος παρ᾽ ἡμῖν ποικίλος
κεκλήσεται
"he will be called by us a many-colored
francolin"

(59) Ar. *Ra.* 910 μώρους λαβὼν παρὰ Φρυνίχῳ τραφέντας
"after taking the fools brought up by
Phrynichus"

---

[18] See lines 13, 170, 213, 240, 524, 624, 640, 725, 947, 948, 997, 1341.
[19] ὑπό at lines 114, 164, 216, 630, 678, 680, 699, 707, 824, 1194; παρά⁺ᴳ at 226.
[20] ὑπό at lines 285, 338, 355, 456, 1070, 1086, 1229, 1382, 1447, 1492; παρά⁺ᴰ at 761.
[21] See lines 386, 399.

In stark contrast to the PACs in tragedy with non-standard agent markers, these five form a coherent group based on the semantics of the verb. In the first two, the verb is νομίζω, a verb found frequently with παρά$^{+D}$ in prose. In the second two, the verb is καλέω; it is not too different from νομίζω, just as "to think that something is so" is not far removed from "to call something so." One may compare Herodotus, who uses πρός as an agent marker with both of these verbs. Finally, the use of παρά$^{+D}$ with τρέφω in (59) may be compared to its use with παιδεύω in Xenophon at *Cyr.* 1.2.15. In both cases, the agentive sense of the preposition is derived from the ambiguity of marking the person by whom one is raised as opposed to the person in whose establishment one is raised.

For the parallel with prose to be good, one would also expect to see PACs with παρά$^{+G}$. Only one occurs, however:

(60) Ar. *Ach.* 226   οἶσι παρ' ἐμοῦ πόλεμος ἐχθοδοπὸς αὔξεται
   "against whom hateful war is raised by me"

Although αὔξω is not a verb that has come up already as construing with παρά$^{+G}$ in prose, it is not surprising to find that a verb of initiating here takes an ablatival agent marker, just as verbs of accomplishing do: one may compare the use of ἐκ with ποιέω in Herodotus, inasmuch as Herodotus uses ἐκ in much the same way later authors use παρά$^{+G}$. It should not, however, be understood as a significant difference from prose that παρά$^{+G}$ is only found this one time in Aristophanes. The verbs that most commonly construe with παρά$^{+G}$ in prose – πέμπω, ἀποστέλλω, δίδωμι – simply do not occur in PACs in Aristophanes. Certainly a construction like the following suggests that Aristophanes might have used παρά$^{+G}$ to mark the agent with one of these verbs:

(61) Ar. *Ach.* 61   οἱ πρέσβεις οἱ παρὰ βασιλέως
   "the representatives from the king"

As for the other agent markers of tragedy, ἐκ is not found in any PACs in Aristophanes. Finally, πρός does occur once, but with a suppletive passive:

(62) Ar. *Nu.* 1122   πρὸς ἡμῶν οἷα πείσεται κακά
   "what sort of sufferings he would be dealt by us"

This line recalls the fact that Sophocles regularly used πρός with suppletive passives when ὑπό was not metrically possible.[22] That suppletive passives were treated differently from true passives is also suggested by the data from Menander: of the two PACs with non-standard agent markers in his works, one, with ἐκ, also involves the verb πάσχω:

(63) Men. *Inc.* 1.13 ἀδικεῖ μ' ἐκεῖνος οὐδὲν ἐξ ἐμοῦ παθών
"he wrongs me though he's not been treated thus by me"

The other, with παρά⁺ᴰ, resembles (59) in that the verb is one of educating:

(64) Men. *Asp.* 293 καὶ τὴν ἐμὴν μητέρα παρ' ᾗ παιδεύεται
"and my mother by whom she is being brought up"

It thus falls into line with prose usage.

From the evidence of both Aristophanes and Menander, it appears as though agent marking in comedy was much closer to that of prose than that of tragedy. Whereas tragedy used ἐκ and πρός indiscriminately with all types of verbs simply to fit the meter, comedy restricted the use of agent markers other than ὑπό to the same classes of verbs with which they occur in prose.

Conclusion

What motivated the use of non-standard agent markers in tragedy and comedy? The two genres must be considered separately. In tragedy, on the one hand, meter was the most important factor. Because ὑπό could not fit easily into the constraints of tragic iambic trimeter, ἐκ and πρός were useful alternatives. Now it may be that, in Aeschylus, ἐκ was favored in the same conditions as in prose. In the case of πρός, however, in Aeschylus, and both πρός and ἐκ in Sophocles and Euripides, there are no linguistic conditions that set the PACs with these prepositions off from one another or from those with ὑπό. But if meter is taken into consideration, we find

---

[22] It is not, to be sure, a perfect parallel as ὑπό would fit the meter in (62).

that ὑπό, though not numerically predominant overall, was still the preferred agent marker in positions where both it and another agent marker fit the meter. The preposition παρά$^{+G}$ is also found as an agent marker in Aeschylus and Sophocles, but not in Euripides. Its absence from the later tragedian is probably due to its increasing occurrence in prose: by the time of Euripides, it was of too low a register for use in tragedy.

In comedy, on the other hand, ὑπό prevailed, as it did in prose. Furthermore, when non-standard agent markers are used, they occur with verbs similar to those with which they occur in prose. The difference between comedy and tragedy can be attributed to the relative freedom of the comic trimeter in admitting resolutions.

6

THE DECLINE OF ὑπό IN AGENT CONSTRUCTIONS

In the previous chapters, it was seen that several prepositions, primarily ablatival in sense, competed with ὑπό as means of marking the agent. While ὑπό was clearly the dominant preposition in Attic authors like Plato, Xenophon, or Demosthenes, its position was not particularly stable: especially in Demosthenes, παρά sometimes alternates with ὑπό in apparent free variation. These other prepositions were thus situated in a place from which they could potentially oust ὑπό from its role as the agent marker. And ὑπό did indeed fall out of use in the end. As can be seen from modern Greek, it was ἀπό that eventually replaced ὑπό as the grammaticalized means of marking the agent. Scholarship on this development is scanty. For the most part, it is summarily stated that ἀπό simply took over from ὑπό, primarily on the basis of its occurrence in the Septuagint (LXX) and New Testament (NT). A fuller examination of the evidence, however, suggests that the development was not so straightforward. Although ἀπό does occur suggestively early in the LXX and NT, it is not the dominant agentive preposition in the papyri of late antiquity or the lower-register texts of the Byzantine period. It appears rather that παρά[+G] was the immediate successor of ὑπό, and that ἀπό was not the primary agentive preposition until after the twelfth century AD. Because texts not influenced by classical language are so rare in the relevant period, the details of this change will remain obscure. Still, the hypothesis that the expression of the agent was fluid enough to allow multiple changes in this period is not unparalleled. Old and Middle English and Old Spanish also provide evidence of multiple agent expressions within a short time span.[1] In this chapter, I will begin by discussing earlier accounts of the decline of ὑπό. Next, I will present the data

---

[1] For Old English, see Mitchell 1985: 334–48; for Middle English, see Mustanoja 1960: 442; for Old Spanish, see Penny 1991: 103.

in a chronological sequence from biblical Greek through Digenis Akritis and the poems of Ptochoprodromos. It will emerge that ἀπό played only a marginal role in agent marking when compared to παρά$^{+G}$.

Survey of earlier literature

There has been little academic work on the expression of the agent in the period from the first through twelfth centuries AD. Hatzidakis (1892) and Jannaris (1897) cover the question briefly in their historical grammars of Greek, as does Schwyzer (1943), almost as an afterthought, in his article on agent expressions. Hult (1990) goes into more detail, examining quite closely the agent expressions found in seven fifth-century authors. All four scholars, however, take it for granted that ἀπό is the direct successor of ὑπό as the primary means of marking the agent. This assumption seems to have been bolstered by an excessive emphasis placed on the language of the LXX and NT, where ἀπό occurs more frequently as an agent marker than in other texts.

In a chapter on the general breakdown of the Greek prepositional system, Hatzidakis briefly discusses the prepositions used to express the agent (1892: 211). Giving examples principally from the LXX and NT, he notes that ἀπό was well placed to replace ὑπό as the chief agentive preposition, for it denoted the source or cause of the action, a role quite close to that of the agent. He compares the loss of παρά, stating that it too was replaced by ἀπό, though not in reference to agentive uses in particular. He does not offer any dates for these changes.

This account is unsatisfactory owing to the weight Hatzidakis places on evidence from the LXX and NT. First, he gives two examples of ἀπό in place of ὑπό from the LXX. In the first of these, ἀπό is not even used to mark the agent:

(1) *Exod.* 1.12   וַיָּקֻצוּ מִפְּנֵי בְּנֵי יִשְׂרָאֵל

     way-yāquṣû   *mip-pənê*
     and-felt.loathing.3.M.PL.   from-before
     bənê   *yiśrāʔēl*
     (the.)sons.of   Israel
     ἐβδελύσσοντο οἱ Αἰγύπτιοι ἀπὸ τῶν υἱῶν Ἰσραήλ

The verb βδελύσσομαι most frequently occurs in the middle voice, where it means "to feel loathing at." In the rare instances when it is found in the active, it means "to make loathsome." As the sense of the verse must be "the Egyptians felt loathing at the Israelites" rather than "were made loathsome by the Israelites," ἀπό is not being used to mark an agent, but rather the object of loathing. The use of ἀπό rather than the more normal accusative to mark the object of the verb must be due to the Hebrew use of מִן (min-) "from" after verbs of fearing.[2]

The other LXX example cited by Hatzidakis is also problematic, as it involves a verb that construes with ἀπό in earlier texts as well:

(2) *Prov.* 19.4   וְדָל מֵרֵעֵהוּ יִפָּרֵד

    wə-ḏāl   mē-rēʕ-ēhû   yippārēḏ
    and-a.poor.man   from-friend-his   is.divided
    ὁ δὲ πτωχὸς καὶ ἀπὸ τοῦ ὑπάρχοντος φίλου λείπεται

The semantics of "left by" and "left away from" are quite close. Accordingly, even in earlier Greek ἀπό can be used with λείπω in this manner:

(3) *Il.* 9.437–8   πῶς ἂν ἔπειτ᾽ ἀπὸ σεῖο, φίλον τέκος, αὖθι λιποίμην |
              οἶος; (cf. 444–5)
              "How then could I be left here alone by you *or* away from you, dear child?"

(4) Hdt. 9.66.1   λειπομένου Μαρδονίου ἀπὸ βασιλέος
              "when Mardonius was left by *or* away from the king"

The use of ἀπό is further influenced by the Hebrew construction, which means "separated from" rather than "left by." As an ablatival preposition is thus doubly motivated in this passage, it cannot be understood as a straightforward example of a general replacement of ὑπό by ἀπό.

Turning to the examples from the NT, we find that, there too, Hatzidakis has cited passages that show only ambiguously the use of ἀπό as an agentive preposition. One of the examples, for instance, has ἀπό construed with γίνομαι:

---

[2] See BDB *s.v.* 2.e.c.

(5) *1 Cor.* 1.30 ὃς ἐγενήθη σοφία ἡμῖν ἀπὸ θεοῦ
"who became wisdom for us by God's doing"

One could of course translate this with an English passive construction ("was made wisdom by God"), but, even if we ignore the fact that ἐγενήθη is at best a suppletive passive, here too, as with example (2), there are parallels in earlier Greek, notably Herodotus, for the use of ἀπό with this verb:[3]

(6) Hdt. 1.14.4 ἀλλ' οὐδὲν γὰρ μέγα ἀπ' αὐτοῦ ἄλλο ἔργον ἐγένετο
"but no other great work was done by him"

As for the other three examples from the NT, two show ὑπό as a variant in at least one old papyrus or uncial manuscript:

(7) *Acts* 15.4 παρεδέχθησαν ἀπὸ (BC) / ὑπὸ (p⁷⁴ אAD) τῆς ἐκκλησίας καὶ τῶν ἀποστόλων καὶ τῶν πρεσβυτέρων
"they were received by the church and the apostles and the elders"

(8) *Jas.* 1.13 ἀπὸ (AB) / ὑπὸ (א) θεοῦ πειράζομαι
"I am tempted by God"

Only the third example is uniformly read with ἀπό:

(9) *Lk.* 6.18 καὶ οἱ ἐνοχλούμενοι ἀπὸ πνευμάτων ἀκαθάρτων ἐθεραπεύοντο
"and those disturbed by unclean spirits were cured"

Now it is of course true that passages like those cited in (7) to (9) could illustrate the point when ἀπό began to usurp the place of ὑπό as the chief agentive preposition. The alternative readings with ὑπό in (7) and (8) would then be corrections of the vernacular ἀπό to the high-register agent marker. But another possibility is that the use of ἀπό in the NT was a Semiticism carried over from its use in the LXX. For, even if Hatzidakis' LXX examples of ἀπό as an agent marker do not illustrate the beginning of this preposition's ultimate replacement of ὑπό in this capacity, they and others like

---

[3] For further examples, see Powell 1938 *s.v.* C.IV.1.

them would still suffice as a model for the sporadic use of ἀπό as an agent marker in the NT.

To judge between these two competing explanations, one must look at the expression of the agent in subsequent centuries, to see whether ἀπό rose steadily from its beginnings as a Semiticism until it overtook ὑπό in the end, or whether it remained marginalized for a long period of time after the NT. Although Hatzidakis does present a handful of examples of agentive ἀπό from post-NT texts, they nearly all come from Christian literature and will thus have been influenced by the language of the NT.[4] Moreover, as will be shown below, there is much more evidence for παρά$^{+G}$ than ἀπό as an agentive marker in the first millennium AD. In short, Hatzidakis, anticipating the eventual triumph of ἀπό, assumed that its occurrence in Judeo-Christian literature represents the beginning of this development. That this is an over-simplification will become clear.

Jannaris provides an alternative explanation for the decline of ὑπό in agent expressions (1897: §1507–9). In his view, ἀπό replaced ὑπό because of phonetic confusion and the influence of Latin *ab*. Unlike Hatzidakis, he does give a timeline for this development: in his Transitional period (AD 300–600), ἀπό became more frequent, while in his Byzantine period (AD 600–1000), ὑπό disappeared from common speech. Additionally, he remarks that the occurrence of ἀπό in Thucydides would have been due to copyists of this later period.

This argument is flawed. The first problem is the assumption that ἀπό and ὑπό would have been confused from a phonetic standpoint. The location of the written accent is misleading: these prepositions were probably proclitic, so it is not the case that the first syllable would have been acoustically eclipsed by the second

---

[4] These examples are Chron. Pasch. 608 συσχεθέντας ἀπὸ ἐπάρχου and 669 σφάζεται ἀπὸ ἐπάρχου, and Theophan cont. 410 κατηγορηθῆναι ἀπό τινων. (I have been unable to find the exact location of Hatzidakis' references in Migne's texts.) His other example, ἀναλίσκεσθαι ἀπὸ γαλῶν (MS γαληνῶν) (Boucherie 1872: 511), is exceptionally dubious, as it comes from a bilingual text of Aesop, in which the Greek has been reproduced from a Latin model: "Le texte a été écrit avec beaucoup de soin par un scribe qui connaissait bien le latin et très-peu le grec. Pour lui le latin était le type sur lequel le texte grec devait se mouler" (*ibid.* 495). It is not hard to imagine the influence of *ab*. One inscription, *CIG* 1.1716 τετειμημένον ἀπὸ τῆς Κορινθίων βουλῆς, does appear legitimate. (Hatzidakis quotes its spurious duplicate *IG* XII.7 *4.1.)

(Devine–Stephens 1994: 357).[5] Besides, languages are perfectly capable of maintaining a difference between two semantically and phonetically similar prepositions, as for example Italian *da* "from" and *di* "of." Second, it is unlikely that Latin *ab* would have motivated the use of ἀπό in Greek, because *ab* and *ex* were themselves giving way to *de*. Löfstedt notes that *ab* had already lost a lot of ground by the time of the Peregrinatio Aetheriae (fourth to fifth century AD), that is, roughly the period when Jannaris sees the advance of ἀπό as getting under way (1962: 103). Lastly, the occurrence of ἀπό in Thucydides does not appear to result from the random corruption of a copyist.[6] As discussed in Chapter 4, the use of ἀπό as an agent marker is particularly frequent with the verbs πράσσω and λέγω, and it occurs in specific linguistic contexts: if it were a later scribal introduction, then we would not expect that it would collocate so often with these particular verbs under identifiable conditions. As for Jannaris' dating of the change, it will be seen below that, although ὑπό did wane in the centuries Jannaris proposes, it was not so much ἀπό as παρά that took its place.

Schwyzer provides a slightly more detailed account of the decline of ὑπό in his discussion of agent expressions (1943: 42). He too discusses the problem from the standpoint that it was ἀπό that replaced ὑπό. He notes that one example of ἀπό as an agentive preposition can be found already in papyri of the Ptolemaic era.[7] Furthermore, he draws attention to their frequency in the LXX, often as a variant of ὑπό. To account for this, he rightly points out that ἀπό is used in these passages to translate the Hebrew ablatival expressions מִן (*min-*) and מִפְּנֵי (*mippǝnê*, equivalent to ἀπὸ προσώπου). As the NT continued this use, he concluded that "die Sprache der heiligen Schriften konnte dann auch in diesem Punkte auf die Profanliteratur abfärben." He also correctly, though without explanation, rejects Jannaris' view that Latin *ab* played a role in the spread of ἀπό.

---

[5] Evidence that such prepositions were proclitic include: (i) the apocope of the *second* syllable of prepositions like ἀνά and παρά, (ii) the apocopated pronunciation of these prepositions in modern Greek (see also Horrocks 1997: 216 on ἀπό), and (iii) the loss of their accent when elided (contrast πόλλ').

[6] This objection is already made by Hult 1990: 36 n. 4.

[7] The only example in Mayser (1934: 378) is that given by Schwyzer. Mayser's perception is that it is διά and παρά that are in competition with ὑπό, not ἀπό (*ibid.* 510).

Although Schwyzer's portrayal is accurate as far as it goes, it again overstates the prominence of ἀπό in the LXX and NT and does not take sufficient account of the much greater frequency of παρά in non-Christian writings of the first millennium. For even in the LXX, ὑπό is still more frequent than ἀπό in expressions of the agent. Likewise, the best manuscripts of the NT only have ἀπό in a very limited number of contexts. As there is little evidence for the "Abfärbung" of Judeo-Christian ἀπό on pagan literature of this or the immediately subsequent periods, it would surely be better to explain the eventual Greek development as internally motivated if possible, taking recourse to Semitic influence only if necessary.

Hult, in an study of syntactic variation in seven fifth-century authors, employs a less impressionistic and more data-intensive approach in examining the development of agent marking; as a result, her findings shed a rather different light on the history of the construction (1990: 66–8). One of her seven authors, Procopius of Gaza, has very few agent expressions altogether, but the other six all use both ὑπό and παρά. Interestingly, the three authors writing in a more educated style generally prefer to express human agents with ὑπό rather than παρά:

Author	ὑπό	παρά
Eunapius	15	8
Theodoret	36	8
Marinus	2	2

The three writing in a lower register, however, usually prefer παρά in this context:

Author	ὑπό	παρά
Palladius	3	33
Callinicus	7	9
Mark the Deacon	19	16

However, with non-human agents such as spirits and emotions, all authors, even the latter three, completely avoid using παρά, using ὑπό instead (respectively 15×, 5×, and 3×). She further remarks that παρά is most common with verbs of giving, sending, and speaking "and other verbs where the agent is naturally denoted with a preposition meaning 'from'" (ibid. 66). The use of ἀπό, on the other hand, is quite rare. Even in Callinicus, where it is the most frequent, it only occurs three times. While Hult explains the use of παρά as a stylistic device imitative of classical Attic, she takes this sprinkling of agent expressions with ἀπό to be symptomatic of changes in the spoken language.

Hult's work raises two issues, one regarding her semantic grouping of verbs that would naturally be denoted with an ablatival preposition, the other concerning her assessment of the sociolinguistic status of ἀπό and παρά. While she is undoubtedly right in setting apart some verbs as being particularly likely to have their agent expressed with a preposition like παρά, her criteria for doing so are not well defined. Apparently, she feels that those verbs which in English could be construed with "from" in addition to "by" are those which would also tend to occur with an ablatival preposition in Greek. Consider, for instance, her comment on the following passage:

(10) Pall. 7.3 (25.13)   πολλὰ ὠφεληθεὶς ἀπὸ τῶν μακαρίων πατέρων
"benefited in many respects by the blessed
fathers"

"Of course, with this verb 'from' is a natural agent preposition ('to receive help from')" (ibid. 58). She contrasts such a construction with Callinicus' παρὰ πάντων ἠγαπᾶτο (12.3), which she cites to show the spread of παρά to verbs that would not obviously trigger an ablatival preposition in an agent construction. But if it is valid to translate ὠφεληθείς as "receive help from" so as to incorporate an ablatival preposition into the English, then there is no reason not to treat ἠγαπᾶτο in like manner ("met with love from"). Although Hult is right to distinguish those verbs that are more inclined to construe with an ablatival agent marker than others, one should not rely on the ability to use such a preposition in an English translation in order to identify them.

Instead, to determine whether a verb would naturally construe with an ablatival agent marker, one should look at Greek parallels instead. For example, the passive of the verb in question, ὠφελέω, occurs with ἀπό in Xenophon and Plato as well as in Palladius.[8] Additionally, other classical authors use ἐκ, παρά, and πρός with this verb.[9] It is on the basis of this widespread occurrence in classical Attic of ablatival prepositions with ὠφελέω that one should argue that its use in Palladius with ἀπό does not represent the extension of ablatival prepositions into what was formerly the strict preserve of ὑπό.

When ablatival prepositions do appear, then, what is the relationship between ἀπό and παρά? Hult believes that Callinicus' use of ἀπό mirrors development in the spoken language, whereas παρά represents an attempt to Atticize. If this is so, then their distribution is strange, for we should expect παρά to be more prevalent in the higher-register authors, ἀπό in those of the lower register. Just the opposite is the case, however. Moreover, two of the three PACs with ἀπό in Callinicus resemble passages from the LXX or NT. Consider first:

(11) *Gen.* 6.13   ἐπλήσθη ἡ γῆ ἀδικίας ἀπ᾽ αὐτῶν
                "and the land was filled by them with injustice"
(12) *Call.* 35.12   ἐπληρώθη κατανύξεως ἀπὸ τοῦ θεοῦ
                "and he was filled by God with bewilderment"

In both cases, the aorist passive of a verb based on the root πλη- is followed by a genitive of material and an agent construction with ἀπό. The use of ἀπό in Callinicus could well be an imitation of the language of the LXX rather than a reflection of the vernacular speech. Secondly, there is this passage:

(13) *Lk.* 16.18   ὁ ἀπολελυμένην ἀπὸ ἀνδρὸς γαμῶν
                "one who marries a woman divorced by her
                husband"

---

[8] Cf. example (120) and note 52 in Chapter 4.
[9] Aeschylus and Antiphon have ἐκ, Plato has παρά, and Herodotus has πρός (see LSJ).

(14) Call. 22.10   παραλελυμένους ἀπὸ δαιμόνων
          "paralyzed by demons"

An ablatival preposition is clearly motivated in the example from *Luke*: not only is a distinction between "from" and "by" quite minimal in light of the verb's semantics ("be divorced"), but the verb is even compounded with ἀπο-.[10] As Greek often repeats a preposition, first as a verbal prefix, then as a separate word governing a noun phrase, the occurrence of ἀπό in *Luke* is quite natural.[11] Although the parallel with Callinicus is not perfect – the compound παραλύω does not convey the same spatial significance of separation that ἀπολύω does – it is still possible that NT usage influenced Callinicus, especially considering that example (9) provides a parallel for the agent in (14) as well. His final use of ἀπό to mark the agent does not, admittedly, have any clear parallels in the LXX or NT:

(15) Call. 50.5   ἃ ἐδιδάχθην ἀπὸ τοῦ θεοῦ
          "which I was taught by God"

Instead of assuming that such an isolated example hints at the beginning of the modern Greek agent construction with ἀπό, it is better to compare the use of the similarly ablatival παρά[+G] to mark the agent of (ἀνα)διδάσκω in Xenophon and Plato.[12]

In noticeable contrast to the rare use of ἀπό to mark the agent in these fifth-century authors is the frequency with which authors such as Palladius and Mark the Deacon use παρά. Hult herself notes that its occurrence has extended beyond the verbs of giving, sending, and speaking to which it had earlier been limited. Palladius, for instance, uses it with τιμάω and ζητέω, Callinicus with ἀγαπάω and ἀκούω, and Mark the Deacon with κτίζω and ὑποφθείρω. Rather than seeing this extension of παρά as an example of false Atticization (in relatively low-register authors), it seems better to understand it as a change in the spoken language.

Such a statement, however, might not seem convincing until the agent markers in these authors are seen in the context of their

---

[10] Compare the use of ἀπό with λείπω in (2).
[11] For examples in NT Greek, see Moule 1963: 91.
[12] See examples (106) and (169) in Chapter 4.

development in Greek on a broader scale. I will therefore turn now to a more complete exposition of the data, examining snapshots of Greek from several different texts, starting from the LXX and ending with the vernacular poetry of the twelfth century. Before doing so, one problem must be addressed: how can we be sure that the texts themselves have not suffered corruption of ὑπό to ἀπό or vice versa? Indeed, especially in the NT, they are frequently variant readings of one another. The best answer seems to be as follows: considering that ὑπό is the more common preposition, one must examine the occurrences of ἀπό. If ἀπό is limited to appearing under particular linguistic conditions, such as with certain types of verbs, then it is probably original in those places. If, however, it is scattered randomly, then it is more likely that ὑπό was perceived as the correct literary preposition, but that ἀπό was used in everyday language and was therefore introduced erroneously by scribes.

Septuagint

As the LXX is seen as the starting-point for the spread of ἀπό as an agent marker, it is the best place to begin a close examination of the decline of ὑπό in PACs.[13] By far the most important fact to note about the LXX is that the vast majority of it is a translation from Hebrew. This is particularly relevant to a discussion of PACs because Hebrew hardly ever expressed the agent of a passive verb.[14] All the PACs in the LXX, then, are reworkings of different Hebrew constructions, of which the most common are the construct chain, oblique expressions with the preposition מִן (min-) "from," and clauses with active verbs. The construct chain perhaps requires some explanation. It is a Semitic construction in which two or more nouns are united to form a single phonological and semantic unit. The first noun, acting as the head of the phrase, is phonologically

---

[13] LXX quotations are from Rahlfs' edition.
[14] Lambdin 1971: 176, Waltke–O'Connor 1990: 383. In the latter grammar, six examples of passives with agents are given, three with בְּ (bə) "in," three with לְ (lə) "for." In four cases (Gen. 9.6, Exod. 12.16 (2×), I Sam. 25.7), the agent is not translated into Greek, probably because the functions of these Hebrew prepositions are so varied that the infrequent use to mark the agent was not recognized by the translators. Of the other two examples, one with בְּ becomes ὑπό (Deut. 33.29), and one with לְ becomes a dative of agent with a perfect (Gen. 31.15).

weakened with respect to its vocalic structure and endings, while the second noun, which is dependent on the first noun, retains its stress and endings. Additionally, the entire phrase is either definite or indefinite, and, if definite, only has the definite article in front of the second noun. Most commonly, the construct chain is translated into English by using the preposition "of" to connect the two nouns.

Contrast example (16), in which the Hebrew words for "the words" and "the man" are given in their independent forms, and (17), which shows how "the words of the man" would appear in a construct chain:

(16) had-dəḇārîm   hā-ʔîš
      the-words   the-man
(17) diḇrê   hā-ʔîš
      (the.)words.of the-man

Such a construction may be rendered into the LXX with the preposition ὑπό rather than a genitive when the first noun is translated with a Greek participle:

(18) *Gen.* 45.21 עַל־פִּי פַרְעֹה
      ʕal-pî   p̄arʕōh
      according.to-(the.)mouth.of   Pharaoh
LXX: κατὰ τὰ εἰρημένα ὑπὸ Φαραω

Hebrew can also mark the genitival relationship with suffixed possessive pronouns, and, when translated as PACs in the Greek, these behave like the construct chains:

(19) *Num.* 4.31 מַשָּׂאָם
      maśśāʔ-ām
      carrying-their (= the objects carried by them)
LXX: τῶν αἰρομένων ὑπ' αὐτῶν

The other two Hebrew constructions that may be turned into PACs in Greek are more familiar to the classicist. First is the use of an intransitive verb with מִן (*min-*) "from."

(20) *Lev.* 26.43 וְהָאָרֶץ תֵּעָזֵב מֵהֶם
      wə-hā-ʔāreṣ   tēʕāzēḇ   mē-hem
      and-the-land   was.left   from-them
LXX: καὶ ἡ γῆ ἐγκαταλειφθήσεται ὑπ' (Bᶜ ἀπ') αὐτῶν

Second is the transformation of an active clause in the Hebrew into a passive clause in the Greek:

(21) *Exod.* 5.14   אֲשֶׁר־שָׂמוּ עָלֵהֶם נֹגְשֵׂי פַּרְעֹה

              ʔăšer-śāmû   *ʕălēhem*

              which-placed.3.M.PL.   over.them

              nōḡəśê   *parʕōh*

              (the.)taskmasters.of   Pharaoh

     LXX: οἱ κατασταθέντες ἐπ' αὐτοὺς ὑπὸ τῶν
              ἐπιστατῶν τοῦ Φαραω

Only seldom did the translators of the LXX introduce a passive construction into the Greek in any of these three circumstances. A comparison of the frequency of ὑπό$^{+G}$ in the translated books of the LXX with that in those books of the LXX that were originally written in Greek (2, 3, 4 Maccabees, Wisdom of Solomon) illustrates this point:

Book	no.[a] of ὑπό$^{+G}$	Pages of LXX text	ὑπό$^{+G}$ per page
2 Maccabees	44	39	1.13
3 Maccabees	9	17	0.53
Wisdom	16	32	0.50
4 Maccabees	13	28	0.46
Pentateuch	15	354	0.04
Psalms	2	163	0.01

[a] These figures also include a few instances where ὑπό$^{+G}$ marks cause with a transitive verb.

The preposition ὑπό$^{+G}$, then, is rare in those books of the LXX that have been translated from Hebrew, but it is still more common as an agent marker than ἀπό. In Rahlfs' edition of the Pentateuch, the PACs with ὑπό and ἀπό number as follows:[15]

---

[15] The central column lists instances where one preposition is printed in the text, while the other is listed in the apparatus criticus. In three cases (*Lev.* 10.6, 20.16, 20.43), Rahlfs prints ὑπό, in one, ἀπό (*Deut.* 3.11). The variant reading ἀπό (Gfk) for *Lev.* 10.6 does not come from Rahlfs, but from Johannessohn's study of LXX prepositions (1925: 175).

Preposition	ὑπό	ὑπό/ἀπό	ἀπό
Number of PACs	12	4	7
Hebrew construction	7× const. chain 3× poss. pron. 1× בְּ 1× active verb	2× מִן 2× active verb	6× מִן or compound of מִן 1× active verb

Two facts stand out. First, ὑπό is more common than ἀπό. Second, it is exclusively preferred to ἀπό when the construct chain is translated with a passive construction in Greek. Besides (18) above, other examples occur at *Gen.* 26.29, 45.27, *Exod.* 16.3, *Num.* 26.64, *Deut.* 21.23, 33.12. As in (19), a suffixed possessive pronoun is rendered into Greek with ὑπό at *Num.* 4.32 and *Deut.* 4.21. The latter is particularly interesting, as a Hebrew phrase has been translated literally, thus obscuring its idiomatic meaning. The Hebrew expression עַל־דְּבַר (ʿal-dᵊḇar), while literally meaning "because of the word of," has the weakened idiomatic sense "because of, for the sake of."[16] The Greek, however, translates with the passive participle of λέγω:

(22) *Deut.* 4.21   עַל־דִּבְרֵיכֶם
        ʿal-diḇrê-ḵem
        because.of-words-your.M.PL. *or* for-sakes-your.M.PL.
LXX: περὶ τῶν λεγομένων ὑφ᾽ ὑμῶν
NRSV: "because of you"

Considering the context of the line – Moses is explaining to the Israelites why the Lord is angry with him – the broader translation of the NRSV seems closer to the Hebrew than the literal rendering of the LXX. That ὑπό was chosen to express the agent in neutral passages involving suffixed pronouns and the construct chain suggests that it was the default preposition. Further support for this

---

[16] The word דָּבָר (dāḇār) can mean either "word" or "matter, affair." See BDB *s.v.* IV, especially IV.8. The expression here occurs with the plural rather than singular of דָּבָר, an unusual usage, found elsewhere only at *Jer.* 14.1. In this latter passage, the meaning cannot be literal ("the words of") as the noun found after דְּבָר is חַבַּצָּרֹת (habbaṣṣārôt "destitutions").

assertion is provided by comparison with the contexts in which ἀπό was used.

The preposition ἀπό is used to express the agent in seven clear instances in the Pentateuch. In all cases but one, the Hebrew construction being translated involves the preposition מִן (*min-*) or a compound thereof, such as מִפְּנֵי (*mippǝnê*), literally "from the face of." In the remaining instance of agentive ἀπό, the Greek has rewritten an active construction as a passive, but the verb involved is the anomalous ὑπολείπω, which might have construed with ἀπό even in literature uninfluenced by Hebrew. The examples are as follows:

- ἀπό translates מִן (*min-*)

(23) *Gen.* 47.18

לֹא־נְכַחֵד מֵאֲדֹנִי כִּי אִם־תַּם הַכֶּסֶף

lōʔ-nǝkaḥēd	*mē-ʔăḏōn-î*	
not-we.can.hide	from-lord-my	
kî	*ʔim-tam*	*hak-kesēp*
that	PARTICLE-is.spent	the-money

LXX: μήποτε ἐκτριβῶμεν ἀπὸ τοῦ κυρίου ἡμῶν· εἰ γὰρ ἐκλέλοιπεν τὸ ἀργύριον

NRSV: "We cannot hide from my lord that our money is all spent"

Clearly, the LXX does a poor job of expressing the Hebrew. The pleonastic אִם (*ʔim*), for instance, has been translated literally as εἰ, although there is no conditional sense in the Hebrew.[17] As for the first clause, whatever the Greek was intended to mean, it cannot be construed to be equivalent to the Hebrew, but is presumably a hortatory subjunctive: "Let us not be destroyed utterly by our lord." The origin of this erroneous translation must be the double sense of the verbal root כחד (*kḥd*). According to BDB, while the Niphil stem can mean "be effaced, destroyed," it is the Piel stem of the verb, meaning "hide, conceal," that is found here. In light of the fact that the translation of the passage is both muddled and erroneously literal at the same time, it is not surprising that ἀπό is used here to translate מִן, thereby assuming the role of an agent marker.

---

[17] For pleonastic אִם, see BDB *s.v.* כִּי אִם 2b.

(24) *Lev.* 21.7　וְאִשָּׁה גְּרוּשָׁה מֵאִישָׁהּ

        wə-ʔiššāh   gərûšāh   mē-ʔîš-āh

        and-woman   divorced   from-husband-her

   LXX: γυναῖκα ἐκβεβλημένην ἀπὸ ἀνδρὸς αὐτῆς

   NRSV: "a woman divorced from her husband"

Like the Greek ἐκβάλλω, the Hebrew root גרשׁ (*grš*) literally means "drive, cast out." Hence the use of an ablatival preposition to express the agent is natural in Hebrew, Greek, and English as well.

- ἀπό translates מִפְּנֵי (*mippənê*)

While this preposition literally means "from the face of," "from before," it is its figurative sense "because of" (BDB פנה II.6.c) that becomes agentive when translated with ἀπό in Greek:

(25) *Gen.* 6.13　כִּי־מָלְאָה הָאָרֶץ חָמָס מִפְּנֵיהֶם

        kî-māləʔāh   hā-ʔāreṣ   ħāmās

        for-is.filled   the-earth   (with.)violence

        mippənê-hem

        because.of-them.MASC

   LXX: ἐπλήσθη ἡ γῆ ἀδικίας ἀπ' αὐτῶν

   NRSV: "for the earth is filled with violence because of them"

In such an example, it cannot be determined whether ἀπό has truly agentive force. While the NRSV does not translate the Hebrew preposition as an agent marker, the Greek ἀπό certainly had the potential to be interpreted as one, especially considering later constructions like (12) above.

(26) *Exod.* 8.20　וּבְכָל־אֶרֶץ מִצְרַיִם תִּשָּׁחֵת הָאָרֶץ מִפְּנֵי הֶעָרֹב

        û-bə-kol-ʔereṣ   miṣrayim   tiššāħēt

        and-in-entire-land Egypt   was.ruined

        hā-ʔāreṣ   mippənê   he-ʕārōb

        the-land   because.of   the-swarm

   LXX: καὶ ἐξωλεθρεύθη ἡ γῆ ἀπὸ τῆς κυνομυίης

   NRSV: (*Exod.* 8.24) "in all Egypt the land was ruined because of the flies"

As in the previous example, an expression of cause has been translated with ἀπό in the Greek. In this case, there is a better argument against an agentive reading, inasmuch as God is seen as the ultimate agent of the destruction, with the flies merely as his instrument, in contrast to (25), in which the wicked people are clearly the authors of the injustice that fills the world. Still, while the flies may be caused in turn by God, they themselves are responsible for the destruction, and occur as sentence subjects earlier in *Exod.* 8.20 (παρεγένετο ἡ κυνόμυια πλῆθος εἰς τοὺς οἴκους Φαραω) and in 8.25 (ἀπελεύσεται ἡ κυνόμυια ἀπὸ σοῦ). Once again, then, a causal expression cannot be distinguished from an agentive one.

• ἀπό translates מִלִּפְנֵי (*millip̄nê*)

Like the previous compound preposition, this preposition also means "from the face of," "from before." While it too can have the figurative sense "because of" (BDB פָּנֶה II.5.b), it has in the following example the literal sense, despite its occurrence with the same verb as in (26), ἐξολεθρεύω:

(27) *Lev.* 22.3   וְנִכְרְתָה הַנֶּפֶשׁ הַהִוא מִלְּפָנַי

       wə-niḵrəṯāh   *han-nep̄eš*   *ha-hî?*

       and-shall.be.cut.off   the-person   the-that

       milləp̄ān-ay

       from-me

    LXX: ἐξολεθρευθήσεται ἡ ψυχὴ ἐκείνη ἀπ' ἐμοῦ

    NRSV: "that person shall be cut off from my presence"

In (26), the Hebrew preposition had lost its spatial significance: Egypt was not ruined apart from the flies, but because of them. Here, however, the verb translated by ἐξολεθρεύω is כרת (*krt*), "cut (off)," and the preposition מִלְּפְנֵי denotes separation. The Greek ἀπό, however, is better interpreted as an agent marker than as a spatial preposition because the verb ἐξολεθρεύω does not convey the sense of division that its Hebrew counterpart does.

• ἀπό translates מֵאֵת (*mēʔēt*)

Yet another compound preposition of מִן, מֵאֵת means "from proximity with," and BDB (II.אֵ 4) compares it to French *de chez* and Greek παρά[+G]. In (28), however, it is translated by ἀπό:

(28) *Num.* 3.9   נְתוּנִים נְתוּנִים הֵמָּה לוֹ מֵאֵת בְּנֵי יִשְׂרָאֵל

nəṯûnîm	nəṯûnîm	hēmmāh	lô
given	given	they	to.him
mē-ʔēṯ	bənê	yiśrāʔēl	
from-among	(the.)sons.of	Israel	

LXX: δόμα δεδομένοι οὗτοί μοί εἰσιν ἀπὸ τῶν υἱῶν Ἰσραηλ

NRSV: "they are unreservedly given to him from among the Israelites"

It is curious that ἀπό, not παρά⁺ᴳ, translates מֵאֵת here. BDB's gloss of this preposition by παρά⁺ᴳ is supported by the fact that of the nine instances of מֵאֵת cited under the same heading as that where (28) is found, it is translated in the LXX six times with παρά⁺ᴳ, once with ἐνώπιον, and only once with ἀπό.[18] Possibly, the use of ἀπό here has been influenced by the comparative rarity of παρά⁺ᴳ in the LXX. In *Numbers*, for instance, it occurs only twenty-eight times, compared to 204 instances of ἀπό. The latter preposition was the obvious translation for מִן and its compounds and so might have been used mechanically even when παρά⁺ᴳ would have provided a more nuanced translation.

• active rewritten as passive with ἀπό expressing the agent

In only one of the PACs with ἀπό does the preposition unambiguously translate something other than an ablatival preposition:

(29) *Exod.* 10.15   אֲשֶׁר הוֹתִיר הַבָּרָד

ʔăšer	hôṯîr	hab-bārāḏ
which	left.over	the-hail

LXX: ὃς ὑπελείφθη ἀπὸ τῆς χαλάζης

NRSV: "that the hail had left"

As ἀπό is chosen over ὑπό despite the absence of מִן in the Hebrew, it is possible that the use of ἀπό had spilled over from such cases as (23) to (28) and contaminated a passage where ὑπό would be expected in classical Greek. Johannessohn notes, however, that variation between ἀπό and ὑπό is particularly common

---

[18] In the ninth passage, the translation rewords the original such that the object of מאת becomes the subject of the sentence.

with λείπομαι and its compounds (1925: 174–5, 282). This example should therefore be compared to passages (2) to (4) above, with the presence of ἀπό attributed to the ablatival semantics of the verb. By way of contrast, consider (21), in which an originally active verb without the skewed semantics of "leaving behind" is translated by κατασταθέντες with ὑπό.

In all these instances where ἀπό is used to express the agent, there is always some factor that keeps the environment from being that of an unmarked PAC. Usually the expression is only borderline agentive, with ἀπό translating a Hebrew preposition that was more ablatival or causal in sense, as can be seen from the NRSV translations. By comparison, the constructions with ὑπό are much more neutral, as seen from its use in the majority of the PACs that do not represent the Hebrew preposition מִן. In conclusion, while the LXX does have a greater frequency of PACs with ἀπό than has been seen so far, ἀπό is far from being the unmarked agent expression. Rather, it is generally restricted to conditions under which an ablatival preposition was also employed in Hebrew.

The New Testament

Like the LXX, the New Testament (NT) has a greater frequency of PACs with ἀπό than do the classical Greek texts. The picture is complicated by the great amount of variation in the manuscripts. Still, it can be seen that ὑπό continued to predominate over ἀπό. What, then, accounts for the sporadic instances of ἀπό? Were they motivated by certain linguistic conditions, or are they truly random, representing the occasional incursion of a vernacular ἀπό into a text that primarily used the older, written ὑπό as its agent marker? From the data below, it will be seen that the majority of the PACs with ἀπό do indeed fall into two discrete categories, although there are some instances which do not appear to be linguistically motivated. Nevertheless, in most cases, either the agent is not a typical animate agent marker, or the verb is ablatival in sense, often compounded with the prefix ἀπο-.

From an examination of the bare statistics, it is clear that ὑπό is considerably more frequent than ἀπό as an agent marker, though

Luke, Acts, and Romans do have a significant number of PACs with ἀπό.[19]

	ὑπό	variant readings	ἀπό
Matthew	21	1	2
Mark	7	1	–
John	1	–	–
Luke	19	6	4
Acts	31	6	2
Romans	2	3	–
1 Corinthians	12	–	–

To see whether there is some common property shared by the instances of ἀπό, consider first the eight instances where only ἀπό is found in the early manuscripts, as these provide the soundest evidence. In four cases, the agent is inanimate; in the other four, the verb is a compound verb with the prefix ἀπο-.

First, the four times that ἀπό is unanimously attested as the agent marker, the agent is inanimate:

(30) *Mt.* 11.19   καὶ ἐδικαιώθη ἡ σοφία ἀπὸ τῶν ἔργων αὐτῆς
"and wisdom is shown to be right by her works"

(31) *Mt.* 28.4   ἀπὸ δὲ τοῦ φόβου αὐτοῦ ἐσείσθησαν οἱ τηροῦντες
"and those who watched were shaken by fear of him"

This use of ἀπό to denote the emotion responsible for an event was foreign to classical Greek, which used ὑπό (e.g. X. *Cyn.* 6.25 κατακλίνεται γὰρ ἐν μικρῷ τὸ θηρίον καὶ οὐκ ἀνίσταται ὑπὸ κόπου καὶ φόβου, Pl. *Ion* 535c).

---

[19] There exist many more manuscripts of the NT than of the canonical authors of classical Greece. To avoid needless confusion in trying to separate readings from earlier and later manuscripts, I will limit the scope of this section to the early papyri fragments and the oldest manuscripts, written in uncial script in the fourth and fifth centuries AD (ℵABCD). For a survey of the NT textual tradition, see Metzger 1992. The text used initially for all seven books studied was the Nestle–Aland edition. I subsequently checked for additional variants using Legg 1935 and 1940 for Mark and Matthew, the American and British Committees of the International Greek New Testament Project's edition of Luke, Elliott–Parker 1995 for John, and Nestle 1896 for the readings of D in Acts.

(32) *Lk.* 6.18 καὶ οἱ ἐνοχλούμενοι ἀπὸ πνευμάτων ἀκαθάρτων
ἐθεραπεύοντο
"and those disturbed by unclean spirits were cured"

While the agent in (32) could be considered animate, Hult has
noted that the agentive expressions in Palladius and Callinicus
found with demons and spirits align more closely with those for
inanimate objects than those for humans.[20]

(33) *Lk.* 7.35 καὶ ἐδικαιώθη ἡ σοφία ἀπὸ πάντων τῶν τέκνων αὐτῆς
"and wisdom is shown to be right by all her children"

While children are of course animate, a comparison with the parallel passage (30) and the weakly transitive nature of δικαιόω suggests that the τέκνα are not strongly agentive.

The other four times that ἀπό is unanimously attested as the
agent marker, the verb in the construction begins with the prefix
ἀπο-:

(34) *Acts* 2.22 ἄνδρα ἀποδεδειγμένον ἀπὸ τοῦ θεοῦ εἰς ὑμᾶς
"a man shown to you by God"
(35) *Acts* 15.33 ἀπελύθησαν μετ᾽ εἰρήνης ἀπὸ τῶν ἀδελφῶν πρὸς
τοὺς ἀποστείλαντας αὐτούς
"and they were sent off in peace by their brothers to
those who had sent them"
(36) *Lk.* 16.18 ὁ ἀπολελυμένην ἀπὸ ἀνδρὸς γαμῶν
"one who marries a woman divorced by her husband"
(37) *Lk.* 17.25 πρῶτον δὲ δεῖ αὐτὸν πολλὰ παθεῖν καὶ
ἀποδοκιμασθῆναι ἀπὸ τῆς γενεᾶς ταύτης
"but first he must suffer much and be rejected by this
generation"

The ablatival force of both prefix and preposition can be seen
in all these examples. It is quite clear in both (34) and (35), in
which the destination or target of the action is stated directly after
the phrase with ἀπό. Regarding (36), the similarity in meaning

---

[20] These later authors are different, however, in that the expression found with inanimate
agents is ὑπό, not ἀπό, while παρά is found more frequently with animate agents.

between "divorced by" and "divorced from" has already been mentioned in the discussion of example (24). In (37), the ablatival force of the verb "rejected" is more figurative than literal, but can be compared to (27).

As with the passages where ἀπό is unanimously attested, those in which both ἀπό and ὑπό are variants can, for the most part, be sorted into examples where the agent is inanimate or the verb is ablatival. In the following passages, it is not particularly important which reading has better manuscript support, as the mistakes are potentially an even better indication of changes in the language than the correct readings are.

The three times that ὑπό and ἀπό are both attested as variant readings in a PAC, the agent in question is inanimate:

(38) *Mt.* 8.24 ὥστε τὸ πλοῖον καλύπτεσθαι ὑπό (ἀπὸ B²) τῶν κυμάτων
"that the ship was covered up by the waves"

(39) *Acts* 5.16 ὀχλουμένους ὑπό (ἀπὸ D) πνευμάτων ἀκαθάρτων
"disturbed by unclean spirits"

In both of these passages, Nestle–Aland prints ὑπό. In light of (32), the decision to print ὑπό in (39) must reflect the general unreliability of manuscript D.

(40) *Lk.* 4.2 πειραζόμενος ὑπό (אABD) / ἀπό (p⁴ (3C)) τοῦ διαβόλου
"tempted by the devil"

As with (32) and (39), the demonic agent in this passage is perhaps construed with ἀπό in one early papyrus because it is seen as being somewhat removed from the prototypical human agent.

Another four PACs in which both ὑπό and ἀπό are attested as variant readings are constructions in which the verb begins with the prefix ἀπο-:

(41) *Mk.* 8.31 δεῖ τὸν υἱὸν τοῦ ἀνθρώπου πολλὰ παθεῖν καὶ ἀποδοκιμασθῆναι ὑπό (ἀπὸ A) τῶν πρεσβυτέρων καὶ τῶν ἀρχιερέων καὶ τῶν γραμματέων

"the Son of Man must suffer much and be rejected by
the elders and the chief priests and the scribes"

(42) *Lk.* 9.22   δεῖ τὸν υἱὸν τοῦ ἀνθρώπου πολλὰ παθεῖν καὶ
ἀποδοκιμασθῆναι ἀπὸ (ὑπὸ D) τῶν πρεσβυτέρων καὶ
ἀρχιερέων καὶ γραμματέων
"the Son of Man must suffer much and be rejected by
the elders and the chief priests and the scribes"

In two parallel passages similar to (37), there is fluctuation between
ὑπό and ἀπό. The unanimous reading of ἀπό in that passage suggests that ἀπό is correct at least in (42), as both passages are in
Luke and the reading ὑπό in (42) occurs only in D. It could well
be that Mark has used ὑπό, but Luke ἀπό, considering that agentive ἀπό is generally found more frequently in Luke-Acts than in
Mark.

(43) *Lk.* 1.26   ἀπεστάλη ὁ ἄγγελος Γαβριὴλ ὑπὸ (ACD) / ἀπὸ (אB)
τοῦ θεοῦ εἰς πόλιν τῆς Γαλιλαίας
"the angel Gabriel was sent by God to a city in Galilee"

As in (34) and (35), the occurrence of a local phrase indicating
the destination of the movement would have further motivated the
choice of ἀπό.

(44) *Acts* 10.17   οἱ ἄνδρες οἱ ἀπεσταλμένοι ὑπὸ (ἀπὸ D) τοῦ
Κορνηλίου
"the men sent by Cornelius"

Considering (42) and (44), one must conclude that manuscript D
does not deviate consistently in favor of either ἀπό or ὑπό.

Similar to these constructions with verbs with the ἀπο- prefix
are five PACs that involve other ablatival verbs:

(45) *Lk.* 8.29   ἠλαύνετο ὑπὸ (ἀπὸ B) τοῦ δαιμονίου εἰς τὰς ἐρήμους
"he was driven by the demon into the wilderness"
(46) *Lk.* 10.22   πάντα μοι παρεδόθη ὑπὸ (ἀπὸ D) τοῦ πατρός μου
"everything has been handed over to me by my
father"

244

(47) *Acts* 15.40   παραδοθεὶς τῇ χάριτι τοῦ κυρίου ὑπὸ (ἀπὸ D) τῶν
ἀδελφῶν
"given over by the brothers to the grace of the
Lord"

(48) *Rom.* 15.15   διὰ τὴν χάριν τὴν δοθεῖσάν μοι ὑπὸ (**p**⁴⁶**א**²ACD) /
ἀπὸ (**א***B) τοῦ θεοῦ
"because of the grace given to me by God"

(49) *Rom.* 15.24   ἐλπίζω γὰρ διαπορευόμενος θεάσασθαι ὑμᾶς καὶ ὑφ᾽
(**א**AC) / ἀφ᾽ (**p**⁴⁶BD) ὑμῶν προπεμφθῆναι ἐκεῖ
"for I hope that, when I travel there, I will see you
and be sent forth by you"

In all Greek texts, verbs of giving and sending are those that were
most likely to have an agent expression with an ablatival preposition rather than ὑπό. As has been seen above, the destination of the
action is stated in (45) through (48), either as a local expression or
as an indirect object.

A final five cases do not fit readily into the two categories of
PACs with ἀπό set out above:

(50) *Lk.* 8.43   οὐκ ἴσχυσεν ὑπ᾽ (**א**C) / ἀπ᾽ (**p**⁷⁵AB) οὐδενὸς
θεραπευθῆναι
"she was not able to be cured by anyone"

(51) *Acts* 4.36   ὁ ἐπικληθεὶς Βαρναβᾶς ἀπὸ (ὑπὸ D) τῶν ἀποστόλων
"the one called Barnabas by the apostles"

(52) *Acts* 10.33   τὰ προστεταγμένα σοι ὑπὸ (**א***B) / ἀπὸ
(**p**⁴⁵**p**⁷⁴**א**²ACD) τοῦ κυρίου
"that which you have been ordered to say by the Lord"

(53) *Acts* 15.4   παρεδέχθησαν ὑπὸ (**p**⁷⁴**א**AD) / ἀπὸ (BC) τῆς
ἐκκλησίας
"they were received by the church"

(54) *Rom.* 13.1   οὐ γὰρ ἔστιν ἐξουσία εἰ μὴ ὑπὸ (ἀπὸ D*) θεοῦ, αἱ δὲ
οὖσαι ὑπὸ θεοῦ τεταγμέναι εἰσίν
"for authority does not exist unless it comes from *or* is
given by God, and those authorities that exist have
been set in place by God"

245

In (50), the presence of ἀπό may be due to contamination with a passage like (32), in which the preposition could be construed with the verb of healing ("to be cured of"), although such a reading would leave the participle lacking its natural complement. The collocation θεραπεύεσθαι ἀπό in the sense "be cured of" also occurs at *Lk.* 5.15 and 8.2; a similar passage at 6.18 has ἀπό with the verb ἰαθῆναι. It is possible that examples (51) and (52) represent an extension of the category of ablatival verbs that take ἀπό. Example (51) could be considered ablatival if the naming is conceived of as the punctual act of giving a name (cf. the NRSV translation: "to whom the apostles gave the name Barnabas"), and example (52) is not very different from (48) in this respect. Perhaps (53) could be included in the category of inanimate agents. Even in classical Greek, the construction of (54) would probably be better with ἀπό than with ὑπό, as the latter reading requires the verb to be understood in advance from the following clause.

In conclusion, the NT has a far greater number of PACs with ἀπό than any of the other texts examined in this study. However, they are still significantly fewer in number than those with ὑπό, and their occurrence is not random, but is on the whole limited to constructions involving verbs with ablatival semantics or agents that are not prototypically human. As such, they are not likely to represent the occasional random intrusion of a vernacular whose agent marker had switched wholesale from ὑπό to ἀπό, but rather a limited development under particular grammatical conditions. This use of ἀπό as an agent marker in the NT would have been encouraged by its presence in the LXX, where it also occurs in contexts conducive to an ablatival preposition owing to its use as a translation of מִן and its compounds.

From the New Testament through the fifth century AD

As Hult has already assembled statistics for agent expressions in authors of the fourth and fifth centuries AD, it will not be necessary to examine these in detail here. Nevertheless, I will briefly outline her data, which nearly unanimously point to the increasing use of παρά$^{+G}$ to mark the agent at the expense of ὑπό; during this time, PACs with ἀπό were extremely rare.

Before examining her fifth-century authors, Hult first provides an overview of PACs in the postclassical period (1990: 37–44). When she assesses the role of παρά$^{+G}$, she notes that its use had been extended beyond the classical parameters in the following authors: (4th century BC) Aristotle; (second century BC) Polybius; (first century BC) Diodorus; (second century AD) Lucian, Achilles Tatius; (third century AD) Philostratus; (fourth century AD) Libanius, Julian, Gregory Nazianzen, and Synesius (ὑπό preferred to παρά by only a 3:2 ratio) (1990: 38). In other texts, however, it remained comparable to classical usage: the LXX the NT, and Epictetus. In his article on classicism in the Church Fathers, Fabricius mentions that Basil and John Chrysostom (both fourth century AD) also used παρά$^{+G}$ with greater frequency than in classical texts; Basil preferred παρά to ὑπό by a ratio of over 3:1 (1967: 192 n. 17). As noted above (p. 228), the data are similar for the fifth-century authors Hult studies more closely: παρά to ὑπό ratios range from 1:4.5 and 1:2 for Theodoret and Eunapius, to near parity for Marinus, Mark the Deacon, and Callinicus, to an overwhelming 11:1 preference for παρά in Palladius. While παρά is thus well represented, ἀπό is considerably less frequent. The only text in which Hult says it is common is the NT, in which ὑπό is still more frequent, and ἀπό is limited to particular syntactic environments, as seen in the previous section. Furthermore, ἀπό does not occur in the Atticists or with any great frequency in Hult's fifth-century authors.

The standard interpretation of these data is that the use of παρά$^{+G}$ as an agent marker was considered an Atticism (Hult 1990: 38). Fabricius suggests that it was a reaction against strongly Attic πρός^{+G} on the one hand and vernacular ἀπό on the other. This view is open to criticism on two points: first, it is not explained why παρά, rather than ὑπό, should have been selected as the neutral Attic variant in the middle ground between πρός and ἀπό.[21]

---

[21] I am not convinced by Helbing's view that παρά as an agent marker in authors like Polybius or Diodorus was due to "[das] Streben, das alltägliche ὑπό zu verdrängen und Abwechslung hervorzurufen" (1904: 125). First, it does appear to have occurred primarily with verbs of giving, speaking, and believing: the three examples in Book 3 fall into these categories (44.5, 69.1, 103.5). Second, it is matched by a spread of παρά in the Ptolemaic papyri, in which I would be surprised to find *variatio gratia variationis* (Mayser 1934: 484–6).

Second, evidence that ἀπό was indeed the vernacular agent marker is scanty, being limited primarily to its use in the NT and eventual adoption by modern Greek in this function. As an alternative, I would propose that παρά was the vernacular agent marker at this period, while ἀπό was used only in marginal cases, much as in classical Greek. If παρά was the agent marker of the spoken language, then the concurrent use of ὑπό and παρά in the majority of the texts can be explained quite simply as the tension between older, literary ὑπό and contemporary, spoken παρά – instead of the more complicated traditional view that two older literary agent markers, ὑπό and παρά, were in competition with each other in written texts, while a third preposition, ἀπό, was undermining these other two prepositions from below, a usage for which evidence is primarily limited to the Semitic-influenced LXX and NT as well as the final outcome in modern Greek. This position will be strengthened below by the introduction of evidence from the papyri and later Greek vernacular texts.

The sixth century

To determine what prepositions were used to mark the agent in the sixth century, I examined the works of Malalas and Moschus. Malalas (*c.* 491–578) wrote the *Chronographia*, a chronicle of the entire history of the world, while Moschus (*c.* 550–619), in the *Spiritual Meadow*, presented a collection of anecdotes about the lives of monks.[22] In both works, the predominant marker of the agent is the preposition ὑπό, but there was also much variation besides, with παρά, ἀπό, and ἐκ all found as well. It is possible to glimpse hints of a pattern whereby the semantics of the verb affected the preposition that was used, but the main impression given by the data is one of confusion.

Beginning with Malalas, one may first note that PACs are quite frequent in the *Chronographia*: in Books 10 to 12 (sixty-one pages

---

[22] Initially, I read both authors in Migne's edition. I have since checked his readings of prepositions against Thurn's edition of Malalas (of seventy-six prepositions, only one was different), and have learned by E-mail from P. Pattenden that there is at least one place in Moschus where Migne printed ἀπό that ὑπό should be read.

in Migne's edition), there are seventy-six PACs. The distribution is as follows:

ὑπό	παρά	ἀπό	ἐκ	+D	παρά⁺ᴰ	διά⁺ᴳ	διά⁺ᴬ
51	12	7	2	I	I	I	I

To gain a clear picture of what verbs construed with what prepositions, I shall list the verbs that occur with παρά⁺ᴳ or ἀπό, giving both their frequency with these prepositions, as well as their frequency with ὑπό if they construe with both prepositions:

Verb	παρά⁺ᴳ	ὑπό	ἀπό
κτίζω	3	I I	–
ἐάω	2	I	–
κελεύω	2	–	–
παρακαλέω	2	I	–
παρέχω	I	–	–
πέμπω	I	–	–
συγγράφω	I	–	–
ἀγαπάω	–	I	I
προβάλλω	–	I	I
λέγω	–	–	I
λοιδορέω	–	–	I
ἐπηρεάζω	–	–	I
καταστρέφω	–	–	I
προχειρίζομαι	–	–	I

The presence of the prefix παρα- cannot be assumed to favor the use of παρά as an agent marker, for not only can παρακαλέω take ὑπό, but παραδίδωμι and παραλαμβάνω do as well. About the only conclusion that can be drawn is that verbs of killing consistently construe with ὑπό. None of the verbs in the chart above belong to this semantic field, while the following verbs are found with ὑπό marking the agent: σφάζω (six times), σφαγιάζω, φονεύω (once each). As languages typically treat killing as a highly transitive action, it may be that these verbs were most prone to maintain ὑπό as an agent marker when other prepositions had begun to gain ground in other contexts.[23] The nature of the agent may also have played some role in determining which preposition was used:

Agent	παρά	ὑπό
αὐτοῦ or αὐτῶν	7	4
proper name	3	23

Even though there are fifty-one PACs with ὑπό and only twelve with παρά, the latter preposition is still the more common agent marker when the agent is αὐτοῦ or αὐτῶν. When the agent is a proper name, on the other hand, ὑπό is preferred by a greater ratio than would be expected from its overall numerical predominance. It may be that παρά was sufficient to mark αὐτοῦ as an agent because, as a pronoun, αὐτοῦ is relatively high in the animacy hierarchy; one may compare the use of παρά in Plato to mark pronominal agents in PACs with δίδωμι. As for ἀπό, its agents tend to be common nouns, like βουλή or στρατιῶται. As these are not as high in the animacy hierarchy, many of these nouns might well have a semantic role closer to that of source than that of agent. In this, they resemble some of examples from Herodotus cited in Chapter 4, especially (60) and, to a lesser extent, (62) and (63). One may also compare the use of ἀπό with non-human agents in the NT, e.g. (30) to (33).

Similarly, the data in Moschus do not suggest any obvious conditions under which one preposition was preferred to another, and

---

[23] Bakker makes this claim for Greek in particular (1994: 40–1). It is also mentioned in Hopper and Thompson's article on transitivity (1980: 270).

accounting for the differences is harder than for Malalas as a comparable amount of text, the first sixty pages in Migne's edition, only contains twenty-six PACs:

ὑπό	ἐκ	παρά	-θεν	ἀπό	+D
17	3	2	2	1	1

The three examples with ἐκ might be grouped together insofar as the verbs all involve harm of some sort. Such an interpretation is rather uncertain, however, especially considering that the latter two examples may be better regarded as instrumental than agentive in any case:

(55) Mosch. *prat.* 40   οὐδὲν βλάπτεται ὁ ἀββᾶς Κοσμᾶς ἐκ τοῦ
    (M. 2893b)   αἱρετικοῦ
                   "Abbot Cosmas is not harmed at all by the heretic"

(56) Mosch. *prat.* 107 ὡς ἐκ τούτου ὀγκωθῆναι αὐτοῦ τὸν πόδα
    (M. 2965d)   "as his foot was swollen by this [splinter]"

(57) *ibid.*   τὸν πεπληγμένον πόδα ἐκ τοῦ ἐμπαγέντος
                  αὐτῷ σκώλοπος
                  "the foot that was afflicted by the splinter fixed in it"

As for the two examples with παρά, one PAC is clearly ablatival; the other possibly is as well:

(58) Mosch. *prat.* 29 τὴν σταλεῖσαν αὐτῷ παρὰ τοῦ αἱρετικοῦ
    (M. 2877a)   μερίδα
                  "the piece sent to him by the heretic"

(59) Mosch. *prat.* 24 ἐκ τοῦ ἐπιφερομένου παρ᾽ αὐτοῦ ὕδατος
    (M. 2869c)   "from the water brought by him"

The two examples with -θεν are both construed with θεόθεν (ἐμπνευσθείς and κινηθείς). The sole PAC with ἀπό is ablatival:

(60) Mosch. *prat.* 72   καβαλλάριος πεμφθεὶς ἀπὸ τοῦ
    (M. 2925b)   Αὐγουσταλίου
                    "a knight sent by the prefect"

In conclusion, the data from these two sixth-century authors are not particularly informative. It does appear as if ὑπό was restricted to the literary language at this point; otherwise, it would be hard to account for all the instances of agentive παρά and ἀπό that occur. But, on the basis of these texts alone, one cannot satisfactorily distinguish between the usage of these latter two prepositions. For Moschus, the data are simply too limited, although it may be revealing that the only PAC with ἀπό is strongly ablatival (60). With Malalas, however, the picture is simply confused. Fortunately, enough papyri have survived from this period that it is possible to use them as an additional source of data.

Papyri

Because of the pervasive influence of classical Greek models on later literary Greek, it is difficult to determine the extent to which the texts just discussed reflect the expression of the agent in the spoken language: certainly the presence of an archaic form like θεόθεν (which does not occur in the NT) provides ample warning against assuming that even Moschus' relatively informal diction can be understood as straightforward vernacular Greek. Fortunately, the papyri preserved in Egypt do provide some record of a register unlikely to have been as influenced by Attic Greek. In order to see what light these documents shed on the expression of the agent, I have collected all the PACs with ὑπό, παρά, and ἀπό in the following editions of papyri: from Hunt and Edgar's Selected Papyri (henceforth HE), the Letters and Memoranda sections of the first volume, and the Codes and Regulations, and Edicts and Orders sections of the second; volumes one to three of P. Lond.; volumes I and II of BGU.[24] The figures collected suggest that παρά had replaced

[24] I used the PHI CD-ROM to search P. Lond. and BGU. It omits those papyri which also occur in Mitteis and Wilcken's *Grundzüge und Chrestomathie der Papyruskunde*. There is no overlap between the Hunt–Edgar PACs and the P. Lond. and BGU PACs, as the only PACs found in HE that were taken from the relevant volumes of P. Lond. and BGU were also in Mitteis–Wilcken, and thus not covered by the CD-ROM search.

ὑπό as the most common agent marker by the sixth century AD, while ἀπό is found only in marginal constructions.

First, I shall give the number of PACs found with ὑπό, παρά, and ἀπό in these volumes, sorted by century. The first figures are for the number of distinct papyri in which a given agent marker occurs; the second figures, in brackets, are for the total number of PACs with that agent marker found in those papyri. Because the language of the papyri can be rather repetitive, the first figures should give a more accurate picture of the status of the various agent markers.

Century	ὑπό	παρά[+G]	ἀπό
3C BC	3 (8)	2 (2)	–
2C BC	1 (1)	–	–
1C BC	–	–	–
1C AD	10 (14)	–	–
2C AD	37 (50)	3 (3)	–
3C AD	32 (57)	1 (1)	1 (1)
4C AD	5 (5)	–	–
5C AD	–	1 (2)[a]	–
6C AD	2 (2)	11 (24)	1 (1)
7C AD	–	7 (9)	–
8C AD	1 (4)	1 (4)	–

[a] These two PACs come from HE 166, which is dated to the fifth or sixth century AD.

The eight PACs with παρά that precede the sixth century AD all involve verbs that typically construe with an ablatival agent marker, namely ἀποστέλλω (HE I.166.3, I.166.6, II.203.42.19, II.216.7), δίδωμι (HE II.207.172), and διαγράφω in the sense "pay" (BGU I.102.2, P. Lond. II.318.6, 330.3):

(61) HE II.216.17   τοῖς ἡγεμόσιν τοῖς κατ᾽ ἐπιτροπείας παρ᾽ ἐμοῦ
    ἀπεσταλμένοις   (AD 222)
    "the governors sent by me as procurators"

The frequency of παρά as an agent marker increases greatly in the sixth century. At the same time, it starts to appear with verbs of a much wider semantic range. While most are still verbs of giving, selling, or paying, there is also a diverse group of verbs denoting different forms of communication. An idea of the variety of constructions found with παρά can be obtained by considering some examples.

First, as expected, παρά continues to be used with verbs of giving, selling, and paying:

(62) P. Lond. I.113.1.44–5   νομισμάτων δοθέντων ... παρά
                               Οὐαλεντίνου   (6C AD)
                               "money given by Valentinus"

(63) BGU I.3.r.19   τὰ ἀναλωθέντα παρὰ σοῦ   (AD 605)
                               "what was spent by you"

Other verbs of similar meaning found with παρά are διαπιπράσκω, δωρέω, καταβάλλω, παρέχω, πιπράσκω, πληρόω, προσφέρω, and ὑποτίθημι.

The verbs of communicating form a more disparate collection than the previous category, ranging from verbs of writing, decreeing, ordering, or entreating (γράφω, θεσπίζω, κελεύω, παρακαλέω, αἰτέω) to verbs of agreeing, confirming, reminding, or abusing (διομολογέω, προσκυρόω, ὑπομιμνήσκω, ἐπηρεάζω).

(64) HE II.218.53   τὰ παρ' ἡμῶν νῦν θεσπισθέντα   (AD 551)
                        "what has now been decreed by us"

(65) P. Lond. III.1007a.32   παρακληθεῖσαν αὐτὴν παρ' ἐμοῦ
                                            (AD 558)
                        "that woman, entreated by me"

(66) P. Lond. I.77.85   μαρτ<υρ>ῶ τῇ πράσει αἰτηθεὶς παρὰ
                        τοῦ θεμένου   (8C AD)
                        "I witness the sale as requested by the
                        depositor"

(67) P. Lond. III.1044.15   ἐπὶ τὴν νῦν προσκυρωθεῖσάν σοι παρ'
                                ἐμο(ῦ) δεσποτείαν   (6C AD)
                        "to the ownership that has now been
                        confirmed by me as yours"

(68) HE I.167.10 (sc. ἐγώ) ἐπηρεασθεὶς πάλιν παρὰ τῶν ἀπὸ
Τερύθεω[ς] (6C AD)
"abused again by those from Teruthis"

Yet another verb that occurs with παρά is κωλύω.

(69) P. Lond. III.1073.r.1 οἱ γραμματηφόροι γεωργοὶ λέγουσιν
κωλύεσθαι ἀκαίρως παρά τινων
γιτόνων (6C AD)
"the letter-bearing farmers say
that they are inappropriately
hindered by some of their
neighbors"

In contrast to the wide range of PACs found with παρά, the only
examples with ἀπό are quite marginal:

(70) HE I.149.12 περιεκλείσθημεν ἀπὸ τοῦ δοθέντος [τῷ
παι]δίῳ ὑπὸ τοῦ λαμπροτάτου ἡγεμόνος
κομεάτ[ου] (3C AD)
"we were hindered by the furlough given to the
child by the most illustrious prefect"

(71) P. Lond. II.391.16 πρὸς τὸ ἀπὸ τούτους διαιρεισθέντας κρατεῖν
ἑκάστους (6C AD?)
"with regard to each having control, divided
from these or by these (?)"

Regarding the first example, not only is the agent κομίατον
("furlough") inanimate, but there is also a more standard PAC with
ὑπό and a typical animate agent in the same sentence. As for (71),
the syntax is quite mangled, and it is not certain that it is even a
PAC at all.

Finally, it may be noted that ὑπό is only found six times as an
agent marker in papyri of the sixth century or later. Twice, the agent
is νόμοι, which accords well with Hult's observation that inanimate
agents tended still to be construed with ὑπό even in authors who
generally preferred παρά for animate agents:

(72) P. Lond. I.77.14[25]   ὑπὸ τῶν καλῶς καὶ εὐσεβῶς κειμένων νόμων
διηγορευμένα   (8C AD)
"declared by the well and piously established laws"

A third example occurs with the verb παγαρχέω, and the semantics of a verb of ruling seem to have favored the retention of a preposition denoting subjacency in the marking of the agent:[26]

(73) P. Lond. III.776.r.6   κώμης . . . παγαρχουμένης ὑπὸ τῆς
ὑμετέρα[ς ὑ]περφυίας   (AD 552)
"a village administered by your excellency"

The final three examples all come from the same papyrus and contain the following set phrase:

(74) P. Lond. I.77.18   τὴν καταλειφθησομένην ὑπ᾿ ἐμοῦ . . . ὑπόστασιν
(8C AD)
"the property left behind by me"

Clearly, the papyri show that the use of ὑπό to mark the agent had declined, while παρά, not ἀπό, had come to take its place.

The eighth to eleventh centuries

For the period stretching from the eighth to eleventh centuries, almost no evidence for vernacular Greek survives. One source is the collection of Protobulgarian inscriptions, dating to the ninth century.[27] These are not very useful for the present study, however, first because the rather simplistic syntax contains only one PAC, second because it is quite possible that the Greek of these inscriptions was affected by the language of the local Slavs. A second means of investigating what agent constructions were used is to see what variants were introduced into New Testament manuscripts of this period. Again, these are far from satisfactory, in this case

---

[25] See also P. Lond. I.113.2.r.18.
[26] Elsewhere in this papyrus (as well as in P. Lond. III.774 and 775) the phrase ὑπ᾿ ἐμέ is used to mean "under my charge," for which translation see P.Oxy. I.137.13.
[27] An edition of these inscriptions can be found in Beševliev 1963.

because it cannot be determined whether a reading has been erroneously introduced by contamination from the vernacular or from literary texts. All that can be said for certain is that both ἀπό and παρά occasionally entered the text as replacements for ὑπό. First, consider the single PAC found in the Protobulgarian inscriptions:

(75) 15.6–9   σὺν τῷ ἐκ θ(εο)ῦ δεδομένω αὐτῷ ἔθνει
"with the people given to him by God"

This PAC does not shed much light on agent marking at this time, as the use of ἐκ here is probably motivated by the phrase ὁ ἐκ θεοῦ ἄρχων, which occurs frequently in these inscriptions as a title of the Bulgarian rulers (Beševliev 1963: 74–7). This title is itself patterned on that of the Byzantine emperor, ὁ ἐκ θεοῦ βασιλεύς, which calls to mind the older usage of ἐκ with a divine agent. The only other noteworthy phenomenon is that ὑπό does occur once, with the accusative:

(76) 41.9   τὸν ὄντον ὑπὸ τ[ὸ]ν β[ασιλέαν
"those who are subject to the king"

Even at this late date, ὑπό was still present in a lower register, if perhaps only with the accusative in the sense "subject to."
    The data provided by the later manuscripts of the NT are equally inconclusive. According to the apparatus found in Legg 1935 and 1940 (for Matthew and Mark) and that of the American and British Committees of the International Greek New Testament Project (for Luke), there are seven PACs where ἀπό or παρά is read in a manuscript of these centuries, but not in any earlier manuscripts. In four cases (*Mt.* 16.21, 20.23, 27.12, *Lk.* 4.15), παρά is found; in three cases, with one instance of overlap, ἀπό is found (*Mt.* 20.23, 24.9, *Lk.* 2.29). If, on the one hand, one wishes to maintain the hypothesis that ἀπό had become the vernacular agent marker by this time, then one must explain the instances of παρά as contamination from literary texts. But it is hard to see how παρά could have become common enough in the written language to have had such influence unless it had been the agent marker of the spoken language at some point. On the other hand, if one assumes that

παρά was the preposition used in the spoken language at this time, the occasional instances of ἀπό can be explained as extensions of the earlier presence of ἀπό in the NT.[28] In short, while these data do not on their own indicate unambiguously how agents were marked in this period, they are nevertheless most easily explained by supposing that παρά preceded ἀπό in replacing ὑπό as the default agent marker.

The twelfth century

While evidence for vernacular Greek is scanty for the centuries just covered, the twelfth century does offer us two texts that are relatively representative of the language as it was spoken: the epic of Digenis Akritis and the poems of Ptochoprodromos.[29] Although classical models will inevitably have exercised some influence over the language of these works, there are several features which show clear modernization in comparison to the classical language, such as the reduction of μετά and εἰς to μέ and 'ς, and the expansion of νά-clauses to express what had earlier been the domain of the infinitive (Horrocks 1997: 264, 269). Because PACs are quite rare in both of these works, it is difficult to determine the conditions which favored one agent marker over another with certainty. What is clear, however, is that both ὑπό and παρά are relatively frequent as agent markers, while ἀπό is not found at all.

There are two major manuscripts of Digenis Akritis, both dating from the fifteenth century. One, the Escorial manuscript (E), is generally agreed to be more vernacular, the other, the Grottaferrata (G), of a higher register.[30] In all of E (sixty-nine pages in Jeffreys' edition), there is only one PAC, with παρά[+G]:

(77) Dig. Akr. E1565   παρὰ σαλῶν καὶ ἄτακτων ἀνθρώπων
                                        ἐδιδάχθην
                   "I was taught by mad and disorderly men"

---

[28] Admittedly, of the three additional occurrences of ἀπό, it is only in *Lk.* 2.29 that the conditions for ἀπό proposed above are met. (The agent is the inanimate πνευμάτων.)

[29] For an introduction to the language of these works, see Horrocks 1997: 261–71, Jeffreys 1998: xlix–lii.

[30] Jeffreys 1998: xiv.

PACs are more frequent in G; there are twenty in the first five books (seventy-five pages in Jeffreys' edition):

παρά⁺ᴳ	ὑπό	διά⁺ᴳ	διά⁺ᴬ	ἐκ	παρά⁺ᴬ
9	7	I	I	I	I

Of the four agent markers that only occur once each, the following points may be made. First, both instances of διά are with verbs of saving or rescuing:

(78) Dig. Akr. G3.65   οὗ πολλάκις ἐρρύσθητε δι᾽ ἐμὲ ἐκ κινδύνων
"where you were often saved by me from dangers"

(79) Dig. Akr. G5.214   τοῦ δι᾽ ἐμοῦ σωθέντος
"of the one who was saved by me"

Second, in the PAC with ἐκ, the agent is God. As ἐκ frequently marks divine agents in earlier Greek, its presence in this passage as well can be ascribed to the nature of the agent:

(80) Dig. Akr. G5.47   ἀλλ᾽ ἐπειδή, ὡς ἔοικεν, ἐκ Θεοῦ ὡδηγήθης
"but since, as it seems, you were guided by God"

As for the PAC with παρά⁺ᴬ, it is reminiscent of the earlier PACs with παρά⁺ᴰ, for the sense is strongly local:

(81) Dig. Akr. G2.81   ὅταν ἤθελες δοξασθῆν παρ᾽ ὅλην τὴν Συρίαν
"when you were about to be glorified by all Syria"

These minor prepositions aside, the PACs are fairly evenly split between παρά⁺ᴳ and ὑπό. The verbs found with each are:

259

παρά$^{+G}$	ὑπό
• ἀφαιρέω	• βιβρώσκω
• δείκνυμι	• γιγνώσκω
• δίδωμι (2×)	• γνωρίζω
• κατηγορέω	• δαπανάω
• κελεύω	• καλύπτω
• λέγω	• καταβάλλω
• τιμάω	• σφάζω
• φημίζω	

As with earlier authors, verbs of giving and speaking occur with παρά, while the one instance of a verb of killing is with ὑπό. Furthermore, both verbs of eating and knowing are also found with ὑπό. It therefore seems reasonable to see the semantics of the verb as having influenced which preposition is used to express the agent.

The preposition ἀπό does not occur in a true agent expression in either manuscript. Once, however, it is found with a verbal adjective in a context that approximates to a PAC:

(82) Dig. Akr. G2.56   βδελυκτοὶ δὲ γεγόναμεν ἀπὸ παντὸς
ἀνθρώπου
"and we have become loathed by every man"

Once more, it occurs with an inanimate object that might be regarded as an agent:

(83) Dig. Akr. G5.247   καὶ ἐμιάνθη ἡ ὁδὸς ἀπὸ τῆς ἀνομίας
"and the road was defiled by lawlessness"

In these two passages, one may detect faint echoes of passages from the LXX, examples (1) and (25) respectively. More frequently, ἀπό is used with emotions to denote cause:[31]

(84) Dig. Akr. G2.224   ἀναιρέσει ἑαυτὸν ἀπὸ παραπληξίας
"he will kill himself from madness"

---

[31] Additional examples are found at 3.272, 3.283, 4.837.

There is also one instance of ὑπό being used in this manner:

(85) Dig. Akr. G4.592   ὁ δέ γε παῖς ὑπὸ χαρᾶς κινηθεὶς καὶ ἀνδρείας
"but the son, moved by joy and courage"

The coexistence of passages like (84) and (85) renders it difficult to determine exactly what stage Greek had reached at this point. Nevertheless, because ἀπό is the preposition most commonly used to mark emotional cause, both in this poem and in the Ptochoprodromos poems, it was presumably the usual vernacular preposition for this function by this time, with ὑπό in (85) to be explained as influenced by classical usage. It is also likely that this regular use of ἀπό in a function that belonged to ὑπό in earlier Greek marks the beginning of its rise as the agent marker of modern Greek.

Like the Escorial manuscript of Digenis Akritis, the Ptochoprodromos poems have very few PACs. There are only three good examples, two with παρά⁺ᴳ, one with ἐκ:³²

(86) Ptoch. 4.352   ἀναίτιοι καὶ δίκαιοι παρὰ πολλῶν ὁρῶνται
"they are seen to be blameless and just by many"
(87) Ptoch. 4.628   ὑπνιάρης δὲ καλούμενος καὶ πάλιν παρ' ἐκείνων
"yet again called a heavy sleeper by them"
(88) Ptoch. 4.616   καὶ μεθυστὴς ἀδόμενος ἐκ πάντων καὶ οἰνοπότης
"and called in song a drunkard and an alcoholic by them all"

All three come from the fourth poem, and all three have the same syntactic structure, in that the patient is labeled as some predicate noun by the agent. As in Digenis Akritis, ἀπό is used to denote cause, but here it is found both with the genitive (2.14, 2.18, 2.71, 3.105, 3.222, 4.101, 4.231, 4.244, 4.393, 4.629, 4.630) and in the modern construction with the accusative (1.138, 1.259, 3.106, 4.299, 4.627). In one passage, its construction with an inanimate noun approaches that of a PAC, much as in (83):

³² I use Eideneier's numbering.

(89) Ptoch. 3.35 καθώσπερ τήκεται κηρὸς ἀπὸ πυρὸς προσώπου
"just as wax melts from the presence of fire"

Like ἀπό, the preposition ἐκ, found always with the genitive, could be used to express cause (2.18, 4.619, 4.623, 4.625, 4.631, 4.632). The absence of ὑπό from the Escorial manuscript of Digenis Akritis as well as its near absence from Ptochoprodromos – it occurs once at 4.10 with the accusative in the sense "fleeing to" – suggests that it had dropped out of the lowest register of speech by that point. Its presence in the Grottaferrata version of Digenis Akritis should therefore be understood as due to the influence of the classical language. The modern preposition ἀπό had still not established itself as the clear agent marker, but the beginning of this development can be seen. If any preposition can be regarded as the unmarked agent marker, it would be παρά, although even it is rare enough that it might be better to describe the passive of this stage of Greek as not having had any agent markers at all.

Conclusion

From the data presented in this chapter, it is clear that we cannot assume that the classical Greek agent expression with ὑπό simply gave way to the modern Greek expression with ἀπό. Instead, there was an intermediate period during which παρά was the predominant agent marker. The development may be outlined as follows:

- Koine: ὑπό was the most common agent marker; παρά was used with ablatival verbs like πέμπω.
- Septuagint: ὑπό was the most common agent marker; ἀπό was used to translate Hebrew expressions involving ablatival prepositions.
- New Testament: ὑπό was the most common agent marker; ἀπό was sometimes used when the verb was ablatival (especially when compounded with ἀπο-) or when the agent was inanimate; this use of ἀπό would have been prompted at least in part by its presence as a marginal agent marker in the LXX.
- fourth through seventh centuries: According to the data from papyri, ὑπό was the most common agent marker in the fourth

century, παρά in the sixth and seventh centuries; ἀπό is very rare, suggesting that its use in literary Greek of the period should be attributed to the influence of Judeo-Christian literature. Data assembled by Hult from fourth- and fifth-century texts show that παρά had gained ground as an agentive preposition; they do not provide any evidence that ἀπό had become a prominent agent marker. Sixth-century data from Malalas and Moschus show that both ἀπό and παρά were found as agent markers, though neither was as common as ὑπό. The most economical explanation is that ὑπό was seen as the correct preposition to use for literary Greek, that ἀπό shows the influence of biblical language, and that παρά was the preposition used in vernacular Greek.

- eighth through eleventh centuries: Hardly any vernacular Greek of the period survives; both παρά and ἀπό are occasionally introduced by copyists into the manuscripts of the NT that date from this period.
- twelfth century: While the Escorial manuscript of Digenis Akritis only has one PAC, with παρά as the agent marker, the Grottaferrata manuscript has both ὑπό and παρά competing in this function; ἀπό is not found in either manuscript in agent expressions. The Ptochoprodromos poems only provide three PACs, two with παρά and one with ἐκ.

As the agentive use of ἀπό can always be attributed to biblical language, and that of ὑπό to classical models, it seems likely that παρά was the preposition used by the vernacular to denote the agent during the period from the sixth through twelfth centuries. An ablatival preposition is always a natural candidate to express the agent, and a look at the difference between ἀπό and παρά in the papyri reveals why παρά would have been preferred. While ἀπό is predominantly used with inanimate objects – in two common formulaic uses, it expresses either the location from which a letter is sent or the time at which an action began – παρά is mostly found with human objects. In the introductory formula in a letter, for example, the sender is denoted by παρά. As the agent of a verb is prototypically human, παρά was naturally preferred to ἀπό in marking this role.

SUMMARY

At this point, it will be useful to summarize the main arguments presented in this investigation of the ways in which Ancient Greek expressed the agents of passive verbs. For the purposes of this study, the agent is defined in syntactic terms as that constituent of the clause that would be the subject if the clause were reformulated with an active verb (pp. 17–19). Before looking at the different agent markers in question, it is first necessary to consider why agents should be marked in the first place (pp. 19–28). After all, it is somewhat odd that a language would take the trouble to demote the agent with the passive voice, only to reintroduce it as an oblique element. Several factors, however, account for this. First, it may be necessary to promote the patient to the subject relation for syntactic reasons, as is commonly the case with participles (pp. 21–2). Second, there can be pragmatic reasons for using a passive construction. Writers of Greek prose tended to structure their sentences such that the narrative theme of a passage was the subject of its clause. If, then, that narrative theme was the patient of the verb, then a passive would be used, thus necessitating an oblique expression should the author wish to express the agent (pp. 22–8). Third, the passive emphasizes the state of the patient that results from the action as against the agent's performing the action; while this motivation for the passive often operates jointly with the previous one and is accordingly difficult to detect independently, on occasion it does seem to have been the deciding factor (p. 26). In these circumstances too, the author would have to mark the agent in an oblique expression.

As for the agents themselves, their status is, at least in Greek prose, different from that of agents in English. In particular, agents of Greek passive verbs are far more likely than in English to be pronouns, and far less likely to be new information (pp. 28–32). The agents in Aristophanes, on the other hand, are more like those of

English (p. 32). This difference is due in part to the fact that Greek used the instrumental dative with inanimate nouns that English would treat as agents (pp. 32–3). But it is also important that Greek has freer word order than English. Thus, while English speakers are almost forced to use a PAC if they wish both to front the patient and to state the agent, Greek can use OVS word order to achieve this same end (pp. 34–7). As a result, writers of Greek prose were able to choose between using the OVS construction if they wanted to emphasize the agent's role in the action, and the PAC if it was the result of the action on the patient that was to be highlighted. A difference can also be detected between the pragmatic status of agents introduced by ὑπό and those marked by the dative: with the latter, even in Aristophanes, the agents are typically pronominal, and, as the dative of agent is used with the perfect passive, the verb is a stative, precisely the nuance also given to the verb in the ὑπό constructions in the prose authors (pp. 37–9). In Aristophanes, then, there is a pragmatic split between two different uses of PACs: this can be paralleled in the Mayan language K'iche', which has two passives, one of which, like the Aristophanic construction with ὑπό, avoids pronominal agents and does not lend a stative quality to the verb, the other of which, like the dative of agent in Greek, readily construes with pronominal agents and occurs with stative verbs (p. 39). There remains the question of the frequency of PACs in the various Greek authors (pp. 39–42). The construction is least common in poetry, especially in Homer, in which there is a pronounced tendency to use active verbs, even at the expense of having to change frequently from one sentence subject to another (p. 43). In prose, there is not a close correlation between genre and frequency, although within the works of Xenophon, some evidence indicates that the PAC was less common in narrative than in direct speech, especially in contexts where the speaker is employing mannered rhetorical devices like anaphora and antithesis (pp. 41–2).

PACs in Homer are best considered apart from those of later Greek: there are fewer of them, and the formulaic nature of epic poetry skews their distribution (p. 43). Thus, the dative of agent, though the most common agent marker, should hardly be considered a default agent marker, because it occurs with a circumscribed set of verbs, especially δάμνημι (pp. 51–60). The standard agent marker in classical Greek, ὑπό, already performs this function in Homer, though not only with the genitive, but also with the dative. Like the dative of agent, ὑπό$^{+D}$ is mostly limited to constructions with δάμνημι, while ὑπό$^{+G}$ collocates with a slightly broader range of verbs, thus looking ahead to its status in classical Greek (pp. 61–7). A number of ablatival prepositions, notably ἐκ and πρός, are also found as agent markers in Homer, especially with verbs of bringing about and accomplishing (pp. 67–71). That the semantics of a verb played a major role in determining which agent marker was chosen again anticipates the situation in classical Greek. Later epic poets (Apollonius, Quintus, Nonnus) avoided ὑπό$^{+G}$ and favored ὑπό$^{+D}$ as agent markers, no doubt because in doing so they could impart a Homeric color to their language (pp. 71–6).

On turning to classical Greek, we find that the most frequent agent marker other than ὑπό$^{+G}$ is the dative of agent, found especially with the perfect passive. The use of the anomalous agent marker was motivated by the unusual nature of the perfect passive, which – at least in the earliest Greek – did not, like the present and aorist passive, describe a dynamic action ("The door was opened"), but rather an unchanging state ("The door was open") (pp. 79–81). It was thus incompatible with an agent marker like ὑπό. Later, by the fifth century BC, as the transitive perfect active became more widespread, the perfect passive, increasingly viewed as its intransitive counterpart, came into closer alignment with the present and aorist passive ("The door has been opened") (pp. 81–3). At this point, because it was no longer purely stative, the perfect passive could construe with ὑπό. But ὑπό at first only occurred with the perfect passive in two environments (pp. 84–8). First, it was used when a noun in the dative might have been interpreted as something other than an agent. Second, it was used when the patient of the verb was animate, e.g. "The man has been sent by the king." To account for the prevalence of ὑπό in this second case, one may draw upon the concept of the animacy hierarchy. The combination of an animate agent and an inanimate patient is natural enough that the dative, though potentially ambiguous, is nevertheless sufficient to mark the agent. But when both agent and patient are animate, then there is a greater number of potential types of interaction between them, and the relations between the two participants need further clarification: hence, the use of ὑπό, the agent marker *par excellence*.

Furthermore, as the perfect passive became more closely aligned with the present and aorist passive in classical Attic, the dative of agent also became less common: it occurs more frequently in Thucydides and Lysias, less so in Xenophon and Plato (though it is anomalously common in Demosthenes) (pp. 88–94). It goes on to be quite rare in Polybius, the New Testament (in the whole of which it occurs only once), and, though to a lesser extent, Plutarch (pp. 94–100). In these authors, its decline seems largely due to an increased use of the perfect active (pp. 100–1): εὕρηταί μοι gives way to εὕρηκα.

But non-standard agent marking in Greek is not limited to the dative of agent. There are also PACs in which prepositions other than ὑπό mark the agent. Which preposition is chosen depends to a large extent on the semantics of the verb (pp. 113–15; for Herodotus in particular, see pp. 128–30; for Xenophon, pp. 140–6). Verbs denoting motion of the patient away from the agent, such as those of sending and giving, mark the agent with an ablatival preposition, usually ἐκ in Herodotus and παρά$^{+G}$ in Attic prose. Examples include the PACs with δίδωμι in Herodotus (pp. 125–6) and those with δίδωμι and πέμπω in Xenophon (pp. 146–7, 151–2). On the other hand, verbs that do not depict the patient as moving away from the agent, especially those of thinking or believing, use locatival prepositions, most often πρός^{+G} in Herodotus and παρά$^{+D}$ in Attic prose. Such is the case with γινώσκω, νομίζω, and τιμάω in Herodotus (pp. 122–6) and with νομίζω in Xenophon (pp. 149–50).

It can be difficult to decide in particular passages whether the preposition is truly being used to mark the agent, as opposed to a concrete spatial role like source or location. One factor, however, that can help determine between the two is the regularity with which the verb construes with ὑπό. If a verb usually construes with ὑπό, then it is more likely that a noun marked by a different preposition is not in fact an agent. If, however, the verb construes only rarely with ὑπό, then such a noun has a greater chance of being an agent.

Examples of the former include ὠφελέω in Xenophon and Plato (pp. 147–9, 167–8) and διδάσκω in Xenophon (pp. 152–3). The latter situation can be seen with γινώσκω and νομίζω in Herodotus (pp. 122–4), δωρέομαι in Plato (pp. 174–5), and δίδωμι in Demosthenes (pp. 181–2). In such cases, ὑπό is used to clarify the role of the agent, much as when it is used with perfect passives instead of the dative of agent. Verbs do not always clearly fall into one category or the other, however, as is illustrated by the behavior of δίδωμι in Plato (pp. 169–74).

Apart from this general explanation for non-standard prepositional agent markers in classical prose, there are two further points to be made about Thucydides and Demosthenes in particular. First, Thucydides is peculiar in his use of ἀπό as an agent marker, which is motivated by two different factors, as exemplified by the two verbs with which it construes most frequently, λέγω and πράσσω (pp. 134–8). On the one hand, λέγω also occurs in regular PACs with ὑπό, and, when its agent is marked by ἀπό, the latter preposition lends a contrastive sense in which one agent is opposed to the workings of another. On the other, the agent of πράσσω is never marked by ὑπό, but instead by an anomalous dative of agent, even when the verb is not a perfect passive. Here, the PACs with ἀπό show that the agent is an indirect agent, while those with the dative have agents that are so directly responsible for the action that they can, in fact, be treated as instruments and thus marked with the dative. Second, in Demosthenes, there are no longer readily apparent conditions to account for the use of παρά (both with the genitive (pp. 189–92) and with the dative (pp. 185–6)) as opposed to ὑπό. Accordingly, the language has reached a state of free variation, in which παρά has begun to replace ὑπό as the standard agent marker.

Unlike in prose, ὑπό[+G] was not the most common agent marker in Attic tragedy (p. 40). Instead, ἐκ and πρός[+G] were used with as much or greater frequency (pp. 197 (Aeschylus), 202 (*Prometheus Bound*), 204 (Sophocles), 213 (Euripides)). Again in contrast to prose, these prepositions were not favored as agent markers with verbs of particular semantics (pp. 199–200 (A.), 211 (S.), 216 (E.)). Nor were they triggered by the nature of the agent (pp. 200 (A.), 210–11 (S.)), aside from the fact that ἐκ in Aeschylus collocates frequently with θεῶν (p. 198). The use of ἐκ and πρός⁺ᴳ in tragedy instead is a result of their metrical utility, as monosyllables are much easier to fit into iambic trimeter than ὑπό, which was not allowed to count as a single long syllable by resolution in tragic iambs. Instead, it had to be either elided, placed in anastrophe at the end of a line, or used before a word that began with a double consonant. That metrical factors account for the predominance of ἐκ and πρός⁺ᴳ as agent markers in tragedy can be seen by singling out the PACs in which both ὑπό and one of the monosyllabic prepositions would be metrically interchangeable. In such cases, ὑπό is preferred almost invariably (pp. 201 (A.), 204–5, 211–12 (S.), 213–15 (E.)). The situation in tragedy can be contrasted with that in comedy, where freer metrical rules allowed ὑπό to stand by resolution for a long syllable. In Aristophanes and Menander, ὑπό is used with the same preponderance as in prose (pp. 217–20).

As for the decline of ὑπό in post-classical Greek, while it is generally thought that ὑπό was merely replaced by ἀπό, the agent marker of modern Greek, this view relies too much on the evidence of Judeo-Christian writings (pp. 223–32). Indeed, even in the Septuagint and the New Testament, while ἀπό does occur more frequently than in classical Greek as an agent marker, such examples are limited to special circumstances. In the Septuagint, the use of ἀπό as an agent marker is almost entirely restricted to PACs in which the agent in the Hebrew original was marked by the preposition *min* "from" or one of its compounds. Otherwise, ὑπό is still favored (pp. 232–40). So too in the New Testament, ἀπό primarily occurs when marking inanimate agents or with verbs that have the prefix ἀπο-. Though there are some instances that cannot be explained thus, even here the use of ἀπό can be attributed to the influence of the Septuagint (pp. 240–6). That ἀπό had not gained widespread currency as an agent marker can be seen both by examining agent marking in literary texts of the fifth and sixth centuries AD (pp. 246–52) and also in papyri from the third century BC to the eighth century AD, in which ὑπό predominates until the fifth to sixth centuries AD, when παρά⁺ᴳ becomes more common. Throughout this period, ἀπό is almost never used as an agent marker (pp. 252–6). Even in the twelfth-century poems of Digenis Akritis and Ptochoprodromos, παρά$^{+G}$ is still far more common than ἀπό, though the latter was by this point used to mark the emotion that causes an action (as in "to shake *from fear*") (pp. 258–62). As this function had belonged to ὑπό in classical Greek, we may see here the beginning of the rise of ἀπό as the agent marker of modern Greek.

BIBLIOGRAPHY

Allen, W. S. (1964) "Transitivity and possession," *Language* 40: 337–43.

American and British Committees of the International Greek New Testament Project (1984–7) *The New Testament in Greek: The Gospel According to St. Luke.* Oxford.

Andersen, P. K. (1993) "Zur Diathese," *Historische Sprachforschung* 106: 177–231.

(1994) *Empirical Studies in Diathesis.* Münster.

Arce-Arenales, M., M. Axelrod, and B. A. Fox (1994) "Active voice and middle diathesis: a cross-linguistic perspective," in Fox and Hopper: 1–21.

Bakker, E. J. (1994) "Voice, aspect, and Aktionsart: Middle and passive in ancient Greek," in Fox and Hopper: 23–47.

Barber, E. J. W. (1975) "Voice – Beyond the passive," *Berkeley Linguistics Society* 1: 16–24.

Bauer, B. L. M. (1996) "Residues of non-nominative syntax in Latin: the *mihi est* construction," *Historische Sprachforschung* 109: 241–56.

(1997) "Nominal syntax in Italic: a diachronic perspective," in *Language Change and Functional Explanations*, ed. J. Gvozdanović. Berlin and New York: 273–301.

Benveniste, E. (1950) "Actif et moyen dans le verbe," *Journal de Psychologie* 43: 121–9.

Bernert, E. (1943) "Das Verbalsubstantiv und Verbaladjektiv auf *-to-*," *Glotta* 30: 1–14.

Berrettoni, P. (1972) "L'uso del perfetto nel greco omerico," *Studi e saggi linguistici* 12: 25–170.

Bertinetto, P. M. and D. Delfitto (2000) "Aspect vs. actionality: Why they should be kept apart," in *Tense and Aspect in the Languages of Europe*, ed. Ö. Dahl. Berlin: 189–225.

Beševliev, V. (1963) *Die protobulgarischen Inschriften.* Berlin.

Blake, B. (1994) *Case.* Cambridge.

Blass, F. and A. Debrunner (1961) *A Greek Grammar of the New Testament and Other Early Christian Literature*, trans. R. W. Funk. Chicago.

Boucherie, A. (1872) "ΕΡΜΗΝΕΥΜΑΤΑ ΚΑΙ ΚΑΘΗΜΕΡΙΝΗ ΟΜΙΛΙΑ de Julius Pollux," *Notices et Extraits des Manuscrits* 23/2: 277–605.

Brugmann, K. (1916) *Grundriß der vergleichenden Grammatik der indogermanischen Sprachen* vol. II. part III. Strasburg.

Burnyeat, M. (1990) *The Theaetetus of Plato.* Indianapolis and Cambridge.

Calhoun, G. M. (1938) "ΟΡΜΗΘΕΙΣ ΘΕΟΥ ΑΡΧΕΤΟ," *Classical Philology* 33: 205–6.

Campbell, L. (1883) *The Theaetetus of Plato.* Oxford.

Campbell, L. (2000) "Valency-changing derivations in K'iche'," in Dixon and Aikhenvald: 236–81.

Chadwick, J. (1996–7) "Three temporal clauses," *Minos* 31–2: 293–301.

Chantraine, P. (1927) *Histoire du parfait grec.* Paris.

(1963) *Grammaire homérique* vol. II. Paris.

(1967) "Le parfait mycénien," *Studi micenei ed egeo-anatolici* 3: 19–27.

Chomsky, N. (1957) *Syntactic Structures.* 's-Gravenhage.

(1965) *Aspects of the Theory of Syntax.* Cambridge, Mass.

Classen, J. and J. Steup (1914) *Thukydides* vol. II, 5th edn. Berlin.

De La Villa, J. (1998) "La agentividad en la lengua homérica," in *Nombres y funciones: Estudios de sintaxis griega y latina,* ed. M. E. Torrego. Madrid: 147–80.

Delbrück, B. (1879) *Die Grundlagen der griechischen Syntax.* Halle.

(1888) *Altindische Syntax.* Halle.

(1897) *Vergleichende Syntax der indogermanischen Sprachen* part II. Strasburg.

Desclés, J.-P., Z. Guentchéva, and S. Shaumyan (1985) *Theoretical Aspects of Passivization in the Framework of Applicative Grammar.* Amsterdam and Philadelphia.

Devine, A. M. and L. D. Stephens (1994) *The Prosody of Greek Speech.* New York and Oxford.

Dickey, E. (1996) *Greek Forms of Address.* Oxford.

Diès, A. (1924) *Platon: Œuvres complètes* vol. VIII. part II. Paris.

Dik, S. C. (1978) *Functional Grammar.* Amsterdam.

Dixon, R. M. W. (1979) "Ergativity," *Language* 55: 59–138.

(1994) *Ergativity.* Cambridge.

Dixon, R. M. W. and A. Y. Aikhenvald (eds.) (2000) *Changing Valency: Case Studies in Transitivity.* Cambridge.

Eideneier, H. (1991) *Ptochoprodromos: Einführung, kritische Ausgabe, deutsche Übersetzung, Glossar.* Cologne.

Elliott, W. J. and D. C. Parker (1995) *The New Testament in Greek IV: The Gospel According to St. John. Vol. 1: The Papyri.* Leiden.

Fabricius, C. (1967) "Der sprachliche Klassizismus der griechischen Kirchenväter: ein philologisches und geistesgeschichtliches Problem," *Jahrbuch für Antike & Christentum* 10: 187–99.

Fillmore, C. J. (1968) "The case for case," in *Universals in Linguistic Theory,* ed. E. Bach and R. T. Harms. London: 1–88.

Fox, B. and P. J. Hopper (eds.) (1994) *Voice: Form and Function.* Amsterdam and Philadelphia.

Fraenkel, E. (1950) *Aeschylus: Agamemnon* vol. III. Oxford.

Garvie, A. F. (1994) *Homer: Odyssey Books VI–VIII.* Cambridge.

Gildersleeve, B. L. and G. Lodge (1895) *Latin Grammar*, 3rd edn. London.

Givón, T. (1979) *On Understanding Grammar.* New York.

Grahame, K. (1908) *The Wind in the Willows.* London.

Green, A. (1913) *The Dative of Agency.* New York.

Griffith, M. (1977) *The Authenticity of "Prometheus Bound".* Cambridge.

Hartmann, F. (1935) "Zur Frage der Aspektbildung beim griechischen Futurum," *Zeitschrift für Vergleichende Sprachforschung* 62: 116–31.

Hatzidakis, G. N. (1892) *Einleitung in die neugriechische Grammatik.* Leipzig.

Helbing, R. (1904) *Die Präpositionen bei Herodot und andern Historikern.* Würzburg.

Hettrich, H. (1990) "Der Agens in passivischen Sätzen altindogermanischer Sprachen," *Nachrichten der Akademie der Wissenschaften in Göttingen* 1990: 57–108.

Heubeck, A., S. West, and J. P. Hainsworth (1988) *A Commentary on Homer's Odyssey* vol. I. Oxford.

Hoffmann, O. and A. Debrunner (1969) *Geschichte der griechischen Sprache* vol. I, 4th edn, ed. A. Scherer. Berlin.

Hofmann, J. B. and A. Szantyr (1965) *Lateinische Syntax und Stilistik.* Munich.

Hopper, P. J. and S. A. Thompson (1980) "Transitivity in grammar and discourse," *Language* 56: 251–99.

Horrocks, G. C. (1997) *Greek: A History of the Language and its Speakers.* London.

Hult, K. (1990) *Syntactic Variation in Greek of the 5th Century A. D.* Gothenburg.

Humbert, J. (1960) *Syntaxe grecque*, 3rd edn. Paris.

Jamison, S. W. (1979a) "The case of the agent in Indo-European," *Sprache* 25: 129–43.

(1979b) "Remarks on the expression of agency with the passive in Vedic and Indo-European," *Zeitschrift für Vergleichende Sprachforschung* 93: 196–219.

Jankuhn, H. (1969) *Die passive Bedeutung medialer Formen untersucht an der Sprache Homers.* ZVS Ergänzungsheft 21. Göttingen.

Jannaris, A. N. (1897) *An Historical Greek Grammar, chiefly of the Attic Dialect.* London.

Jeffreys, E. (1998) *Digenis Akritis: The Grottaferrata and Escorial Versions.* Cambridge.

Joffre, M.-D. (1995) *Le verbe latin: voix et diathèse.* Louvain.

Johannessohn, M. (1925) "Der Gebrauch der Präpositionen in der Septuaginta," *Nachrichten von der Gesellschaft der Wissenschaften zu Göttingen* (Phil.-hist. Kl.).

Jowett, B. (1953) *The Dialogues of Plato* vol. III, 4th edn. Oxford.

Keil, F. (1963) "Untersuchungen zum Perfektgebrauch Herodots," *Glotta* 41: 10–51.

Kemmer, S. (1993) *The Middle Voice.* Amsterdam and Philadelphia.

Kemple, B. (1993) *Essential Russian Grammar.* New York.

Kennedy, B. H. (1894) *The Theaetetus of Plato*. Cambridge.

King, R. T. (1988) "Spatial metaphor in German causative constructions," in *Topics in Cognitive Linguistics*, ed. B. Rudzka-Ostyn. Amsterdam and Philadelphia: 555–85.

Kirk, G. S. (1985) *The Iliad: A Commentary* vol. I: books I–IV. Cambridge.

Klaiman, M. H. (1991) *Grammatical Voice*. Cambridge.

Koster, W. J. W. (1952) "De graecorum genitivo, qui dicitur auctoris; de *Od.* θ 499," *Mnemosyne* (4th series) 5: 89–93.

Kühner, R. and B. Gerth (1898) *Ausführliche Grammatik der griechischen Sprache* part II. vol. I. Hanover and Leipzig.

(1904) *Ausführliche Grammatik der griechischen Sprache* part II. vol. II. Hanover and Leipzig.

Kuryłowicz, J. (1932) "Les désinences moyennes de l'indo-européen et du hittite," *Bulletin de la Société de linguistique de Paris* 33: 1–4.

(1964) *The Inflectional Categories of Indo-European*. Heidelberg.

La Roche, J. (1861) "Beobachtungen über den Gebrauch von ὑπό bei Homer," *Zeitschrift für die österreichischen Gymnasien* 12: 337–77.

Lambdin, T. O. (1971) *Introduction to Biblical Hebrew*. New York.

Leaf, W. (1900) *The Iliad* vol. I, 2nd edn. London.

Legg, S. C. E. (1935) *Novum Testamentum graece: Euangelium secundum Marcum*. Oxford.

(1940) *Novum Testamentum graece: Euangelium secundum Matthaeum*. Oxford.

Lejeune, M. (1939) *Les adverbes grecs en -θεν*. Bordeaux.

Löfstedt, E. (1962) *Philologischer Kommentar zur Peregrinatio Aetheriae*. Darmstadt.

Luraghi, S. (1986) "On the distribution of instrumental and agentive markers for human and non-human agents of passive verbs in some Indo-European languages," *Indogermanische Forschungen* 91: 48–66.

(1989) "Cause and instrument expression in Classical Greek," *Mnemosyne* 42: 294–307.

(1994) "Animate nouns in cause expression," in *Cas et prépositions en grec ancien*, ed. B. Jacquinod. St-Etienne: 227–37.

(1995) "Prototypicality and agenthood in Indo-European," in *Historical Linguistics 1993*, ed. H. Andersen. Amsterdam and Philadelphia: 259–68.

(2000) "Spatial metaphors and agenthood in Ancient Greek," in *125 Jahre Indogermanistik in Graz*, ed. M. Ofitsch and C. Zinko. Graz: 275–90.

(2001) "Some remarks on Instrument, Comitative, and Agent in Indo-European," *Sprachtypologie und Universalienforschung* 54: 385–401.

(2003) *On the Meaning of Prepositions and Cases: The Expression of Semantic Roles in Ancient Greek*. Amsterdam and Philadelphia.

Lyons, J. (1968) *Introduction to Theoretical Linguistics*. Cambridge.

MacDonell, A. A. (1916) *A Vedic Grammar for Students*. Oxford.

Maiden, M. (1995) *A Linguistic History of Italian*. London and New York.

Mallinson, G. and B. J. Blake (1981) *Language Typology: Cross-cultural Studies in Syntax*. Amsterdam.

Mandilaras, B. G. (1973) *The Verb in the Greek Non-literary Papyri*. Athens.

Matthews, P. H. (1981) *Syntax*. Cambridge.

Mayser, E. (1934) *Grammatik der griechischen Papyri aus der Ptolemäerzeit. Vol 2.2. Satzlehre. Analytischer Teil. 2. Hälfte.* Berlin and Leipzig.

McKay, K. L. (1965) "The use of the Ancient Greek perfect down to the second century A. D.," *Bulletin of the Institute of Classical Studies of the University of London* 12: 1–21.

—— (1980) "On the perfect and other aspects in the Greek non-literary papyri," *Bulletin of the Institute of Classical Studies of the University of London* 27: 23–49.

Meid, W. (1971) *Das germanische Präteritum*. Innsbruck.

Menge, H., T. Burkard, and M. Schauer (2000) *Lehrbuch der lateinischen Syntax und Semantik*. Darmstadt.

Metzger, B. M. (1992) *The Text of the New Testament: Its Transmission, Corruption, and Restoration*, 3rd edn. New York and Oxford.

Mitchell, B. (1985) *Old English Syntax* vol. I. Oxford.

Monro, D. B. (1891) *Homeric Grammar*, 2nd edn. Oxford.

Moorhouse, A. C. (1982) *The Syntax of Sophocles*. Leiden.

Moule, C. F. D. (1963) *An Idiom Book of New Testament Greek*. Cambridge.

Moulton, J. H. (1976) *A Grammar of New Testament Greek*. Edinburgh.

Müller, G. (1968) *Studien zu den platonischen Nomoi*. Munich.

Müller, N. (1999) *Agents in Early Welsh and Early Irish*. Oxford.

Mustanoja, T. F. (1960) *A Middle English Syntax* part I. Helsinki.

Nau, N. (1998) *Latvian*. Munich.

Nestle, E. (1896) *Novi Testamenti Graeci supplementum*. Leipzig.

Palmer, F. R. (1994) *Grammatical Roles and Relations*. Cambridge.

Palmer, L. R. (1963) *The Interpretation of Mycenaean Greek Texts*. Oxford.

Panhuis, D. (1984) "Topic shift and other discourse functions of passives in Latin narratives," *Glotta* 62: 232–40.

Penny, R. (1991) *A History of the Spanish Language*. Cambridge.

Powell, J. E. (1938) *A Lexicon to Herodotus*. Cambridge.

Radford, A. (1988) *Transformational Grammar: A First Course*. Cambridge.

Risselada, R. (1991) "Passive, perspective and textual cohesion," in *New Studies in Latin Linguistics*, ed. R. Coleman. Amsterdam and Philadelphia: 401–14.

Rix, H. (1988) "The Proto-Indo-European middle: Content, forms, and origin," *Münchener Studien zur Sprachwissenschaft* 49: 101–19.

Rosén, H. (1999) *Latine loqui*. Munich.

Rusten, J. S. (1989) *Thucydides: The Peloponnesian War Book II*. Cambridge.

Rutherford, R. B. (1995) *The Art of Plato*. London.

Sauge, A. (2000) *Les degrés du verbe: Sens et formation du parfait en grec ancien*. Berne.

Schmid, W. (1948) *Geschichte der griechischen Literatur* part I. vol. V. Munich.

BIBLIOGRAPHY

Schmidt, K. H. (1963) "Zum Agens beim Passiv," *Indogermanische Forschungen* 68: 1–12.

Schwyzer, E. (1939) *Griechische Grammatik* vol. I. Munich.

(1943) "Zum persönlichen Agens beim Passiv, besonders im Griechischen," *Abhandlungen der Preußischen Akademie der Wissenschaften* (Phil.-hist. Kl.) 1942/10.

Schwyzer, E. and A. Debrunner (1950) *Griechische Grammatik* vol. II. Munich.

Siewierska, A. (1984) *The Passive: A Comparative Linguistic Analysis.* London.

Silverstein, M. (1976) "Hierarchy of features and ergativity," in *Grammatical Categories in Australian Languages*, ed. R. M. W. Dixon. Canberra: 112–71.

Slings, S. R. (1986) "ΕΙΛΗΦΑ," *Glotta* 64: 9–14.

Smyth, H. W. (1920) *Greek Grammar.* Cambridge, Mass.

Snell, B. (1937) *Euripides Alexandros und andere Straßburger Papyri mit Fragmenten griechischer Dichter.* Hermes Einzelschrift 5. Berlin.

Stang, C. (1932) "Perfektum und Medium," *Norsk Tidsskrift for Sprogvidenskap* 6: 29–39.

Stempel, R. (1995) "Stative, Perfekt und Medium: Eine vergleichende Analyse für das Indogermanische und Semitische," in *Kuryłowicz Memorial Volume* part I, ed. W. Smoczyński. Cracow: 517–28.

(1996) *Die Diathese im Indogermanischen.* Innsbruck.

Strunk, K. (1980) "Zum idg. Medium und konkurrierenden Kategorien," in *Wege zur Universalienforschung*, ed. G. Brettschneider and C. Lehrmann. Tübingen: 321–37.

Szemerényi, O. J. L. (1996) *Introduction to Indo-European Linguistics.* Oxford.

Touratier, C. (1994) *Syntaxe latine.* Louvain.

Tucker, E. F. (1990) *The Creation of Morphological Regularity: Early Greek Verbs in -έω, -άω, -όω, -ύω, -ίω.* Göttingen.

Van Valin, R. D., Jr. (2001) *An Introduction to Syntax.* Cambridge.

Ventris, M. and J. Chadwick (1973) *Documents in Mycenaean Greek*, 2nd edn. Cambridge.

Wackernagel, J. (1904) *Studien zum griechischen Perfektum.* Göttingen.

(1950) *Vorlesungen über Syntax* vol. I, 2nd edn. Basel.

Waltke, B. K. and M. O'Connor (1990) *An Introduction to Biblical Hebrew Syntax.* Winona Lake, Ind.

Waterfield, R. A. H. (1987) *Plato: Theaetetus.* Harmondsworth.

West, M. L. (1987) *Introduction to Greek Metre.* Oxford.

Whitney, W. D. (1889) *Sanskrit Grammar*, 2nd edn. Cambridge, Mass.

Wierzbicka, A. (1981) "Case marking and human nature," *Australian Journal of Linguistics* 1: 43–80.

Wohlrab, M. (1891) *Platonis Theaetetus.* Leipzig.

GENERAL INDEX

INDEX OF GREEK WORDS

281

INDEX OF PASSAGES DISCUSSED